T0323800

SINGLE-SESSION THERAPY (SST)

Even in one session a therapist can make a difference. The second edition of *Single-Session Therapy* enables therapists to work with clients for one session and achieve possible and realistic results.

This book presents the 100 main features of the approach, providing an accessible, succinct overview. Based on the author's extensive work demonstrating the effectiveness of Single-Session Therapy (SST), this concise and practical book covers topics such as

- The goals of SST
- Characteristics of 'good' SST clients
- Responding effectively to the client's very first contact
- Creating and maintaining a working focus
- Making an emotional impact.

Updated with refocused key points and references, this second edition will also include new information about therapists' misconceptions of SST, the single-session mindset, and the working alliance.

Both concise and practical, the book will be invaluable to psychotherapists and counsellors in training and practice.

Windy Dryden is in clinical and consultative practice and is an international authority on Single-Session Therapy. He is Emeritus Professor of Psychotherapeutic Studies at Goldsmiths, University of London. He has worked in psychotherapy for more than 45 years and is the author or editor of over 265 books.

100 Key Points and Techniques
Series Editor: Windy Dryden

ALSO IN THIS SERIES:

COGNITIVE BEHAVIOUR THERAPY: 100 KEY POINTS
AND TECHNIQUES, 2ND EDITION
Michael Neenan and Windy Dryden

RATIONAL EMOTIVE BEHAVIOUR THERAPY: 100 KEY
POINTS AND TECHNIQUES, 2ND EDITION
Windy Dryden and Michael Neenan

EXISTENTIAL THERAPY: 100 KEY POINTS AND
TECHNIQUES
Susan Iacovou and Karen Weixel-Dixon

PERSON-CENTRED THERAPY: 100 KEY POINTS AND
TECHNIQUES, 2ND EDITION
Paul Wilkins

SINGLE-SESSION THERAPY (SST): 100 KEY POINTS
AND TECHNIQUES
Windy Dryden

ACCEPTANCE AND COMMITMENT THERAPY: 100
KEY POINTS AND TECHNIQUES
Richard Bennett and Joseph E. Oliver

GESTALT THERAPY: 100 KEY POINTS AND
TECHNIQUES
Dave Mann

SINGLE-SESSION THERAPY (SST): 100 KEY POINTS
AND TECHNIQUES, 2ND EDITION
Windy Dryden

SINGLE-SESSION THERAPY (SST)

100 KEY POINTS AND TECHNIQUES

SECOND EDITION

Windy Dryden

Routledge
Taylor & Francis Group

LONDON AND NEW YORK

Second edition published 2024
by Routledge
4 Park Square, Milton Park, Abingdon, Oxon, OX14 4RN

and by Routledge
605 Third Avenue, New York, NY 10158

Routledge is an imprint of the Taylor & Francis Group, an informa business

First edition published by Routledge 2019

British Library Cataloguing-in-Publication Data
A catalogue record for this book is available from the British Library

Library of Congress Cataloging-in-Publication Data
Names: Dryden, Windy, author.
Title: Single-session therapy (SST) : 100 key points and techniques / Windy Dryden.
Description: Second edition. | Milton Park, Abingdon, Oxon ; New York, NY :
Routledge, 2024. | Series: 100 key points and techniques |
Includes bibliographical references.
Identifiers: LCCN 2023010258 (print) | LCCN 2023010259 (ebook) |
ISBN 9781032478791 (hardback) | ISBN 9781032478784 (paperback) |
ISBN 9781003386353 (ebook)
Subjects: LCSH: Single-session psychotherapy. |
Psychotherapist and patient.
Classification: LCC RC480.55 .D78 2024 (print) |
LCC RC480.55 (ebook) | DDC 616.89/14–dc23/eng/20230527
LC record available at https://lccn.loc.gov/2023010258
LC ebook record available at https://lccn.loc.gov/2023010259

ISBN: 9781032478791 (hbk)
ISBN: 9781032478784 (pbk)
ISBN: 9781003386353 (ebk)

DOI: 10.4324/9781003386353

Typeset in Aldus
by Newgen Publishing UK

CONTENTS

Preface   xi

Part 1
THE NATURE AND FOUNDATIONS OF SST   1

1   What is SST?   3
2   The development of SST   9
3   What SST is not   17
4   Even a brief encounter can be therapeutic   20
5   The expandable nature of therapy length   22
6   The modal number of therapy sessions
    internationally is 'one', and the majority of
    people who attend for one session are satisfied   24
7   It is difficult to predict, with accuracy, how many
    therapy sessions a client will attend   27
8   What is a 'drop-out'?   28
9   Intermittent therapy through the life cycle   30
10 Sooner is better and less is more   32
11 Human beings can help themselves quickly
    under specific circumstances   34
12 The choice of SST is the client's, but sometimes
    this choice is limited   38
13 Time in SST   40
14 The SST mindset and its practical implications   42
15 Client empowerment   48
16 Service delivery   49
17 The diverse nature of SST   52
18 The goals of SST   57
19 SST challenges established beliefs about
    therapy and change   61

20	The length of SST	65
21	Different approaches to SST	67
22	Different types of help in SST	69

Part 2
THE ASSUMPTIONS OF SST 71

23	Client-centred and client-driven	73
24	Reciprocity in openness and feedback	76
25	Future-oriented, but present and past sensitive	78
26	Readiness	80
27	Strengths-based	83
28	Use of external resources	86
29	Complex problems do not always require complex solutions	88
30	The journey begins with the first few steps	90

Part 3
FACILITATIVE CONDITIONS FOR SST 93

31	Intentionality	95
32	Expect change	97
33	Clarity	99
34	Effective session structure	101
35	Effective goal-setting	104
36	The therapist's use of expertise rather than being the expert	107
37	Helpful attitudes for SST therapists	109
38	Characteristics of 'good' SST therapists	112
39	SST: The dos	116
40	SST: The don'ts	119
41	A conducive environment for SST	122
42	The pluralistic nature of SST	125
43	Characteristics of 'good' SST clients	127
44	The process of SST	131

Part 4
CRITERIA FOR SST   **135**

45   The client criteria question   137
46   Therapist indications and contra-indications
     for SST   139
47   Service indications and contra-indications
     for SST   142

Part 5
GETTING SST OFF ON THE RIGHT FOOT   **147**

48   Respond effectively to the person's very first
     contact   149
49   Helping the client to prepare for the session   151

Part 6
GETTING THE MOST FROM THE SESSION   **155**

50   Agree or review parameters   157
51   Be mindful of the working alliance in SST   160
52   Begin the session   162
53   Focus on a problem that can be solved,
     not one that can't be solved   165
54   Create and maintain a working focus   168
55   Help clients deal with adversity, if possible   172
56   Negotiate a goal   175
57   Understand how clients unwittingly maintain
     their problems and use this understanding to
     help them solve these problems   179
58   What to change, I: Individual-focused change   184
59   What to change, II: Environment-focused
     change   190
60   Focus on and use pivot chords   192
61   Agree markers for change   194
62   Notice and encourage change   196
63   Focus on the second response not the first   197

64	Look for exceptions to the problem	200
65	Look for instances of the goal already happening	202
66	Encourage the client to do more of what works or might work and less of what doesn't work	204
67	Make an emotional impact	207
68	Utilise the client's internal strengths and external resources	210
69	Identify and utilise the client's role model	212
70	Utilise topophilia in SST	214
71	The use of stories and parables	216
72	Use humour	220
73	Use paradox	222
74	Use the 'friend technique'	224
75	The use of chairwork in SST	226
76	Convert meaning into a useful and memorable phrase	229
77	Educate when clients appear to lack information or have faulty information	231
78	Agree on the solution	233
79	Encourage the client to practise the solution in the session, if possible	236
80	Have the client summarise the process	239
81	Take-aways	241
82	Action planning and implementation	243
83	End the session, I: General points	246
84	End the session, II: Accessing further help	248
85	After the session, I: Reflection, the recording and the transcript	250
86	After the session, II: Client feedback	252
87	Follow-up: Outcome and service evaluation	255
88	Example of an SST structure	259

Part 7
WALK-IN THERAPY **263**

89	Two pathways to help	265
90	The nature of walk-in therapy	268

91   The case for walk-in therapy   270
92   Foster an alliance with the service rather than
     with a specific therapist   272
93   How walk-in services are advertised   274
94   A guideline for walk-in session structure
     influenced by brief narrative therapy   278

Part 8
OTHER FORMS OF SST   **281**

95   Therapy demonstrations   283
96   Filmed training tapes   285
97   Second opinions   288

Part 9
**SST COMMON ERRORS, COMMON CONCERNS
AND FREQUENTLY ASKED QUESTIONS**   **293**

98   Common errors made in SST   295
99   Common concerns therapists have about SST   300
100   Frequently asked questions about SST and
      walk-in therapy   306

Afterword   **311**
References   **315**
Index   **326**

PREFACE

In the early 1990s, when I heard of new work that was being done in the field of single-session therapy[1], I was sceptical like many psychotherapists at the time. After all, what productive work could be done in one session? 'Not much' was the general conclusion, and although I was curious enough to buy Moshe Talmon's (1990) book on the subject, I was only sufficiently interested to skim read it, and the book lay on my bookshelves until I retired from my university post in 2014. Then, fuelled by the desire to explore something new (to me) in the field of psychotherapy and excited by the single demonstration sessions I had been doing while running training courses, I decided to read Talmon's book more thoroughly. I read it again straight-away and then read it for the third time. It was as if a light bulb lit up in my head. This was the challenge I had been looking for. So, I embarked on an intensive journey into the relevant literature which included a published copy of the proceedings of the first international symposium on single-session therapy and walk-in services held in Melbourne, Australia in 2012 (Hoyt & Talmon, 2014a) and a pre-publication copy of the second international symposium held in Banff, Canada in 2015 (Hoyt et al., 2018a). I created my CBT-flavoured way of prac-tising SST (Dryden, 2017, 2022a) and developed my approach to single-session demonstration sessions, lasting 30 minutes or less which I termed 'Very Brief Therapeutic Conversations' (Dryden, 2018a). Since then, I have given many one-day and two-day training workshops on SST and have run certificate-length training courses in the UK, India, Russia and Azerbaijan.

---

1   In this book I will use the term 'therapy' to refer to work that includes counselling and other related terms.

I have also published a number of books on SST which feature with verbatim transcripts of actual sessions with commentary by myself and reflections by my clients (Dryden, 2021a, 2022b, 2023).

I must say at the outset that I love working in a single-session and brief manner. It energises me, I think more creatively, and, in my humble view, I think I am quite good at it. Given my passion for this field, I could not wait to write the second edition of this book. Let me say a little bit about it before I start.

100 KEY POINTS

The book is in the series that I edit for Routledge entitled '100 Key Points'. The books in this series are concise and practical introductions to approaches and modalities in counselling and psychotherapy. As such they are ideal for those in training, or for professionals wishing to improve their practice. The books in this series contain brief descriptions of points of theory and practice and are meant to be read and digested a few at a time. So, resist the urge to read this book in one sitting. As you read and digest a point, ask yourself how it might broaden your practice. Really interact with the material.

MY EXPERIENCE IS IN USING SST WITH INDIVIDUALS

While a lot of what I have to say about SST can be applied to working with individuals, couples, families and groups, my own experience is with working in this way with individuals, and thus this emphasis will be apparent. It is good practice to be as transparent as possible in practising SST, and I think the same is true when writing a book on it.

BE SELECTIVE

As you will see if you take a look at the contents page, I cover a lot of ground here, particularly in Part 6 of the book. I do want to make one thing crystal clear. I do not expect anyone to use all the techniques described with any given client. Indeed, to do so would be bad practice. Use this book as a handyperson uses the tools in their toolbox. The person has access to all their tools, but will only use those they need when working to solve a problem. Be parsimonious in your use of methods in SST.

DEVELOP YOUR OWN STYLE

It is very important that you be yourself when practising as an SST therapist. Do not try to imitate the style of any of the leading figures in the field that you may see live or on DVD.

THE IMPORTANCE OF TRAINING AND SUPERVISION

My view is that given the fact that SST is not generally covered in professional counselling and psychotherapy training courses, it does require specialised training and supervision. I decry the practice that practitioners start practising SST after attending a one-day SST workshop and without being supervised by someone experienced in SST. Learning to be an effective SST therapist means, in my opinion, that you will be learning and developing high-level skills. Thus, with your clients' permission, record your work and get feedback in supervision on what you actually did, not just on what you said you did by someone with SST expertise.

GET FEEDBACK FROM YOUR CLIENTS

While getting expert supervision of your SST work is vital, you can also learn about becoming an SST therapist by getting feedback from your client at the end of the session and/or at any scheduled follow-up session. To paraphrase George Kelly, 'If you want to know how you are doing as an SST therapist ask your clients, they will tell you'.

ALLOW YOURSELF TO FALL IN LOVE WITH SST

My final point is this: immerse yourself in the world of SST. It is a gift that keeps on giving (J. Young, 2018). If you do so, then you might find that you have fallen in love with SST – as I have done.

Part 1

THE NATURE AND FOUNDATIONS OF SST

WHAT IS SST?

In this opening chapter, I will consider what is meant by single-session therapy. It may seem, at first sight, that it is obvious what it is, but as with other seemingly simple concepts in psychotherapy, the situation is more complex.

THE RONSEAL APPROACH

In 1994, a British company called Ronseal that manufactures wood stain, paint and preservatives developed a slogan to explain and demystify its products. It was 'Ronseal. It does exactly what it says on the tin'. This caught the public imagination to the extent that the phrase is used internationally and is now a commonly used slogan. The Ronseal approach to the question 'What is SST?', then, is: 'Single-session therapy is a therapy that lasts for one session.'

While this approach appears clear, it begs several important questions such as: 'What constitutes a session?'; 'Does this term apply to therapy that lasts for one session by default as well as therapy that is designed to last for one session?' and 'Does SST preclude a follow-up session?' Hymmen and colleagues provide answers to some of these questions in their 'Ronseal' definition. They say that:

> SST refers to a planned single-session intervention – not to the situation where a client is offered more sessions but chooses to attend just one. The single session may be previously scheduled or provided in a 'walk-in counselling clinic.' Previously scheduled SST involves clients being offered a specific date and time that can be set from a few days to a month in advance; single-session walk-in clinics offer one or more days a week when clients can see

a counsellor for a single session without an appointment, after a relatively short wait.

(Hymmen, Stalker and Cait, 2013: 61)

TALMON'S (1990) DEFINITION

In Chapter 2, I will make the point that the publication of Moshe Talmon's (1990) book on SST was a key moment in its development. As such, it is important to consider his definition of SST. He said: 'Single-session therapy is defined here as one face-to-face meeting between a therapist and a patient with no previous or subsequent sessions within one year' (Talmon, 1990: xv).

Talmon's definition raises several issues:

- As with the Ronseal approach, it calls into question what a 'session' is.
- It allows for there to be other meetings between a therapist and a client that are *not* face-to-face but does not make this clear. Talmon (1990) mentions elsewhere a preparation or set-up contact between the therapist and the client and also mentions a follow-up session, both of which can occur on the telephone to preserve the single-session nature of the face-to-face session.
- It poses a problem for therapy that takes place over the telephone, on platforms such as Zoom or online. If there has to be a face-to-face session, it calls into question whether or not it is possible to have SST by Zoom, telephone or online. To be fair to Talmon, when he wrote his book in 1990, Zoom had not been developed, and online therapy was largely unknown. Now, of course, after the Coronavirus pandemic much therapy is conducted over Zoom (or similar platforms) so the face-to-face requirement in the definition is largely redundant.
- It implies that if a client has a second face-to-face (or online) session before the interval of a year has elapsed, the entire therapy cannot be regarded as single-session therapy.

This shows that what appears to be a simple issue is quite complex and that there does not exist a definition of SST with which all workers in the field can agree. In the next section, I will discuss the approach to the issue of the nature of SST that is currently in vogue.

MAXIMISING WHAT MAY BE THE ONLY SESSION WITH THE POSSIBILITY OF MORE

Hoyt et al. (2018b) note that Talmon's (1990) definition that there should be no other sessions in the year before or after is arbitrary and was used for research purposes. They make the point that the work discussed in Talmon's book was based on the fact that many people attend only one session, and, consequently, the therapist and the client are advised to approach the first session *as if* it were going to be the last. Twenty-eight years after the publication of Talmon's book, Hoyt et al. (2018b: 18, footnote) say the following:

> SST clients may be seen more than once in a year (nowadays either face-to-face or via telephone or online), and the basic SST desideratum is that a session be approached as though it could be the only (single) session, complete unto itself.

Again, to be fair to Talmon, he did recognise this as the subtitle of his book was *Maximizing the Effect of the First (and Often Only) Therapeutic Encounter*.

The movement away from the 'Ronseal' response, where single-session therapy is confined to a single session, to the more pluralistic position where it may be one session but more sessions may take place is summed up by Weir and colleagues. They say about SST:

> It is not a 'one-off' therapy but rather a structured first session which attempts to maximise the client's first therapeutic encounter, understanding that it may be the only appointment the client chooses to attend while entertaining the possibility of ongoing work.

(Weir et al., 2008: 12)

THE PARADOXICAL NATURE OF SST

The above pluralistic position also details what can be seen as the paradoxical nature where SST is more likely if clients appreciate that further sessions are possible. Thus, if clients have a sense that they are in control over whether or not they can have further sessions, then they are more likely to be happy with a single session than when they lack such control (Baumeister & Bushman, 2017). As Hoyt (2018: 157) says:

> Insistence produces resistance, imposition produces opposition, push produces pushback—so I think it is important to offer and invite, but not demand, one visit. In our studies of SST, we have been careful to refer to the 'POSSIBILITY of one session being enough' and to say 'When the first session MAY be the last'.

ONE-AT-A-TIME THERAPY

Several therapy agencies – particularly in UK higher education – offer what Hoyt (2011) referred to as *One-at-a-time therapy (OAATT)*. This term refers to the idea that therapy 'takes place one contact at a time, and one contact may be all the time that is needed'. While different agencies implement OAATT in different ways, its defining feature is to exclude access to ways of delivering therapy services such as 'blocks' of therapy sessions or ongoing therapy. Indeed, in some services, the introduction of OAATT has meant that these other forms of service delivery have been withdrawn. Some agencies enable clients to book as many sessions as they want, but they can only do so 'one session at a time', usually with a prescribed interval between sessions (e.g., two weeks). Other agencies place a cap on the number of OAATT sessions that a client can have in a one year period.

MY OWN DEFINITION OF SST AND ONEPLUS THERAPY

I have reservations about both the terms 'single-session therapy'[1] and 'one-at-a-time therapy'. In the workshops that

---

1　Despite my reservations about the term 'single-session therapy', I continue to use it in my writings because it is now embedded in the language of our field.

I give on SST, despite making the point numerous times that SST does NOT preclude the client having more sessions if they need them, the term 'single-session therapy' leaves the impression in the minds of people that what is being offered in SST is one session and one session only. The term 'one-at-a-time therapy' means that while again the therapist and client will endeavour to help the client with their stated wants in one session, if the client wants more help they can have it but they can only access it one session at a time. OAATT is problematic because it means that if the client and therapist decide that the client would benefit from ongoing therapy, they could not have it, even if it were available.

For these reasons, I personally refer to my work as *ONEplus Therapy*. The word 'ONE' again makes clear that the therapist and client have decided to work together to help the client with their stated wants in one session. It is in capital letters to indicate that endeavouring to help the client in one session is what both therapist and client would like to happen. The word 'plus' indicates explicitly that more help is available to the client, if required. However, unlike in one-at-a-time therapy, no restrictions are placed in ONEplus therapy concerning what form the additional help will take. If needed, the client can have access to whatever mode of therapy delivery the practitioner or agency offers.

Although I personally prefer the term ONEplus therapy, I will use the term single-session therapy in this book because it is in common use. I define single-session therapy[2] as:

> a purposeful endeavour where both therapist and client contract to work together with the intention of helping the client in one session knowing that more help is available, if needed.

The important elements of this definition are as follows:

- The work is contracted. Both client and therapist give their informed consent to proceed. They both understand the nature of SST and what it can do and what it cannot do.

2 This definition also applies to ONEplus therapy.

- The purpose of SST is to help the client, if possible, to achieve their stated wants in one session. While the *consequence* of SST is that it brings down waiting lists and reduces waiting time for an appointment in services where SST is by appointment, this is the not the purpose of SST. Its purpose is as stated above.
- SST does not serve as a barrier to the client from getting the help that they require as determined by themself in consultation with the therapist. If the client wants to access a different mode of therapy delivery and the practitioner and/or agency offers this, then they can do so. However, they need to know how long it will take for this help to become available.
- Thus, the therapist in SST strives to integrate two seemingly different foci. The therapist is saying to the client, in effect: 'Let's work together to see if we can help you to achieve your stated wants in one session. However, if you wish you can have access to further help'.

SST endeavours to offer the client the help that they need: a single session for those who would prefer, if possible, to come to only one session and more help for those who request it. The first group has been poorly served by our field. SST seeks to provide the help that they need rather than offering them more help than they want.

THE DEVELOPMENT OF SST

While it is not possible to detail the exact date when single-session therapy (SST) was created, it is easier to chart its development by highlighting key contributions to its growth. Although the publication of Moshe Talmon's (1990) seminal book, entitled *Single Session Therapy: Maximizing the Effect of the First (and Often Only) Therapeutic Encounter* is an important event in the history of SST, the following might be said to have cleared the path for its current popularity.

SIGMUND FREUD'S SINGLE SESSIONS

Psychoanalysis is usually a long-term therapy, but its founder, Sigmund Freud, did conduct two single sessions which showed what could be achieved in a short period of time.

Freud's single session with Aurelia Öhm-Kronich ('Katharina')

Aurelia, an 18-year-old inn-keeper's daughter, informally consulted Freud in 1893 when he was vacationing in the Rax mountains in Austria. She complained of a suffocating feeling, accompanied by the vision of a terrifying face. These feelings started after she had witnessed her uncle[1] having sex with a maid. Freud helped Aurelia to trace these feelings back to times when her 'uncle' made sexual advances to her and latterly when he showed her that he was angry with her. Having been helped to make sense of her feelings in a single session, Aurelia's anxiety symptoms abated (Freud & Breuer, 1895).

---

1 It transpired that this 'uncle' was really Aurelia's father.

DOI: 10.4324/9781003386353-3   9

Freud's single session with Gustav Mahler

Mahler contacted Sigmund Freud for an appointment even though he was aware that Freud was on vacation. Significantly, Mahler missed several appointments and was given one last chance to see Freud in Leiden in the Netherlands before the latter left for Sicily. Freud conducted a four-hour 'walking consultation' in the Dutch university town on 26 August 1910. In a paper on this 'treatment', Kuehn (1965: 358) notes that 'Freud's diagnosis and reassurance seemed to be very helpful. At least no more was heard from the manifest problem[2] throughout the remaining eight months of Mahler's life'.

ALFRED ADLER'S DEMONSTRATION SESSIONS

Just after the First World War, in 1922, Alfred Adler, a previous disciple of Freud and founder of what came to be known as 'Individual Psychology', established a number of child guidance clinics in the public schools of Vienna. At those clinics, Adler would hold public demonstrations of therapy with parents and children, separately and together, in front of a mixed professional and lay audience. These single sessions had both therapeutic and educational value for those present and influenced Albert Ellis who, in 1965, established his popular 'Problems of Everyday Living' events that came to be known as the 'Friday Night Workshop'.

ALBERT ELLIS'S FRIDAY NIGHT WORKSHOP

At these workshops, which began in 1965 and ran until 2005,[3, 4] Albert Ellis interviewed two members of the audience who volunteered to discuss an emotional problem for which they needed help. Ellis would interview the volunteer

2 Of not being able to have relations with his wife.
3 Today, this workshop is known as 'Friday Night Live' and is held at the Albert Ellis Institute, where it retains its original format.
4 At the time of writing (December 2022).

for about 30 minutes and then invite members of the audience to ask questions of him and the volunteer as well as to make observations on the therapy session. The volunteer would then be given a recording of the session for their later review. Ellis & Joffe (2002) discovered that the vast majority of volunteers found these single sessions a helpful experience and most of them also benefited from the audience comments.

I have been influenced by Ellis's work and have conducted over 700 single sessions of therapy that I have referred to as 'Very Brief Therapeutic Conversations' (Dryden, 2018a).

MILTON ERICKSON'S SINGLE SESSIONS

Milton Erickson is considered the father of modern hypnotherapy and as one of the most innovative of psychotherapists. A single session was the most common length in all of Erickson's known cases (O'Hanlon & Hexum, 1990) and, thus, he can be said to have significantly contributed to the development of SST. Perhaps the most famous of Erickson's single-session cases was as follows.

Milton Erickson's single session with the 'African violet queen' (O'Hanlon, 1999)

Erickson was asked to see a depressed woman in her sixties by her nephew. She was withdrawn and confined to a wheelchair. During a single visit to her home, Erickson noticed the pride that the woman derived from taking cuttings from her African violets and repotting them. Using this observation, Erickson helped the woman by encouraging her to act in ways consistent with her Christian values, which she had not been doing. He suggested that she first notice who in her local church community had experienced a significant event in their life (e.g., birth, death or marriage), as detailed in her church's bulletin, and then offer them a pot with an African violet as a mark of comfort, condolence or congratulation. She did this consistently and doing so both revitalised her life and reconnected her with the community in which she lived. On her death, she was mourned by many as the 'African Violet Queen of Milwaukee'.

THREE APPROACHES TO PSYCHOTHERAPY (GLORIA)

In 1965, Everett Shostrom, a well-known American psychotherapist, produced a series of filmed therapy demonstration sessions where one patient, known as 'Gloria', was seen by three therapists who had originated specific systems of psychotherapy. These were: Carl Rogers (creator of what is currently known as 'Person Centred Therapy'), Fritz Perls (creator of 'Gestalt Therapy') and Albert Ellis (creator of what is currently known as 'Rational Emotive Behaviour Therapy'). These sessions lasted for 30 minutes or less. While not promoted as examples of SST, this is precisely what they were, and each session showed clearly what could be gained from a very brief therapeutic conversation. As such, the 'Gloria trilogy' (as the films are colloquially known) warrants an important place in the development of SST.

DAVID MALAN AND THE UNEXPECTED EFFECTS OF SINGLE DYNAMIC INTERVIEWS

David Malan and his colleagues (Malan et al.,1975) at the Tavistock Clinic, London, reported on a study of 11 patients who attended for one intake consultation, but did not, for one reason or another, have ongoing therapy. In effect, they had a single therapeutic consultation but made dynamic rather than symptomatic changes, what Malan et al. (1975) called 'apparently genuine improvements'. Another group of 13 patients made symptomatic, but not dynamic, changes as a result of a single intake session (Malan et al., 1968). Taken together, Malan et al.'s (1968, 1975) data show that people can experience a range of benefits from one intake interview to see if they were suitable for dynamic psychotherapy; the effects of this therapy are meant to be evident over a much longer period. Rather than being welcomed, these findings were met with some consternation in the field of psychodynamic therapy as it challenged cherished ideas.

BERNARD BLOOM

Bloom (1981) was one of the first to offer a coherent, focused approach to SST. His approach was informed by psycho-dynamic therapy, and therapy sessions lasted from between 60 and 80 minutes (Bloom, 1992). Like most approaches to SST that came after, Bloom stressed to his SST clients that more sessions would be provided if required.

In his early publication, Bloom (1981) outlined a number of therapeutic factors that characterised his focused approach to SST. These were:

- identify a focal problem;
- do not underestimate the patient's strengths;
- be prudently active;
- explore then present interpretations tentatively;
- encourage the expression of affect;
- use the interview to start a problem-solving process;
- keep track of time;
- do not be overambitious;
- keep factual questions to a minimum;
- do not be overly concerned about the precipitating event;
- avoid detours;
- do not overestimate a client's self-awareness (i.e., don't ignore stating the obvious).

In his later work, Bloom (1992) added the following principles:

- help mobilise social supports;
- educate when patients appear to lack information;
- build in a follow-up plan.

Many of Bloom's principles are present in others' contributions to SST and yet, in my view, his contributions have not been sufficiently well recognised.

MOSHE TALMON

As noted at the beginning of this chapter, the publication of Moshe Talmon's (1990) seminal book on SST was a key moment in its development. In the book, Talmon reports how, when he worked at Kaiser Permanente Medical Center in California during the mid-1980s, he found that a sizeable number of his family clients did not return for a second session despite being offered one (i.e., their single session was often unplanned). Rather than settle for the usual explanations for such a common phenomenon (e.g., 'they are drop-outs', 'these things happen' or 'they weren't ready to change'), Talmon took an unusual step. He contacted the 200 cases he had seen for one session to find out from them what accounted for their single clinic attendance. To his astonishment, he found that '78 percent of the 200 patients I called said that they had got what they wanted out of the single session and felt better or much better about the problem that had led them to seek therapy' (Talmon, 1990: 9). This finding prompted him to team up with two colleagues at Kaiser Permanente, Michael Hoyt and Robert Rosenbaum, who worked primarily with individuals, and the three of them were awarded a research grant to study the effects of planned (rather than unplanned) SST, one of the first studies on this approach.

MICHAEL HOYT, ROBERT ROSENBAUM AND MOSHE TALMON

In the study that Hoyt et al. (1992) conducted, first clients were told that it was their therapist's intention to see if they could be helped in a single session, but that they could have more sessions if needed. The results showed that (a) over half of the 58 patients in the study (58.6%) chose to have only one session; (b) more than 88% reported significant improvement in the problem for which they sought help; (c) more than 65% also reported improvements in other areas; and (d) and there was no difference in outcome and satisfaction between those who elected to have one session and those who chose to have more sessions.

ARNOLD SLIVE AND MONTE BOBELE

Twenty-one years after the publication of Talmon's (1990) seminal text, Slive and Bobele (2011a) published a text on walk-in therapy entitled *When One Hour is All You Have: Effective Therapy for Walk-In Clients*. Interestingly, although walk-in therapy was first documented in Minnesota in 1969, it is not mentioned in Talmon's (1990) book. Slive and Bobele's publication helped put walk-in[5] therapy on the therapeutic map and it has informed later developments in SST.

As the name implies 'walk-in therapy' occurs when a person or group of persons walk in to a service, requesting to see a therapist and is/are able do so almost immediately. It is therapy that seeks to meet a client's 'need' to be helped when the client experiences that 'need' and with minimal intake if any at all. After four general chapters on setting up and delivering walk-in services, Slive and Bobele's book gives six examples of walk-in therapy in various locations in North America.

INTERNATIONAL SYMPOSIA

The development of SST and walk-in therapy has picked up momentum in the second decade of the 21st century. This is evident by the holding of three international symposia. The first was called 'Capturing the Moment' and was held in 2012 in Victoria, Australia, hosted by the Bouverie Centre, part of La Trobe University in Melbourne. The second was called 'Capturing the Moment 2' and was held in 2015 in Banff, Canada, hosted by Wood's Homes, Calgary. The third was called 'Single-Session Thinking: Going Global One Step at a Time' and was held in 2019, again in Victoria, Australia, and hosted for the second time by the Bouverie Centre. All of these

---

5 Recently, the term 'walk-in' has been criticised as excluding those unable to walk and the term 'open-access therapy' is being promoted (Slive, personal communication, 27/9/2022).

symposia spawned edited books (Hoyt & Talmon, 2014a; Hoyt et al., 2018a; Hoyt, Young & Rycroft, 2021) which detail the work that is going on internationally in the SST and walk-in therapy field. Having said that, SST and walk-in therapy services have been particularly widely adopted in Australia and Canada, and it is only fitting that the three international conferences were hosted in these two countries.[6]

---

6 The fourth international symposium, scheduled to take place in Rome in November 2023, was entitled, 'Single-Session Therapies: What, Why and How Single-Session Mindset and Practices are Effective, Effective and Excellent'.

WHAT SST IS NOT

It is also useful to understand the nature of SST by considering what it is not and this will be the focus of this chapter.

SST IS NOT A MODEL OF THERAPY IN ITSELF

It is important to realise that SST is not a therapeutic model. In fact, as Hoyt et al. (2018b) note, there is not one approach to SST. Rather, SST can be practised by therapists from a range of different approaches. Thus, it is best viewed as a way of delivering therapeutic services rather than as a therapeutic approach or model such as CBT or Ericksonian therapy.

SST IS NOT THE ANSWER TO EVERYTHING

When people are first enthused by SST, it is easy for them to think that SST is the answer to everything. It is decidedly not. It has its place, but it is best seen as standing alongside other ways of delivering therapeutic services rather than replacing them.

SST IS NOT A QUICK FIX

The term 'quick fix' in the field of psychotherapy is often used disparagingly to describe a temporary, but ineffective, approach to solving a problem. The implication is that the problem has not been solved, but rather patched up and will return as soon as the temporary solution fails to work. Another derogatory phrase that is used to describe SST is that it is akin to 'putting a sticking plaster over a wound'. Again, the implication is that without properly addressing the wound, the plaster will not work for long.

DOI: 10.4324/9781003386353-4

Using the latter analogy, when it works well, SST does effectively deal with the wound so that subsequent healing can take place. In fact, I see SST as a way of helping a person to get unstuck by encouraging them to find a constructive way forward on which they can capitalise and, thus, move towards solving their problem.

SST IS NOT BETTER BECAUSE IT SAVES MONEY

Some people see SST as an attractive intervention because it saves money. Even if this were to be the case, this is not the prime reason for this way of delivering therapeutic services. What is more important is that SST meets a lot of clients' needs in that 'one' is the most frequently occurring number of sessions people have (see Chapter 6) and it aims to encourage people to help themselves immediately.

SST IS NOT A RESTRICTION ON THE AVAILABILITY OF THERAPY

As discussed in Chapter 1, SST therapists strive to help their clients in one session, but if some of these clients need more sessions, then these are made available to them. It does not place restrictions on the availability of therapy. Rather, it encourages clients to get the most out of what is often the only session they choose to have.

SST IS NOT FIVE, TEN OR MORE SESSIONS DISTILLED INTO ONE

Some people think that SST is like 'therapy speeded up' where the therapist attempts to cram numerous sessions into one session. This is not the case. In fact, if a therapist attempts to do this, it often renders SST ineffective. While it is tempting to give the client as much as possible to take away with them, such an approach often means that the person takes nothing away with them. Because they are overwhelmed with 'thera-peutic goodies', they end up by being dazzled or confused and thus remember very little of the session. As I will discuss in

Chapter 10, 'less is often more' in SST which aims to help the person get the most out of the single session rather than to provide a truncated experience where several sessions are crammed into one.

SST IS NOT THE SAME AS CRISIS INTERVENTION

While a single session can help people with crises, SST is not the same as crisis intervention. Thus, a person does not have to be in crisis to benefit from SST.

SST IS NOT EASY BECAUSE IT IS BRIEF AND FOCUSED

As I will discuss presently, SST is often a very brief, focused mode of intervention. Given this, it is understandable when people think that SST is easy to practise. I tend to think the opposite. Given its brevity and focused nature, it is quite difficult to practise well and SST therapists require high-level therapeutic skills.

SST IS NOT FOR EVERYONE

While SST can be very effective, it is not for everyone. Thus, some clients want ongoing therapy and would not respond well to the offer of a single session even if further sessions may be available. Such clients want the security of an ongoing relationship with a therapist, and their clinical preferences should be respected. Also, SST is not for all therapists. Thus, some therapists like to take their time in planning and carrying out their therapeutic tasks concerning assessment and intervention and would not thrive in practising SST, where such time is at a premium (Dryden, 2016). CBT therapists who believe that intervention can only be meaningfully based on a careful case formulation would, in particular, be hard-pressed to practise SST. Thus, SST should not be foisted on reluctant therapists, nor on reluctant clients. It is best practised when clients see the potential in it, and therapists embrace the challenge of helping clients in the shortest possible period.

4

EVEN A BRIEF ENCOUNTER
CAN BE THERAPEUTIC

Single-session therapy is predicated on the idea that it is possible for therapeutic change to occur when one person has a brief encounter with another person. While this can and does occur in a formal setting, it may also occur as a result of a more informal, even casual, encounter between two people. As an example of the latter, consider what is known as the 'stranger on the train phenomenon' (Rubin, 1973). Here, Person A (let's call him Gavin) meets Person B (let's call him Philip) on a long train journey. Because Philip shows a genuine interest in Gavin, the latter opens up and tells Philip what he is worried about in life, knowing that he will probably never see Philip again. Quite often in such circumstances, people like Gavin gain benefit from talking to people like Philip. This is so for a number of reasons. First, they find the experience of opening up to someone who is genuinely interested in what they have to say therapeutic. Second, in talking to that other person, they may be able to see a solution to their problem that they did not see beforehand. Third, in the course of the conversation, the other person may have said something that they found useful and could implement subsequently. Also, a combination of these factors may have been in play.

While the above shows that people can find a direct brief contact with another person therapeutic, this can also be the case when the contact is brief and indirect. Let me give a personal example of this. I have always had a stammer which was particularly bad in my teenage years, and I was, at that time, quite anxious about speaking in public, or so I thought. One day, I was listening to a radio programme where Michael

  DOI: 10.4324/9781003386353-5

Bentine, a well-known comedian when I was a boy, was being interviewed. In the course of this interview, Bentine mentioned that he too had a bad stammer when he was younger but that he had learned to speak up despite this because he developed the following attitude towards stammering: 'If I stammer, I stammer – too bad!' This struck a chord with me at the time, and I resolved to develop this attitude for myself, by rehearsing it while speaking up without avoiding any problematic words. This approach was very helpful to me, and after a while I was able to speak in public without anxiety; although I still stammered, my stutter was far less pronounced than hitherto. The relevant segment of the radio interview only lasted for a few minutes, but in that time, I strongly resonated with the anti-anxiety attitude he spelt out and my subsequent use of that attitude resulted in long-term benefit.

If personal change only occurred after lengthy therapy, then SST would not exist. The fact that personal change can occur as a result of a brief, and even a very brief, exposure to what other people have to offer us in both direct or indirect form indicates important possibilities for SST.

In SST, therapeutic change is rarely profound (what Miller & C' de Baca, 2001, refer to as 'quantum change'). Rather, it is often small. However, taking a small step forward may help the person see what is possible and provide hope that with continued small steps forward the person may make a meaningful change.

THE EXPANDABLE NATURE
OF THERAPY LENGTH

Therapy takes exactly the length of time allocated for it. When the
therapist and client expect change to happen now, it often does.
(Talmon, 1993: 135)

Several years ago, I was involved in a consultative capacity
helping a student counselling service in a UK university to
adopt an SST approach to its work with students. Originally
this service offered all students 12 sessions of counselling. This
resulted in a very long waiting list for those wishing to use the
service, as existing clients tended to utilise *all* their sessions
because they felt that they were entitled to them. After some
discussion, the service decided to reduce the number of sessions
offered to students to six. Initially, there was outrage that the
number of counselling sessions had been reduced, but things
settled down once a new group of incoming students came to
expect to have six sessions of counselling rather than the previous allocation of 12 sessions. While this new policy reduced
the very long waiting list that had built up in the '12 sessions for
all' arrangement, students who wanted to use the service still
had to wait a long time for an initial counselling appointment.

The service then took the bold step of offering students
'one-at-a-time' counselling. As explained in Chapter 1, this
meant that a student who wanted counselling would initially
be offered one session. If that was sufficient, the counselling
would end there, but if not then the student could book another
single session. As before, existing students used to having six
sessions complained, but once again when the next group of

     DOI: 10.4324/9781003386353-6

incoming students came to expect sessions on a one-at-a-time basis, the service was able to reduce its waiting list to a minimum and students who had a problem requiring counselling could be seen almost immediately.

In this way, the university's counselling service was transformed from one that offered students 12 sessions but had a very long wait to commence counselling to one which offered students a single session at a time when they needed it. When it was introduced, the new single-session, one-at-a-time service was welcomed by students once it became clear that counselling sessions would be immediately available to students when they needed them.

This situation shows that the length of therapy expands according to the expectations set. This has been called 'Parkinson's law of psychotherapy' (Appelbaum, 1975). When the university students discussed above were told that they would receive up to 12 sessions each, those who decided to have more than one session took up their full complement of 12 sessions. When they were then told that they would receive up to six sessions, again those who decided to have more than one session took up their full entitlement to six sessions. Finally, when they were told that they would receive one session at a time when they needed it, with the possibility of booking further sessions, but only one at a time, then counselling tended to last for a single session in most cases.

What this shows is how important structuring clients' expectations is concerning therapy length and that when a client expects therapy to last for a single session, then there is a good chance that the therapist and the client will accomplish what the client is looking for in one session.

THE MODAL NUMBER OF THERAPY SESSIONS INTERNATIONALLY IS 'ONE', AND THE MAJORITY OF PEOPLE WHO ATTEND FOR ONE SESSION ARE SATISFIED

Most training programmes in counselling and psychotherapy are based on the premise that the therapeutic process involves a beginning, middle and end, and extends over time. The assumption is that therapy certainly lasts for more than one session. In fact, in the programmes that I trained in, SST was not even mentioned.

THE MODAL NUMBER OF THERAPY SESSIONS INTERNATIONALLY IS 'ONE'

While it is clear that many therapies last for more than one session, with some extending over many years, it is also true that the modal number of sessions is 'one'. This means that the most frequently occurring number of sessions that people have is 'one'.

Moshe Talmon (1990) discovered that this was the case while working at the Kaiser Permanente Medical Center in California. There, he examined the patterns of practice of individual therapists and found that for every single therapist the modal length of therapy was one session and that this was consistent across a five-year period from 1983 to 1988. Talmon (1990) also reviewed the literature and found that other people had discovered the same thing.

 DOI: 10.4324/9781003386353-7

This single-session mode appears to be the case internationally. For example, J. Young (2018) cites data provided by the Victoria Department of Human Services in Australia. Their client contact data showed that for three years in a row between 2002 and 2005, 42% of over 115,206 clients in community health counselling centres attended only one session; 18% two sessions; and 10% three sessions. These percentages were almost identical for each of the three years.

THE MAJORITY OF PEOPLE WHO ATTEND FOR ONE SESSION ARE SATISFIED

The most frequently occurring number of sessions that clients have may be 'one', but are they happy with the 'one' session that they have? As discussed in Chapter 2, there is certainly evidence that clients are happy with SST. If you remember, Talmon (1990) reported that 78% of the 200 of his one-session clients were satisfied with the one session that they had with him. Also, of Hoyt et al.'s (1992) sample of 58 clients, more than 88% reported significant improvement in the problem for which they sought help and more than 65% also reported improvements in other areas.

Now, given that Talmon, Hoyt and Rosenbaum are competent therapists and had a special interest in SST, it may be that the level of reported client satisfaction can be attributed to such variables. Indeed, Simon et al. (2012) in a study of clients who did or did not return for a second session found that the single-session clients had either the best outcomes or the worse outcomes. The best outcome SST clients were most satisfied with treatment and reported a good working alliance with their therapists. By contrast, the worst outcome SST clients were least satisfied with treatment and reported a poor working alliance with their therapists. Taken together, the research discussed in this chapter indicates that while clients are often satisfied with SST, this is not universally the case.

If the modal number of therapy sessions is 'one' and clients are generally happy with this single session, but therapists are not adequately prepared to offer SST, then we have a serious gap between what clients are seeking (according to their behaviour) and what therapists are providing for them. As I detailed in Chapter 1, while SST is developing, training courses in SST are thin on the ground, and thus there is a need both for therapists to be trained in SST and for therapy services to offer SST as a part of what they provide for their clients.

IT IS DIFFICULT TO PREDICT, WITH ACCURACY, HOW MANY THERAPY SESSIONS A CLIENT WILL ATTEND

You may think that with all the progress that has been made in developing scales and measures to be used in psychotherapy research and from all we know about the effectiveness of psychotherapy that we should be able to predict with accuracy how many therapy sessions specific clients are likely to attend. If we were able to do this, it would enable us to refer clients to therapies of appropriate length, safe in the knowledge that they would be receiving the appropriate 'dose' of psychotherapy and that scarce therapy resources were being well deployed. Sadly, the reality is that our attempts to predict, with accuracy, how many therapy sessions clients will attend have not proven successful (Quick, 2012). This means that while you may think that a specific client may benefit from 12 sessions of psychotherapy, for example, based on a full assessment of their problems and coping skills and also of their treatment length preferences, the truth is that this person may only attend a single therapy session.

Given this, it might well be sensible for you to approach this client as if you are only going to see them once. This does not mean that you will only see them once, but that you approach the session as if this is going to happen because the research literature (reviewed in Chapter 6) indicates that this is the most likely scenario.

DOI: 10.4324/9781003386353-8

8

WHAT IS A 'DROP-OUT'?

Traditionally, a client who does not attend for a second session or subsequent sessions of psychotherapy, when it is indicated that they do so, is regarded as a 'drop-out' from treatment. The term 'drop-out' is generally viewed in a negative light. In the clinician's mind, it indicates that the fault may lie with one or more of three factors. First, the fault may lie with the client (e.g., 'The client wasn't ready to change'). Second, the fault may lie with the therapist (e.g., 'The therapist failed to understand the client'). Third, the fault may lie in the therapeutic relationship (e.g., 'The therapeutic alliance between the therapist and the client was poor'). Other terms that describe the same phenomenon also point to the negative connotations placed on this phenomenon (e.g., 'psychotherapy attrition', 'premature termination', 'psychotherapy discontinuation' and 'unilateral termination').

In Chapter 2, I discussed Talmon's (1990) discovery that of 200 clients whom he saw for one session, 78% indicated that they were helped by this session and required no further treatment. What Talmon did was to question the received wisdom that 'psychotherapy drop-outs' is evidence of treatment failure. Rather, he suggested that the situation where the client decides that they do not need further treatment was an indication that something positive had transpired. If so, then it makes no sense to refer to this phenomenon as indicating that the client had 'dropped out' of treatment, but that the client had got what they wanted from treatment.

It is my view that the term 'drop-out' should not be used in psychotherapy because it is biased and value-laden. The term is often used to indicate that the client, in choosing not

 DOI: 10.4324/9781003386353-9

to return for a second session of psychotherapy, has decided to leave the process earlier than their therapist thinks they should. By contrast, my suggestion is that when a client does not attend a second session of psychotherapy, we should conclude that we do not know what this means. It may mean that they did not find the process helpful and thus decided to leave an unhelpful process. However, it could equally mean that they did find the process helpful and thus decided to leave a helpful process because they did not require further help. The research that I mentioned in Chapter 6 by Simon et al. (2012) indicates that this is the more accurate view despite the title of their paper: 'Is dropout after a first psychotherapy visit always a bad outcome?'

In conclusion, when a client does not return for a second therapy session, it is far from indicating a bad outcome. It may indicate a good outcome, as demonstrated by a client perspective study of self-termination carried out by Scamardo, Bobele and Biever (2004). Further investigation is generally needed to discover the meaning of the non-attendance.

INTERMITTENT THERAPY
THROUGH THE LIFE CYCLE

If you are ill, you go and see your GP who will diagnose the problem and offer you medical treatment via prescription. Alternatively, they may send you for further investigation if they are uncertain about the nature of your illness. The goal of all this is to restore you to your pre-illness state. Most frequently you will have a single consultation with your GP and go some time again in the future when you are ill again. This pattern may be described as you having intermittent consultations with your GP.

Nicholas Cummings (e.g., Cummings, 1990; Cummings & Sayama, 1995) has argued for a similar model in mental health. Rather than sign up for lengthy and time-consuming psychotherapy, Cummings advocated that people should consult a therapist when they have a problem and leave therapy when that problem has been solved. Then, when they experience another problem, they should consult a therapist again, and this process should continue throughout their lifetime. Cummings referred to this as 'brief intermittent psychotherapy throughout the life cycle'. The major difference between the medical context and the therapy context in this respect is as follows. In the latter, the person can learn to become their own therapist and apply what they have learned from specific help-seeking episodes to other problems that they may have, only seeking help from a therapist when their efforts at self-help fail.

This model of brief intermittent therapy through the life cycle sits easily with SST. Here, Cummings (1990) would recommend the use of targeted, focused interventions and when the client's goal has been achieved treatment is 'interrupted'

 DOI: 10.4324/9781003386353-10

rather than terminated. The therapist is urged to do something novel in the first (and perhaps only) session, and the client is encouraged to take whatever they have learned in the session and to apply it to their life outside the session. To Cummings's suggestions, I would add that clients can be encouraged to utilise their internal strengths and external resources in addressing their psychological problems again within a single-session framework.

SOONER IS BETTER AND
LESS IS MORE

In this chapter, I will discuss two important principles that, in my view, help to underpin the theory and practice of SST. The first relates to the timing of therapy sessions ('sooner is better') and the second relates to what is done in therapy sessions ('less is more').

SOONER IS BETTER

In Chapter 5, I mentioned the work that I did at a UK university, helping it to establish a one-at-a-time counselling service where students could book one single session at a time rather than be offered a six-session or 12-session contract as a matter of course as happened hitherto. There were two immediate effects of this new service. First, the waiting list for counselling virtually disappeared and students were able to be seen at the point of need. Second, the students themselves gave positive feedback, saying how much they appreciated being seen when they needed to be seen. For these students, sooner was decidedly better.

LESS IS MORE

When I started to implement SST in my practice, I experienced internal pressure to give my SST clients as much as I could so that they could get the most out of the session. I call this 'Jewish Mother Syndrome'. When I used to visit my mother, she would only be happy if, when I left, I took as much food away with me as I could carry. Only then would she feel that she was being a good mother. As I became more experienced at

  DOI: 10.4324/9781003386353-11

SST, I found out that giving clients as many ways of helping themselves as possible was counterproductive. They reported that they felt overwhelmed, with the result that they could not apply anything I gave them. Alternatively, when I reduced my expectations for myself and helped my clients take away one thing that they could apply immediately in their lives, they reported greater satisfaction with the SST experience than they did when I 'threw the therapeutic kitchen sink' at them. What these experiences taught me is that as well as 'sooner is better', in SST 'less is more'.

HUMAN BEINGS CAN HELP THEMSELVES QUICKLY UNDER SPECIFIC CIRCUMSTANCES

SST is predicated on the notion that human beings are capable of helping themselves quickly in a short period and can develop and maintain what they have found to be self-helping. If personal change could only be initiated after, say, a year, then SST would not exist. In my view, to initiate self-help quickly, four important conditions need to be present: (1) knowledge; (2) a committed reason to change; (3) taking appropriate action; and (4) preparedness to accept the costs of change, if any. If all four ingredients are present, then the person will be able to initiate change in a short period. Let me deal with these conditions one at a time. In doing so, I will discuss the case of 'Vera' a client of Albert Ellis and discussed in Dryden (2022a) and compare this with the case of the 'African Violet Queen', a person whom Erickson saw for a single session (O'Hanlon, 1999)[1] as first mentioned in Chapter 2.

> Vera, had sought help for her elevator phobia from Albert Ellis and because she could not afford individual therapy sessions she joined one of Ellis's groups. While Vera accepted the idea that she needed to confront her fear by going on elevators, she resisted acting on this idea and the efforts of Ellis and her fellow group members to identify and deal with all the obstacles that she erected

---

1 Strictly speaking, the 'African Violet Queen' was not a client of Erickson's. Her nephew, who knew Erickson, asked him to visit when he was in Milwaukee because he was worried about his aunt who was depressed and withdrawn.

     DOI: 10.4324/9781003386353-12

to prevent her from actually entering an elevator. Throughout this, Vera maintained that she really wanted to overcome her elevator phobia.

One day, Vera booked an individual session with Ellis on a late Friday afternoon, which was a very unusual occurrence. She had just heard that the company she worked for was moving their office suite from the fifth floor of a skyscraper to the 105th floor of the same building. Moreover, they were moving over the weekend and planned to be up and running in their new suite early Monday morning. Hitherto, Vera had been able to climb the five flights of stairs, but there was no way, she reasoned, that she could climb 105 flights of stairs every day. Vera was desperate to keep her job and implored Ellis to help her deal with her fear so that she could take the elevator to the 105th floor on Monday morning. Ellis told her that if she wanted to achieve her goal then she would have to commit herself to going up and down elevators in tall skyscrapers all weekend and to accept the great discomfort of doing so. Vera did just that until she had got over her fear. Repeated practice proved effective as it would have done years earlier when Vera first sought therapy, but she did not engage with it at that time.

Dryden (2022a: 50–51)

KNOWING WHAT TO DO TO CHANGE

It is important that a person has some understanding of what they need to do to change. This knowledge can be explicit or implicit. Such explicit knowledge is a feature of SST based on CBT, for example (Dryden, 2022a), or it can be implicit as in the single-session work of Milton Erickson (O'Hanlon & Hexum, 1990).

As discussed above, Vera had an elevator phobia and explicitly knew that to deal constructively with this problem, she had to ride on elevators frequently. The 'African Violet Queen' probably knew, implicitly, that acting according to her Christian values (by sending pots of African violets to members of her local church) would be helpful to her as well as to them. Thus, I would argue that both 'knew' what they needed to do to change.

HAVING A COMMITTED REASON TO CHANGE

Unless the person has a reason to change and this reason is important for the person then the person will probably not change. Prior to her office move, Vera never really had to use elevators. The office where she worked was on the 5th floor of a building, and she was able to walk up five flights of stairs. Thus, for a good while, she flirted with the idea of change but did not go through with it. When the office moved to the 105th floor she had a committed reason to change because she needed to keep her job. Effectively, she had to change over the weekend, or she was out of a job. The Christian value of giving to her community was very important to the 'African Violet Queen', and Erickson found a way for her to practise this value. He showed her the link between actualising this value and the giving of African violets which was her passion.

TAKING APPROPRIATE ACTION

A person may have a committed reason to change, but unless they take appropriate action, then change won't happen. In order to keep her job Vera took action by taking many elevator rides over a short period. If she hadn't, she would not have addressed her problem effectively. If the 'African Violet Queen' had acknowledged that giving pots of African violets to members of her church's congregation was a good idea, but had not done so, then it would have been unlikely that her depressed mood would have abated.

BEING PREPARED TO ACCEPT THE COSTS OF PERSONAL CHANGE, IF ANY

Change is often painful. It involves some discomfort and may involve the loss of certain benefits. If the person is not prepared to accept these costs, then they will soon stop taking appropriate action discussed above, and any change that they may have made may well evaporate. Vera was prepared to tolerate the considerable discomfort that she experienced while embarking on her exposure programme. She did this to keep her job. By contrast, it is not clear from O'Hanlon's account what were the costs of change for the 'African Violet Queen'. It may have been that she had to give up the comfort of staying away from people. Such withdrawal may have become familiar to her and, as we all know, surrendering the familiar, even though it is healthy for us to do, so can be painful.

THE CHOICE OF SST IS THE CLIENT'S, BUT SOMETIMES THIS CHOICE IS LIMITED

By and large, the field of SST emphasises the importance of client determination, and this is especially true concerning who is responsible for choosing whether or not a therapy is to be single-session or not. This is clearly the case when *SST is by default*. Here, the therapist recommends that the client has a further session or sessions and one of two things happen. First, the client decides not to follow the therapist's recommendation and does not make an appointment. Second, the client makes an appointment for a further session, but either cancels it later or does not show up for it. Thus, SST by default is the client's choice.

Then we have *the possibility of SST*. Here, the therapist mentions that it is *possible* to get the work done in one session, but, if not, then further sessions are available. The onus is on the client to choose whether SST meets their needs or not and does so after the session has been conducted. In this scenario, clients may be told something like:

> We have found that a large number of our patients can benefit from a single visit here. Of course, if you need more therapy, we can provide it. But I want you to know that I am willing to work with you hard today to help resolve your problem quickly, perhaps even in this single visit, as long as you are ready to start doing whatever is necessary.
>
> (Hoyt, Rosenbaum & Talmon, 1990: 37–38)

When *SST is planned*, the client exercises their choice at the outset. They either agree to attend a planned single-session

 DOI: 10.4324/9781003386353-13

intervention (organised in advance), or they attend a 'walk-in' service where they are seen immediately (Hymmen, Stalker & Cait, 2013). Here, there is no expectation that there will be further therapy.

Finally, we have *one-at-a-time therapy (OAATT)*. As discussed earlier, this concept was first used by Hoyt (2011) to refer to the idea that therapy 'takes place one contact at a time, and one contact may be all the time that is needed'. In practice, this concept has been utilised by numerous university counselling services in the UK, one of which I referred to in Chapter 5. To address the problem of waiting lists and offer help to students when they need it, services are restructured so that students can make an appointment for an immediate single counselling session. If they need a further session, they can book one, but what they cannot do is book a series of counselling sessions. This shows that while students can choose to have one or more sessions of counselling, these can only be booked one at a time. Client choice here is still present but limited by the exigencies of supply of and demand for therapy sessions in a student population.

TIME IN SST

Talmon and Hoyt (2014: 469) note that 'Single-session therapy is predicated on the belief and expectation that change can occur *in the moment*'. Thus, in Chapter 4, I spoke of my shift of perspective on my stammer after listening to Michael Bentine discuss the importance of de-catastrophising stammering to deal constructively with it. Although I had to act on this shift in perspective for it to affect my feelings and behaviour, something fundamental in me changed *the moment* I heard Bentine talk on this subject. As St Augustine noted in the fourth century, the present is all we have. So, when a client is talking about their past or possible future, they are doing so in that moment. As such, SST seeks to effect change in the moment. This is why skilled SST therapists do not deter clients from discussing the past since they know that change about the past happens in the present moment.

Time is relevant in SST in the following ways.

HELP AT THE POINT OF NEED

Virtually, all therapists wish to help people in distress as quickly as possible. I have not heard a therapist say that they would prefer to try and help someone only when they have been on a long waiting list for therapy! Single-session therapy is more likely than ongoing therapy to enable therapists to offer clients help quickly since SST is based on providing help at the point of client need. If the person is seen quickly then they are more likely to be ready to make personal changes than if they have applied for help and are only seen after being placed on a lengthy waiting list.

DOI: 10.4324/9781003386353-14

PROVIDE HELP IMMEDIATELY

In ongoing therapy, actual therapy tends to start after the therapist has taken a case history, carried out an assessment of the client and, if relevant, has conducted a case formulation. By contrast in SST, therapy begins from moment one and thus the SST therapist makes efficient use of time.

USE SESSION TIME EFFICIENTLY

Another way that the single-session therapist uses time efficiently is by helping the client to identify what they want to take from the session and by focusing the work to that end. Much can be achieved when both therapist and client proceed on this basis.

TIME PERCEPTION

As will be discussed in Chapter 20, the time allocated to the session in SST varies. Some therapists think that the 50 minutes allocated to the session (for example) is short, while others consider it ample to help the client achieve their session goal. Therefore, it is the therapist's relationship with time that is more important than the time itself. I sometimes suggest to therapists who think that the period of 50 minutes is short that they sit in a room for that length of time with no distractions and set a time to go off at the end of this period. Invariably, such therapists realise that this time period is actually much longer than they previously thought and thus they have more time to help the client achieve their stated wants than they think they have.

THE SST MINDSET AND ITS PRACTICAL IMPLICATIONS

As discussed in Chapter 1, there is no consensus as to the nature of SST. However, there is a widespread acceptance in the field that SST is characterised more by mindset than by approach. This means that the SST therapist approaches therapy with a new client with a way of thinking that is distinct from thinking that is more closely associated with ongoing therapy. The following ideas characterise the SST mindset. Cannistrà (2022: 1) states that a mindset is 'the therapist's series of beliefs which influence the actions and decisions taken in the course of their work'.

THINK MAYBE ONE, MAYBE MORE, BUT BE OPEN TO BOTH

Perhaps the main principle within the mindset is where the therapist approaches the first session with a client thinking that this may be the only session that the client will have and, consequently, they will endeavour to help the client get the most from the session even though the client may choose to have more sessions. However, there are SST therapists who dissent, arguing that it describes a situation that the client has a single session and that is that.

My view on this issue is that the SST mindset is more flexible than the 'only one session' view of SST and thus suits better therapists with a pluralistic perspective on therapy. Thus, the SST mindset incorporates *both* a one-session approach to therapy *and* an approach where a client may have an additional session or sessions. Its key factor for me is that it advocates

DOI: 10.4324/9781003386353-15

helping the client get the most out of the session that they attend whether it is the first session or not. Since the therapist does not know whether the client will return for additional sessions, whether they have only had one session or whether they have had more, the best approach is to help them to maximise the session that they are having. By contrast, it is difficult to conceive of a one-session approach to SST that is not based on an SST mindset, particularly if we are talking about SST by design.

Jeff Young (2018) has recommended that the single-session therapist keeps this 'maybe one, maybe more' principle in mind regardless of the severity or complexity of the client's problem and regardless of any diagnosis the client may have received. This is controversial because when first exposed to SST clinicians often ask about the contra-indications for SST. Young's point is that people with a variety of complex problems do seem to benefit from SST and just because someone has severe or complex problems, it does not mean that they are going to attend more than one session. Hoyt & Talmon (2014b: 503), in a review of the literature, present evidence that shows that 'the efficacy of SSTs is not restricted to 'easy' cases but can have more far-reaching effects in many areas, including treatment of alcohol and substance abuse as well as self-harming behavior'.

THE WORK IS CLIENT-LED

One of the guiding principles of SST is that it is structured according to the client's stated wants. Thus, the therapist approaches the session with this principle in mind and focuses on what the client wants to discuss and provides the type of help that the client wants with respect to this issue. The only exception to this is where the client wants to achieve something that is, in the therapist's view, harmful to them. In this case, the therapist will raise their concerns about the client's stated wants in a transparent way and facilitate a discussion on this point.

One of the difficulties that therapists new to SST have here occurs when the client in the course of discussing what they have come to talk about mentions something that the therapist regards as more significant than the presenting issue. Such therapists have been educated to distinguish between the client's 'presenting' issue and their 'real' issue. Consequently, they are sceptical about working with the client's 'presenting' issue even though this issue is the client's priority. When such therapists bring the SST mindset to SST they follow the client's lead.

IDENTIFY AND MEET THE CLIENT'S PREFERENCES FOR BEING HELPED

In Chapter 22, I will discuss the different types of help that clients seek from single-session therapy. The important point from the perspective of the single-session mindset is that the therapist keeps in mind the importance of the client's preferences for being helped and of meeting these preferences unless there is a good reason not to do so. This is an important point for the therapist to bear in mind because while most SST clients seek help for emotional/behavioural problems, not all do. Thus, it would not be good practice to offer a client emotional problem-solving, for example, when they want to have an opportunity to get things offer their chest and express their feelings about an issue.

HOLD IN MIND THE IMPORTANCE OF NEGOTIATING AN END-OF-SESSION GOAL WITH THE CLIENT

While it is not uncommon for a therapist with an 'ongoing therapy' mindset to ask a client what they would like to achieve by the end of therapy, it is rarer for such a therapist to ask the client what they would like to achieve from the end of the first session. However, this is the norm in SST. Thus, the therapist would discuss with the client what they would want to achieve by the end of the session rather than by the end of therapy. This encourages the client to specify a goal that is immediate rather than one that is a long way into the future. Doing this makes it more likely that the person would achieve their goal and be satisfied with the first session. As such the client may be less likely to request further sessions than they may do when the therapist does not ask them for an end-of-session goal.

If the client in SST sets more than one goal, then the therapist would work with the client to prioritise on which goal they should focus. Such negotiation tends to be client-led.

KEEP IN MIND THE CO-CREATION OF A THERAPEUTIC FOCUS AND MAINTAIN IT ONCE CREATED

Aside from when a client says that they want to use the session to just talk about whatever they want to talk about, the SST therapist will keep in mind the importance of co-creating a therapeutic focus with the client. The creation of such a focus increases the chances that the client will take away from the session what they have come for.

To ensure that the negotiated focus is maintained, the therapist would check in with the client at various points to ensure that therapy is on the right track. Also, the therapist would tactfully interrupt the client and gently bring them back to the agreed focus when their mind wanders onto other matters.

FOCUS ON CLIENT STRENGTHS AND ENVIRONMENTAL RESOURCES

As I have stressed in this book, the SST therapist integrates two seemingly different ideas: that they will work with the client to help them achieve what they want from the session and they will provide the client with more help if needed. Given the therapist does not know at the outset which of these two outcomes will transpire, they will use the session to help the client to achieve their stated wants by utilising the client's internal strengths and external resources (see Chapters 27 and 28).

THINK ABOUT THE CLIENT'S TAKE-AWAY(S)

It is important for the SST therapist to keep in mind that it is crucial for the client to take away something meaningful from the session. This is particularly relevant if the client decides to seek no further help. Ideally, a take-away is a broad helping principle that the client can use across relevant situations. In this way, it differs from a homework assignment which tends to be more specific and checked by the therapist at the next session. In SST, there may be no next session.

HELP THE CLIENT LEAVE THE SESSION WITH THEIR MORALE RESTORED: END THE SESSION WELL

Jerome Frank (1961) argued that while people seeking therapy come with a multitude of symptoms, what unites them is that they tend to come in a state of demoralisation. Consequently, SST therapists keep it in mind that it is important to help the client leave the session with their morale restored, if at all possible. This involves ending the session well. When this is done the client takes away something meaningful from the session that will make a difference to their life, have had an opportunity to tell the therapist everything that they needed to say on the presented issue and to ask everything they needed, to ask and have a clear idea how to access further help if needed.

Table 14.1 Fourteen principles identified by Cannistrà (2022) as comprising the typical mindset of a single-session therapist

1.	A single session may be enough
2.	The therapist can play an active role
3.	People have resources they can use to feel better
4.	The client is the expert in their own life
5.	Different methods may be used
6.	Further sessions may be needed
7.	SST is suitable for different contexts and needs
8.	It's fine to aim for small or simple interventions
9.	It's fine to have less prior knowledge
10.	It's best to stick with process and the here and now
11.	Results are mainly achieved outside the session
12.	A structure is needed for the single session
13.	A client–therapist relationship can be established rapidly
14.	Nothing is taken for granted

In conclusion, Cannistrà (2022) in a recent review of the literature identified fourteen principles which make up the typical mindset of a single-session therapist. These are listed in Table 14.1.

CLIENT EMPOWERMENT

Talmon and Hoyt (2014: 471) state that SST is based firmly on the idea that 'clients/patients have the capacity to alter their thoughts, emotions, and behaviors to bring about significant changes'. Thus, despite the SST therapist's contribution, it is what the client takes away from the process that matters, as we have seen in the previous chapter. This is why SST therapists sometimes note that what they regard as a brilliant session has had little effect on the client while what they consider to be a mundane session has led the client to make significant changes. Concerning client change, the power is with the client, rather than with the therapist. The skill of the therapist is to encourage the client to use their power in order to actualise their capacity for self-change.

As noted in the previous chapter, SST is also based on the idea that once clients have made a change, they can maintain and enhance their gains by utilising both their inner strengths and external resources so that a virtuous cycle of change is initiated. Talmon and Hoyt (2014: 471) refer to this as a 'positive cascade of "ripple effects"'. In short, SST stresses client empowerment both in the initiation of change *and* in its maintenance and enhancement.

DOI: 10.4324/9781003386353-16

SERVICE DELIVERY

As I have stressed, SST is not an approach to psychotherapy as CBT or person-centred therapy are. Rather it is both a way of thinking about therapy, more formally referred to as the SST mindset (see Chapter 14), and it is a way of delivering services. In this chapter, I will focus on the latter.

Here I will discuss ways in which SST can be delivered. First, I will first discuss how SST can be delivered by appointment Then, I will discuss open access SST (more commonly known as walk-in therapy). Finally, I will discuss the different formats in which SST can be delivered.

SST BY APPOINTMENT

As the term makes clear, when SST is delivered by appointment, the person makes an appointment, waits for a short period and then attends the appointment. It is important that the time between the making of the appointment and the attending of the appointment is used well. Thus, it is typical for single-session minded agencies and therapists to ask the client to pre-pare for the session by completing a pre-session questionnaire and sharing it with the agency/therapist before the session takes place (see Chapter 49).

I will now discuss three ways that SST by appointment can be implemented.

SST is offered alongside other modes of therapy delivery: I. The client chooses which mode to access

When SST is offered alongside other modes of therapy delivery, before making a decision, clients are provided with

DOI: 10.4324/9781003386353-17

clear descriptions of the nature of each available mode and, more importantly, how much time they will have to wait to access each one. Once the client has made their decision the agency/therapist accepts this unless there is a good reason for this to be questioned.

SST is offered alongside other modes of therapy delivery: II. The agency determines whether a client should be referred for SST

Here, the agency determines to which mode of therapy delivery a person should be referred based on a set of criteria determined by the agency. While the person will be consulted the final decision is usually the agency's. This option is the least favoured by the SST community because it is therapist/agency-centred rather than client-centred.

The embedded approach

The embedded approach to SST (also known as the gateway approach), as the term signifies, embeds SST as central to the offerings of the agency. In most traditional therapy agencies, when attending their first appointment, the client is assessed for their suitability for one of several modes of therapy delivery offered by the agency. Thus, the first appointment routinely involves assessment, not therapy. In the embedded approach to SST, the client's first appointment involves the delivery of a single session of therapy, not a single session of assessment. Ethically, the client should be informed of this before attending the session with any alternatives being outlined if they are not happy to proceed with this way of working. As has already been mentioned, the client should also be informed that more help is available if needed after the single session and typically such clients are contacted two to three weeks after the session to see whether they require more help.

OPEN-ACCESS SST

More commonly known as 'walk-in SST', the term 'open-access SST' is used to highlight the fact that not everybody can walk into a service offering a single session that day without an appointment. Open access also makes it clear that anybody can access the service and that there are no barriers to receiving SST. Given the fact that there is a short wait before a person seeking help from an open access SST agency, the person can still complete a form designed to help them to prepare for their session so that they get the most from it. It should be made clear, however, that the completion of the form is voluntary, not mandatory, but when it is completed it can be shared with the therapist so that the latter knows what the client wants to gain from the session and a little about the context of the issue for which the person is seeking help.

DELIVERY FORMAT

Single-session therapy can be delivered in a variety of formats: face-to-face in person, face-to-face online (e.g., by Zoom), by email or by text-based communication. Ideally, the fundamental principle of SST can be maintained across these formats (i.e., let's work together to help you achieve what you want to achieve today, but more help is available if needed. However, the 'further help' part of the principle will be dependent upon what particular agencies can offer.

THE DIVERSE NATURE OF SST

As you have probably gathered by now, SST is quite a diverse field and, in this chapter, I will demonstrate just how diverse it is.

WHO INITIATES SST?

SST can be initiated by the client, by both the therapist and the client jointly, by the therapist or by an interested third party.

Client-initiated SST

The client may initiate SST before the session begins, after it finishes or books another session and either cancels it or does not show up for it. Please note that in this section, SST can be both one session and where the client accesses more help.

The client initiates SST at the outset. When the client initiates SST at the outset, they announce that they will only be attending therapy for that one session. In this situation, SST is a fait accompli, and thus, it is not an example of therapist–client jointly initiated SST (see below). Client-initiated SST at the outset may happen for a variety of reasons:

- The client may have a clear purpose in mind and decides that they will only need a single session to achieve that purpose.
- For practical reasons, the person can only attend a single session of therapy. This may be due to geographical reasons or financial reasons, amongst other practical factors. Thus, geographically, the person may live a long way from the therapist and cannot travel to the therapist for more than one session. Financially, the person may only be able to afford one session of therapy.

 DOI: 10.4324/9781003386353-18

- Somebody has insisted that the person consults a therapist and to satisfy this other person, the client attends for a single session of therapy and announces this at the beginning of the session.

The client initiates SST after the session finishes. At the end of the session, the client may decide that they do not need to book another appointment. When the client announces this, it usually is because the person has found the session helpful and has got what they were looking for from the appointment. However, it may be that the person has not found the session helpful and decides not to make another appointment for this reason. Occasionally, they may tell the therapist this, but more frequently they may express equivocation about booking another session.

The client cancels or does not show for a second booked session. The situation where a client makes an appointment for a second session, but either cancels it ahead of time or does not show up for it, without cancelling it, may be referred to as 'unplanned SST' (Talmon, 1990). This situation is typically regarded as an indication that the patient has 'dropped out of treatment' or 'terminated treatment prematurely'. As discussed in Chapter 2, one of the key factors in the development of SST was Talmon's (1990) discovery that 78% of 200 of his patients who only had one session with him, *the majority of them unplanned,* found that single session helpful to them.

Therapist–client jointly initiated SST

Therapist–client jointly initiated SST occurs in one of two situations. First, it occurs when both the client and the therapist agree that they will only meet for one session. Second, it occurs when they agree that they will try to get the work done in that one session, but that a further session (or sessions) is (are) available should the client indicate the need.

In my clinical practice, when a person seeks my help, I first outline the range of therapeutic services that I offer including SST. Then, if they indicate a preference for SST, we have a brief conversation where I discuss how I practise SST and detail the practicalities involved (e.g., scheduling and fees). If the client wishes to proceed and I concur then SST has been initiated by both of us.

Therapist-initiated SST

Occasionally, the therapist will initiate SST. This may occur before the session occurs or after it has taken place.

The therapist initiates SST at the outset. An example, of this, might be where the therapist may want to give the client a flavour of the broad approach taken by the therapist (e.g., CBT), but will then refer the person on to a therapist practising the approach for ongoing therapy. This may happen because the consulting therapist is too busy to take on another ongoing client, but is prepared to see the client once so that they can decide if the approach is for them. Of course, if the client agrees, it could be said that this is an example of therapist–client-initiated SST, but as the therapist is setting the agenda and the client agrees reluctantly, it is best viewed as an example of therapist-initiated SST at the outset.

The therapist initiates SST at the end of the session. At the end of the session, the therapist may decide to offer the client no further sessions and thus initiates SST themselves. This may be for the following reasons:

- The therapist may think that the client can utilise the session and needs no further session.
- The therapist thinks that the client is not suitable for the approach that the therapist practises.
- The therapist thinks that the client would not benefit from therapy per se.

In each of these situations, the therapist explains the reason why they are not going to offer the client more sessions. If at all possible, SST therapists tend to eschew making such unilateral decisions, but there may be times when some would choose to do so.

DIFFERENT TYPES OF SST

As I will discuss in greater detail in Parts 7 and 8 of this book, there are different types of SST. I mention them in brief here to show the diverse nature of SST.

Walk-in therapy

As the name makes clear, walk-in therapy describes a situation where a person 'walks into' a therapy service and is seen for a single session of therapy. As Slive, McElheran and Lawson (2008: 6) say:

> walk-in therapy enables clients to meet with a mental health professional at their moment of choosing. There is no red tape, no triage, no intake process, no waiting list, and no wait. There is no formal assessment, no formal diagnostic process, just one hour of therapy focused on clients' stated wants.

However, Slive and Bobele (2011c: 38), echoing the single-session mindset discussed in Chapter 13, note that:

> walk-in counselling does not necessarily mean a single session … However, with a walk-in mindset, therapists are always thinking that the current session is potentially the final one. We organize our sessions with that thought in mind and strive to be maximally effective in every session.

Clinical demonstrations

Clinical demonstrations are single sessions of therapy where the therapist demonstrates their approach to therapy with a volunteer from the audience. The audience is usually comprised of trained and trainee therapists when the demonstrations occur in a professional workshop setting (Barber, 1990) or of a mixture of therapists and interested lay people when the demonstrations occur in workshops open to a mixed audience (Dryden, 2018a; Ellis & Joffe, 2002).

Filmed training tapes

As discussed in Chapter 1, one of the important landmarks in the development of SST was the so-called 'Gloria' films where Carl Rogers, Albert Ellis and Fritz Perls counselled a client named 'Gloria' (not her real name). The purpose of this series of films and the two further series which were produced subsequently was educational, to show therapists how leading practitioners practised their craft. The sessions were, in fact, examples of SST as the client only saw each therapist for a single session. This tradition of filmed training tapes has continued. For example, the American Psychological Association (APA) produces a large number of such DVDs for use in clinical training and as continuing professional development (see www.apa.org/pubs/videos).

Second opinions

In medicine, it is not uncommon for a patient to be sent for or request a second opinion if they are not progressing as well as might be expected from their consultations with their original physician or specialist. The same is also true in the field of psychotherapy. Thus, I have sometimes been asked to offer a second opinion by a fellow therapist, and I invariably see the client only once. I provide an example of this form of SST in Chapter 97.

THE GOALS OF SST

What can be realistically achieved in SST? In addressing this issue, I will first consider the therapist's goals in SST and then the client's.

THE THERAPIST'S GOALS

Slive and Bobele (2014), writing primarily about walk-in therapy, mention numerous factors that they hope that clients will gain at the end of a single session of therapy and that the therapist should aim to promote. Different factors may be appropriate for different clients.

A sense of emotional relief

Quite often people 'bottle up' their feelings about their problems and the act of voicing their concerns to a professional who listens intently to them and gives them an opportunity to speak about their concerns in their own way can lead to a sense of emotional relief which may be all the person may need.

A sense of hope

If a person comes to SST with a sense of hopelessness, then the therapist should strive to help the person gain a sense of hope by the end of the session. This is best done by listening to the person, accepting their distress, helping them to identify their strengths, which they may have forgotten about, and encouraging them to think of ways to apply these strengths to the problem about which they feel hopeless.

DOI: 10.4324/9781003386353-19

A change of perspective

A person may maintain their problem because of how they think of the problem or about the situation that gives rise to the problem. Helping the person to think differently about the problem or the situation can provide them with a new perspective that may help them to solve the problem.

Doing something different

I mentioned above that a person might maintain their problem through the perspective that they have taken towards the problem and/or situation. Similarly, they may unwittingly maintain their problem by their behaviour in problem-related situations. Consequently, helping the person to try something different through a mutually agreed task may be useful.

Utilising resources

The client may benefit from utilising outside resources, and the therapist may be instrumental in helping them to do this.

More prepared to use therapeutic services in future

A person may use a walk-in or single-session therapy service with reluctance and the most useful outcome for such a person may be that they are more likely to seek therapeutic help in future.

Help to get the client unstuck

The way I conceptualise my goal as a single-session therapist is to help the client, who is often stuck with their problem, to get unstuck in some way. This involves me first helping the client to be clear about what being unstuck looks like and then finding out from them what they need to do to make this come to pass.

THE CLIENT'S GOALS

When clients are asked about their therapeutic goals in SST, they often state their goals in broad and general terms. By contrast, workable goals in SST have the following characteristics (de Shazer, 1991). They are:

Salient to the client

If the client is to get the most out of SST, their goal needs to be important to them rather than to other interested people. Sometimes people get 'sent' to therapy to achieve goals that other people want them to achieve. This does not augur well for a good outcome from SST. Thus, the SST needs to help the client set a salient goal.

Small rather than large

The more ambitious the client's goal in SST the less likely they are to achieve it. Given this, the SST therapist needs to help the client set a small, but meaningful goal.

Described in specific, behavioural terms

If the client's goal is specific and expressed in behavioural terms, then this helps the person to achieve it. Thus, the SST therapist needs to help the client specify a broadly expressed goal and to link it to behavioural referents.

Achievable within the practical context of the client's life

It is not only important that the SST therapist ensures that the client's goal is achievable, but also that the client can incorporate it into their life. Otherwise, although their goal is achievable, they won't achieve it.

Perceived by the client as involving their own contribution

It is important that the client sees the link between their goal and what they need to do to achieve it. The SST therapist, therefore, needs to help them make this link. Otherwise, the client may not do what they need to do to achieve their goal.

Described by the client as involving the 'start of something' and not the 'end of something'

It is important that the client sees that there is a process involved in achieving their goal and the more they acknowledge that what they can achieve from SST is to initiate this process rather than to end it, the more they are likely to benefit from the single session. The SST therapist's job, therefore, is to help them take the first steps to goal achievement, not the last steps.

Involving the presence of new feelings and/or behaviour(s) rather than the absence or cessation of existing feelings and behaviour(s)

Often a client may say that their goal is to stop feeling a troublesome feeling or to stop acting in an unconstructive manner. However, human beings do not function well in an emotional and behavioural vacuum, and therefore they need something at which to aim. Therefore, the SST therapist's task is to help the client to set a constructive feeling goal or a constructive behavioural goal instead.

SST CHALLENGES ESTABLISHED BELIEFS ABOUT THERAPY AND CHANGE

When first presented with the concept of SST and the ideas behind it, many therapists have many doubts, reservations and objections (DROs) to SST. On further examination, these DROs are based on the fact that SST appears to challenge several cherished ideas that therapists hold about the nature of therapy and psychotherapeutic change. In this chapter, I will consider some of these beliefs and discuss them as they pertain to SST.

MORE IS BETTER

If something is beneficial, then more of it must be more beneficial than less of it. While this may be true in certain realms of life, it is not the case in the field of psychotherapy. Reviewing the literature on this issue, Lambert (2013) found that there is a diminishing return concerning the effectiveness of the number of therapy sessions that clients have and that the greatest amount of change occurs earlier in treatment rather than later.

OBJECTIVE MEASURES OF DISTURBANCE AND CHANGE ARE BETTER THAN SUBJECTIVE MEASURES

It should be borne in mind that much of the research reviewed by Lambert (2013) employed objective rating scales measuring change rather than subjective measures, meaning what clients say about what they have gained from therapy. When clients are asked about this, they indicate the value of brief forms of

DOI: 10.4324/9781003386353-20

treatment including those lasting for a single session (Hoyt & Talmon, 2014b). While clients who say that they are satisfied with SST may not have made 'clinically meaningful change', as objectively measured, the important point is that *they* are happy with what they received.

It should be remembered that people don't come to therapy because professionals using objective measures of psychological disturbance say that they need therapy. Clients seek help when they are in emotional pain, and they generally stop therapy when the pain stops. What the SST literature challenges us to do is to consider that clients are perhaps the best people to judge when they have gotten what they want from therapy. So, if, objectively, a client has not met the criterion of having made a clinically meaningful change from a single session of therapy, but they are happy with what they have achieved from therapy, how are we going to make sense of this? Is this SST successful or not? 'Yes', according to the client; no according to the objective measure.

MEANINGFUL CHANGE HAPPENS SLOWLY AND GRADUALLY

As discussed above, professionals often distinguish between change that is clinically significant and change that is not. Clinically significant change is change where someone moves outside the range of the dysfunctional population or within the range of the functional population (Jacobson, Follette & Revenstorf, 1984). Critics of SST who recognise that therapeutic change does take place in SST argue that such change is not clinically significant because such change happens slowly and gradually. However, Hayes et al. (2007) have shown that while clinically significant change can be gradual and linear, this is not universally the case and that such change can occur quite quickly. Indeed, there is a concept known as quantum change which shows that meaningful change can occur in a very short period both inside and outside psychotherapy. Quantum change refers to a sudden, dramatic, and enduring change that affects a broad range of emotion, cognition and behaviour (Miller &

C' de Baca, 2001). While this type of change does not often occur in SST, it does not mean that it cannot occur. It is the possibility of meaningful change occurring in a short period in SST that challenges the established idea that real change only occurs slowly and gradually.

The other point that is worth making here reiterates the point I made in the previous section. Who decides what is meaningful change and what isn't? Just because objectively the change a person makes in SST does not meet the criterion of clinically significant or meaningful change does not mean that subjectively it is not meaningful to the person.

EFFECTIVE THERAPY IS BUILT UPON THE THERAPEUTIC RELATIONSHIP WHICH TAKES TIME TO DEVELOP

Studies tend to show that the quality of the relationship that therapists create with their clients is an important factor in determining the effectiveness of psychotherapy (Lambert, 2013). Given this fact, critics of SST doubt its efficacy because they argue that it takes time to develop a good therapeutic relationship with clients. However, SST therapists argue that it is possible to develop a good relationship with clients if both work together to focus on the problem for which the client seeks help and if a goal orientation (or solution focus) is adopted. Indeed, as research shows, when clients benefit from SST, they report a strong working alliance with their therapists while when clients don't benefit from SST, they report a poor alliance with their therapists (Simon et al., 2012). This shows that SST therapists can and do form a good therapeutic relationship with their clients and do so very quickly.

SST IS ONLY SUITABLE FOR CLIENTS FACING SIMPLE PROBLEMS

One of the most common questions asked by therapists first exposed to SST is 'Who is SST suitable for and for whom is it not suitable?' I discuss this issue at length in Chapter 45. Jeff Young (2018: 48) argues that the best response to this question is:

to avoid having to answer it by embedding SST in the total service system so that clients can return if they want to. Embedding SST into the service system so that all services the organization normally provides are available following an initial session, conducted as if it may be the last, allows the practitioner and the organization to avoid the 'difficult if not impossible' decision of who is suitable and who is not suitable for a 'one off' session.

Many SST therapists note that people with complex problems often seek simple solutions to these complex problems and are satisfied when they find such solutions within an SST framework (Hoyt et al., 2018a).

THE LENGTH OF SST

When considering SST, the question is often asked how long the single session should be? If the traditional therapy session lasts for 50 minutes,[1] then should this be the length of the session in SST, or should it be longer or even shorter? The answer is, as elsewhere in therapy, 'it depends' (Dryden, 1991). For some clients, 50 minutes will suffice; for others, it will not be long enough; and for yet others, it will be too long.

Here are some examples of SST at different lengths:

1. The Bouverie Centre is a very well-known family institute in Victoria, Australia, that offers therapy to families in the surrounding area of Brunswick, Victoria. In their letter to families who have initially decided to attend a single session, the Centre tells families to allow at least 90 minutes for the session.

2. One-session treatment (OST) is an intensive form of massed exposure therapy for the treatment of specific phobias devised by Lars-Göran Öst (Davis III, Ollendick & Öst, 2012). OST combines exposure, participant modelling, cognitive challenges, and reinforcement in a single session that lasts for up to three hours. Clients are gradually exposed to steps of their fear hierarchy using therapist-directed behavioural experiments (Zlomke & Davis III, 2008).

3. The 'Gloria' films to be discussed in Chapter 96 are examples of single sessions where different approaches to therapy were demonstrated with the same client 'Gloria' (Daniels,

---

1 Traditionally known as the 50-minute hour.

DOI: 10.4324/9781003386353-21

2012). The films were made for educational purposes. Carl Rogers's session with Gloria lasted 30 minutes 22 seconds, Fritz Perls's session with Gloria lasted 22 minutes 30 seconds, and Albert Ellis's session with Gloria lasted 17 minutes 24 seconds. Given their brevity, I call these examples of 'very brief therapeutic conversations' (VBTCs) where a client discusses a problem with a therapist knowing that they will not see the therapist again and, in this case, knowing that the DVD will be made available for later viewing by a professional audience. I have made four such DVDs myself,[2] the length of these sessions ranging from 28 minutes 27 seconds to 52 minutes 22 seconds.

4. Demonstrations of therapy that are not filmed are VBTCs that are conducted live in front of a professional audience or a mixed professional and lay audience. Here, a therapist works with a volunteer from that audience who is seeking help with a current problem and is prepared to discuss this problem in front of other people. In a book on non-filmed VBTCs, I present eight transcripts of such conversations. These range in duration from 10 minutes 47 seconds to 31 minutes 47 seconds (Dryden, 2018a).

From these examples, it can be seen that a single session of therapy can last anywhere from 10 minutes 47 seconds to three hours depending on the context and the purpose of the session.

2 See https://estore.eclipse.net.uk/epages/colt5155.mobile/en_GB/?Object Path=/Shops/colt5155/Categories/By_Author/Windy_Dryden.

DIFFERENT APPROACHES TO SST

Consistent with the idea that SST is a way of delivering services and is not a therapeutic model or approach in its own right, SST can be practised by therapists from a variety of therapeutic approaches. Thus, in Hoyt and Talmon (2014a), a publication based on the first 'Capturing the Moment' (CTM 1) international conference that took place in Melbourne, Australia, in March 2012, the following therapeutic approaches to SST are represented (Talmon & Hoyt, 2014: 473–478).

- solution-focused approaches
- approaches that create a hypnotic experience
- approaches that help alter the patient's problem-governing rules
- neurolinguistic programming (NLP)
- emotional freedom techniques (EFT)
- equine-assisted therapy.

In their introduction to an edited book that was based on the second 'Capturing the Moment' (CTM 2) conference that took place in Banff, Canada, in September 2015, Hoyt et al. (2018b) appear to argue that there are two different approaches to SST. The first might be termed 'constructive' approaches and the other 'active-directive' approaches.

'CONSTRUCTIVE' APPROACHES TO SST

Constructive approaches to SST include those which are 'non-pathologizing solution-focused, collaborative, or narrative' in nature (Hoyt et al., 2018b: 14). Therapists who are associated with such approaches use their expertise to help clients to

DOI: 10.4324/9781003386353-22

'identify and apply their own pre-existing (albeit sometimes overlooked) abilities' (Hoyt et al., 2018b: 14–15). The majority of contributions to the volume that was derived from the second international symposium are examples of the constructive approaches (Hoyt et al., 2018a).

'ACTIVE-DIRECTIVE' APPROACHES TO SST

In a pre-publication version of their book, Hoyt et al. (2018b) referred to active-directive approaches to SST. In these approaches, Hoyt et al. (2018b: 19, footnote) say that

> change is primarily brought about by the therapist forming an opinion about what is wrong ('How the client is stuck') and then proceeding to provide what the therapist discerns to be the needed remedy— be it insight, explanation and instruction, specific skill training, paradoxical behavioral directives to obviate interpersonal problems, etc.

Examples of such active-directive approaches to SST are 'REBT/ CBT (Dryden, 2016, 2017), psychodynamic, redecision/Gestalt, and some forms of strategic therapy' (Hoyt et al., 2018b: 19, footnote).

My view is that Hoyt et al. (2018b) have presented a bifurcated view of current approaches to SST and have not adequately represented what they initially called the 'active-directive approaches' to SST. While such approaches do present a view of 'what's wrong' and how it can be put right, therapists practising such approaches do so by offering, not imposing, their views and by taking their clients' views on these matters seriously. They also take into account what clients bring to the process of SST concerning the latter's pre-existing abilities. I would say, however, that active-directive SST therapists may be more likely than their 'constructive' colleagues to encourage clients not to use potential solutions that may have negative long-term consequences for them.

DIFFERENT TYPES OF HELP IN SST

It is commonly thought that single-session therapy was designed to help clients find solutions to existing emotional and/or behavioural problems. While the most common form of help that clients seek from SST is emotional/behavioural problem-solving, this is by no means the only type of help that clients seek from SST. Before I briefly list the different types of help that are available in SST, I want to make the point that what is crucial is that the therapist offers the client the help that the client wants, not what the therapist thinks the client needs. When the therapist meets the client's SST helping preferences then this strengthens their working alliance and has a positive impact on what the client takes from SST (Norcross & Cooper, 2021).

The following are the most common types of help that clients seek from SST:

- Help me to solve an emotional or behavioural problem and get unstuck
- Help me to develop a greater understanding of an issue
- Help me to express my feelings about an issue and get things off my chest
- Just listen while I talk about an issue
- Just let me talk about whatever I want to talk about – don't try to focus me
- Help me make a decision
- Help me resolve a dilemma
- Give me your professional opinion on something
- Signpost me to appropriate services.

DOI: 10.4324/9781003386353-23

Part 2

THE ASSUMPTIONS OF SST

CLIENT-CENTRED AND CLIENT-DRIVEN

Effective SST is characterised by being both client-centred and client-driven.

CLIENT-CENTRED

Effective SST is client-centred, but not in the sense that it is based on 'client-centred therapy', the approach to therapy founded by Carl Rogers (1951) and contemporarily known as 'person centred therapy'. Rather, it is centred on where the client is now and where the client wants to be. This means that other than a focused and brief risk assessment carried out before therapy begins, the therapist and the client start work the minute therapy begins. Thus, there tends to be no formal assessment made nor any lengthy case formulation carried out. Indeed, SST poses a particular challenge to some of my CBT colleagues who hold that therapy can only be initiated once a full case formulation has been conducted. Given this position, they would not be able to carry out SST by design.

While all SST therapists share this client-centred focus, some hold that this focus is best implemented concerning the client's preferred solution and that a problem focus only interferes with such solution-focused therapy (Ratner, George & Iveson, 2012). Others including myself (e.g. Dryden, 2017; 2022a) contend that this focus can encompass both a problem and a solution focus, with the latter being a realistic alternative to the former. However, perhaps true client-centredness allows the client to determine their own focus!

Concerning this client-centred focus, Weir et al. (2008: 39) argue that SST therapists tend to believe that 'clients are experts in reporting what kind of and how much change is important to them at any particular time'. They also outline several practices that express this client-centred focus in action. These are:

- ask and explore what a client wants at the outset of the session;
- shift the therapeutic agenda to meet a client's concerns;
- be more overt and collaborative with clients when deciding how much therapeutic contact is required;
- focus on a client's problems, but acknowledge their client's strengths and abilities to cope; and
- create opportunities for the client to try things on their own so that they can judge if they need further help.

CLIENT-DRIVEN

The client largely drives effective SST. Hoyt et al. (2018b: 14–15) argue that the client drives effective SST in four ways.

The client elects and initiates therapy

SST does not work very well with clients who are 'reluctant' or do not want to be there unless such reluctance can be effectively addressed at the outset. By contrast, when the client actively seeks therapy and is keen to 'get the job done' as quickly as possible, effective SST is likely to ensue if the therapist demonstrates similar keenness.

The client defines the goals of therapy

Although the therapist has goals in SST (see Chapters 18 and 56), unless the therapy is focused on what the client wants to achieve from the session then the work will not be very effective, particularly in the longer term. By contrast, when the client sets a goal that they strongly want to achieve and want to achieve quickly, then such motivation brings the process alive and galvanises both parties, with the result that the client may take something away from this process that is meaningful and lasting.

The client's existing internal factors make the most difference

As discussed in Chapter 21, approaches to SST have been grouped by Hoyt et al. (2018b) as falling into two broad camps: the 'constructive' camp and the 'active-directive' camp. In my view, the former argue the following. The process of SST is largely client-driven in the sense that clients get the most out of the process when encouraged by their therapists to identify and use internal factors (e.g., skills, abilities and competencies) that they already have, but have forgotten about, or with which they have lost touch. Therapists in the 'active-directive' camp, while not disagreeing with this position, would argue that clients can also benefit from learning something new which was not present in their pre-SST existing repertoire of internal factors. However, even when the latter approach is taken, what new things are taught to clients in SST will only make a difference to clients if they learn and apply these things in ways that are meaningful to them.

The client decides whether one session is sufficient, or if one or more sessions are needed

Unless the client is seeking help within a context in which they can only have one session, the choice whether to have a single session, for the time being, or whether to request one or further appointments will be determined by the client. This is the case whether it is SST by choice ('I don't need to come back') or by default (making a further appointment which is either cancelled or not kept).

24

RECIPROCITY IN OPENNESS
AND FEEDBACK

Two of the values that underpin SST are openness and feed-back. In effective SST, these values are reciprocally expressed.

OPENNESS

Since the therapist and the client potentially have only one session together, it is important for them both to be honest with one another. Thus, the client needs to be open with the therapist about what they are struggling with and what they want from the process. They also need to be clear with the therapist concerning what they think might help them and what won't. The therapist needs to be clear with the client on the following issues:

• what they can do and cannot do within the SST context;
• whether or not they can help the person; and
• whether or not they have had prior experience in helping people with problems similar to the client's.

Also, the therapist needs to give honest answers to the client's questions. While this does not necessarily mean answering all the client's questions, it does mean giving honest reasons explaining why they will not answer any specific questions.

Finally, therapist openness can be expressed in self-disclosure. However, before disclosing it is important to ask the client if they are interested in the therapist's personal experience. If so, the therapist may disclose that they have encountered a similar problem to the one that the client is experiencing, but

 DOI: 10.4324/9781003386353-26

that they have overcome it. If helpful to the client, the therapist shares how they overcame the problem effectively, since this may help the client to emulate the therapist's problem-solving strategy or stimulate the client to think of their own strategy. Conversely, if the client is not interested in the therapist's personal experience, then the latter should refrain from self-disclosing.

In a study of the implementation of SST and its impact on service delivery in Victoria, Australia, Weir et al. (2008) found that 69% of their respondents agreed that SST had influenced them to be direct and honest with clients. Thus, therapists who value openness are drawn to SST and SST influences therapists to be more open in their work with clients.

FEEDBACK

Weir et al. (2008: 39) also found that

> almost two-thirds of those who claimed to have applied SSW [single session work] principles and practices in their work stated that they encourage feedback about the quality of service received from their clients and, moreover, used this input to shape their work.

Not only do SST therapists elicit feedback about the quality of service delivery they also obtain feedback concerning what clients take away from the session and what they got from the process at a predetermined future date (e.g., three months).

Since feedback is reciprocal, the therapist will give the client feedback periodically in the session regarding where they have reached and what the two of them have yet to do, for example.

25

FUTURE-ORIENTED, BUT PRESENT AND PAST SENSITIVE

As SST is goal-oriented, single-session therapists encourage clients to focus on the future – what they want to get from the process. Some therapists do this by encouraging clients to focus on solutions and not on problems. Other therapists don't discourage clients from outlining problems, but quickly encourage them to specify acceptable goals concerning these problems.

A SOLUTION-FOCUSED APPROACH

A solution-focused approach to therapy helps people to benefit from single sessions in three ways (Iveson, 2002). First, since people get stuck as a result of being preoccupied with their problems, solution-focused therapists help them get disentangled by encouraging them to describe solutions or preferred futures in a detailed way. When this is done, some clients can see quite clearly what they need to do to effect such solutions and need no additional sessions to help them do this. Second, as Iveson (2002) points out, some clients have actually solved their problem but do not realise this. When they hear themselves describe their preferred future they see that sufficient of it is already occurring for them to continue without further therapy sessions. Third, some clients, when asked to focus on the future, come to appreciate their present lives better and realise that what was previously unmanageable is in fact manageable.

Solution-focused therapists would argue that each of the above scenarios is made possible because of the exclusive focus on the future and how clients want their futures to be.

 DOI: 10.4324/9781003386353-27

A PROBLEM-FOCUSED AND SOLUTION-ORIENTED APPROACH

It is possible to take both a problem-focused and a solution-oriented approach to SST. Indeed, when I practise SST, I spend quite a bit of time focusing on the problem so that my client and I can both understand it fully in terms of the factors that both account for it and maintain it. Doing this helps my client and I to find the best solution to the problem based on this full understanding of the problem. Thus, in this approach taking a problem focus facilitates the discovery of the best solution.

Although SST has a future orientation, it does not follow that clients are not permitted to talk about their present or their past. Indeed, as shown above, adopting a problem focus means that the client is discussing how things are for them in the present. However, as we have also seen, this present focus helps the generation of the client's preferred future.

A similar point can be made when the client wants to talk about their past. When this happens, the focus should be on the client's present feelings about their past. When this is done and the present problem about the past is fully understood, both the therapist and the client can take a future focus as discussed above.

READINESS

The concept of readiness is an important one in SST. Let me consider both client readiness and therapist readiness.

CLIENT READINESS

In my view, client readiness is a state of mind. Here the person has decided the following: (1) they have a problem; (2) they want to address the problem; and (3) they want help with this problem now. They are open to the possibility of being helped in a single session. I will now discuss these points one at a time.

The client does think that they have a problem

Clearly, SST will not be effective if the person does not think they have a problem. Indeed, it is unlikely that they will consult a therapist if they do not think that they have a problem. However, if a person does consult a therapist under such conditions, for example at the behest of a partner, relative or friend, the therapist may be able to engage the person in a conversation which may result in them deciding that they do have a problem and, if so, they can address it with the therapist's help in the session itself or later if further help is requested. However, if, after such discussion, the person decides that they do not have a problem, then the session concludes at this point.

The client wants to address the problem

It is quite possible for a person to have a problem and not want to address it. They are living with the problem for better or for worse, but have not reached a tipping point where they

DOI: 10.4324/9781003386353-28

acknowledge the problem *and* want to address it. When they reach this point, they are more likely to benefit from SST than when they have not reached it. However, they need to be clear in their own mind *when* they want to address their problem.

The client wants help with their problem now

It is when the client has decided that they want help with their problem now that they are in a good frame of mind to benefit from SST. In Chapter 11, if you recall, I discussed the case of Vera who had a problem with elevator phobia. She had acknowledged this problem and sought help for it but spent quite a time in group therapy half-heartedly addressing the problem. She entered a state of readiness for change when she learned that her office was to be relocated from the 5th floor of a building to the 105th floor. This relocation meant that she could no longer walk up the stairs to her office, but was forced to take the elevator. When she acted on this state of readiness, she did what she had to do to solve the problem – repeatedly travel on elevators until she was no longer fearful.

The client is open to the possibility of being helped in a single session

When the person wants to address their problem now, we still do not know how long they think it will take to address the problem effectively. When the person is open to the possibility of being helped to do so in a single visit, then this final ingredient is what makes SST a possibility at least from the perspective of the client.

THERAPIST READINESS

In my view, therapist readiness is a combination of the therapist's state of mind and practicalities.

The therapist's state of mind

SST is partly possible because the therapist believes that it is possible. This is part of the SST mindset that I discussed in Chapter 14. Thus, for the therapist to be in the 'readiness' state of mind, they need to believe:

- it is possible to help the client to address their problem in a single session, notwithstanding the fact that additional sessions are available if needed; and
- they are going to do their very best to work with the client to achieve that end.

Practicalities

While it is important that the therapist has the right 'readiness' state of mind, certain practicalities need to be in place for SST to be most effective, even if both parties are 'ready'. Thus, it is important that when the client wants to address their problem 'now', the therapist offers the person an appointment to capitalise on their readiness. Too often in our field, when the client is ready to be helped, the organisation to which they turn for help can only put them on a waiting list and, when this happens, it may be that when the person can be seen, they are no longer in that state of readiness. This is the reasoning behind the provision of walk-in therapy, which I will discuss in Part 7 of this book – helping the person at the point of need for help, not at the point of availability of help.

CONCLUSION

The power of SST is harnessed when the client is ready to be helped, possibly in one session, when the therapist is ready to provide such help and can do so when the person wants to be seen.

27

STRENGTHS-BASED

When people seek therapy for their problems, they are revealing what they are not very good at – what they may regard as their weaknesses. Traditionally, therapists help them to address their weaknesses and develop strengths. Thus, if their problems are due to unrealistic thinking, they are helped to develop realistic thinking. While therapists in the 'active-directive' approaches to SST do something similar (see Chapter 21), most SST therapists help their clients to identify existing strengths that can be used to help solve their problem. A strength has been defined 'as that which helps a person to cope with life or that which makes life more fulfilling for one[self] and [for] others' (Jones-Smith, 2014: 13). In my view 'strengths' are factors that are internal to the person and can be distinguished from 'resources' that are external to the person. I call these external resources (see Chapter 28).

Concerning their position on client strengths, SST therapists share similar ideas to strengths-based therapists (Murphy & Sparks, 2018). Thus, (1) they believe that clients have strengths; (2) they elicit client strengths; and (3) they incorporate client strengths into therapy.

HOW TO DETERMINE CLIENTS' STRENGTHS

Some SST therapists like to invite their clients to prepare for their single session. At this point, the therapist might encourage the client to take a survey of strengths (such as the Via Character Strengths Survey – see www.viacharacter.org/survey) and to send these to the therapist in advance of the session. The resultant information can be used in the single session and applied to help the client solve their problem.

DOI: 10.4324/9781003386353-29

Alternatively, if the therapist asks the client to complete a pre-session preparation questionnaire, they might include an item designed to encourage the client to reflect on their strengths. For example, 'What are the strengths or inner qualities that you have as a person that you could draw on while tackling the issue you are seeking help for? If you struggle to answer this question, think of what people who really know you and who are on your side would say'.

SST therapists who do not have any pre-session contact with their clients will have to rely on asking clients directly for such strengths. Here are some examples of such questions:

- What would you say are your strengths as a person?
- What strengths do you have that could help you to solve your problem?
- If you were at a job interview and were asked what strengths you had, what would you say?
- What would a very good friend who knows you exceptionally well say your strengths are as a person?

Murphy and Sparks (2018) provide some good questions for the SST therapist to ask which focus on clients' resilience-based strengths:

- With everything going on in your life, how do you manage to get up each day and take care of business?
- What keeps you from giving up?
- Where do you find the courage to face these challenges?
- How have you kept things from getting worse?
- What would your friends say they most appreciate about the way you've handled this challenge?

Sometimes in SST, when the therapist encourages the client to focus on their 'problem-solving' strengths, it transpires that this focus is sufficient for the client to take charge of the process and solve their problem. On such occasions, the client has lost touch with their strengths, and the mere reminder of these strengths is all the client needs to address their problem effectively because they can see quite clearly how to do this, and they are confident that they can do so. At other times, the client needs the therapist to help them see how they can use their strengths to solve their problem and to rehearse these in the session if possible. At yet other times, a focus on strengths, while important, is not sufficient to help the client solve the problem because their 'problem-creating' weaknesses need focused attention. In this case, the person needs the therapist's help in addressing the 'weakness' and, if possible, turning it into a strength.

The above shows, in my view, that SST therapists need to be prepared to deal with clients' weaknesses as well as help them apply their strengths and that it will not be clear which approach is needed until the therapist works with the client. Therapist flexibility here, as elsewhere, is an important change-promoting ingredient.

28

USE OF EXTERNAL RESOURCES

In the previous chapter, I distinguished between inner strengths and external resources. I said that a client's strengths are factors that are internal to the person and that external resources are factors that are external to the person. There is a well-known phrase which indicates the role that resources that are available to the client play in SST. It is: 'Only you can do it, but you don't have to do it alone'. This means that while the client's internal efforts are the most important determining factor in the outcome of SST, external factors are important in aiding the person's efforts.

Let me give an example of what I mean. I was contacted by a man who had been struggling with his feelings of grief in response to the loss of his mother and found his feelings a threat to his ideal image of being a man, by which he meant 'being calm and in control'. He knew that I offered a SST programme and signed up for this. As part of this programme, I had a 30-minute pre-therapy phone contact with the man which was designed to help him get the most out of the face-to-face session (see Dryden, 2017).[1] After this telephone call, I arranged to meet him in two days' time. When he arrived for his face-to-face session with me, he seemed much calmer.

1 This occurred before the COVID-19 pandemic moved therapy from face-to-face to online. Pre-pandemic, my preparation for the single session with the client was by phone and the session was face-to-face. During the pandemic, I sent the client a pre-session questionnaire to complete (see Table 49.1) which helped them to prepare for the session, and the session itself was online (e.g., by Zoom). Post-pandemic, I have retained the pre-session questionnaire approach to help the client prepare for the session and the client can choose to see me in person or online. Most choose the latter.

 DOI: 10.4324/9781003386353-30

When I commented on this, he told me the following story. After we had spoken on the telephone, he had a reunion dinner with some old school friends. At this dinner, he plucked up the courage to tell his friends about his feelings of grief and his struggles with his feelings. He was amazed to learn that almost without exception his friends had experienced similar feelings of grief and had struggled with these feelings. As a result of these feelings, my client realised several important points:

- he was not alone in experiencing grief in response to loss – most of his friends had struggled with their feelings of grief too;
- he was still a man even though he was not calm and in control; and
- calmness and being in control are not healthy responses to loss.

My client learned these important lessons not from me in therapy, but from his circle of friends at a reunion dinner. He had made constructive use of the external resources that were available to him – in this case, his old school friends.

This anecdote tells us that it is important for SST therapists to help their clients to identify external resources that they can call upon to help them to solve their problems. Examples of such external resources may be as follows:

- people known to the client who may be useful in some way in helping the client solve their problem (as was the case with my client above);
- people not known by the client but whom the client might consult for help;
- organisations that may be useful to the client in their problem-solving efforts; and
- internet sites that might provide useful problem-solving information.

COMPLEX PROBLEMS DO NOT ALWAYS REQUIRE COMPLEX SOLUTIONS

Psychotherapists rightly see themselves as professionals. They have to be trained and accredited, and their work supervised, and they also are expected to keep up to date with developments in the field of psychotherapy. Given this, they tend to see that their clients' problems are complex. These problems are probably multi-determined and maintained by the complex interaction of intrapersonal, interpersonal and environmental factors. Therapists from diverse approaches now like to develop visual representations of case formulations which show how these complex interacting factors operate to explain the development and perpetuation of clients' problems.

Given this complexity, psychotherapists can be forgiven for thinking that big, complex problems require complex solutions. And, of course, big, complex solutions take time to develop and implement. All of this thinking is, however, anathema to the theory and practice of SST and, often, anathema to what clients want. Do clients want complex or simple solutions to their problems? In my experience they want the latter, but only if the solution works. Hoyt et al. (2018b) have also made this point. While SST therapists may be aware of the complexity of their clients' problems, they look not for complex solutions, but simple solutions that work. Thus, SST therapists and most of their clients are in accord in looking for effective, simple solutions, and this is the case irrespective of the complexity or simplicity of their clients' problems.

 DOI: 10.4324/9781003386353-31

The work of solution-focused therapists demonstrates this search for effective simplicity. Such a therapist would ask their client such questions as: 'What would you notice that would tell you that you were beginning to solve your problem?' Once this sign was identified, then the therapist would then ask the client how they would capitalise on this factor. The client and the therapist would work in this way until the client could see how to solve their problem.

As may be imagined, a simple solution is more likely to be remembered by the client than a complex solution. And if the client can remember a solution, then they have an opportunity to implement it. A more complex solution may be more accurate than the developed simple solution, but if the client is likely to forget it, then they won't implement it.

Some SST therapists favour the technique of giving the client a brief written reminder[1] of what they have agreed to do as a result of the work done in the session. Research on the use of homework assignments in therapy has shown that clients are more likely to carry out such assignments when it is clear to them what they have agreed to do than when this is not clear (Kazantzis, Whittington & Dattilio, 2010).

I finish this chapter with a word of caution. Just because a solution is simple does not mean that it is easy to implement. For example, facing a threat is simple in its conceptualisation, but doing so may mean tolerating much discomfort. Thus, Vera (discussed in Chapter 11) put into practice the simple solution of riding on elevators repeatedly to deal effectively with her elevator phobia, but was it easy for her to do this? Far from it!

---

1 Other SST therapists, including myself, prefer the client to make their own written reminder.

THE JOURNEY BEGINS WITH THE FIRST FEW STEPS

The goal of SST is not to cure the client or even to help the client reach their goals. Its basic goal, in my view, is to help promote movement. Clients often come to therapy because they are stuck. What they don't want necessarily is an elaborate explanation of why they are stuck. Rather they are looking for ways of getting unstuck. If my computer screen is frozen, I don't want an IT consultant only to tell me why it is frozen – I want them to unfreeze it so that I can get on with doing my work.

Stuckness is a state where there is no constructive movement in the client. It does not follow that there is no movement, but that such movement is unconstructive and may embed the stuckness. Imagine, for example, that you are driving your car in the snow and the car becomes stuck in a snow drift. What do you do? The chances are that you will rev the car's engine faster in an attempt to break free. The effect is often the opposite – you get more stuck. In fact, the harder you rev the engine, the more stuck you become. Thus, you need to do something different. If you have a shovel, then you might find it more productive to dig yourself free. If you don't have a shovel, you may ask someone to join forces with you to help you push the car free. When the person has helped you get unstuck, they then stand back so you can drive away.

I think that this is an apt way of thinking about SST. The client is stuck and joins forces with the therapist. As a consequence of their joint efforts, the client becomes unstuck. At this point, the therapist stands back, and the client moves on with their life.

DOI: 10.4324/9781003386353-32

So, the best way to get unstuck is to do something different (O'Hanlon, 1999), and SST therapists are adept at helping clients to look for steps that they can take that will help them eventually get unstuck. It may be that the client has already taken steps that have worked in the past, but which they have forgotten about. In this case, reminding them to use these steps might be all that is required to help them get unstuck. Alternatively, it may be that the therapist can help the client discover steps that they have not tried before that might work for them in the future. Or the therapist may make suggestions themselves about steps that the client might take. The important thing here is that the client sees the value of taking initial steps and can see that taking them will promote change. If the client can take a potentially constructive step, then they will soon discover the results of taking this step. If the step is constructive, this will encourage the person to take another step, and this will help the person initiate a virtuous cycle of change. If the step is not constructive, then such feedback may help the person to stand back, think and find a step that will be more beneficial. Modifying an old adage, in SST the therapist helps the client to develop the following principle: 'If at first, you don't succeed, try something different and keep trying something different until you do succeed'.

Part 3

FACILITATIVE CONDITIONS FOR SST

INTENTIONALITY

There is a distinction that is sometimes made in the SST literature between SST by design (or planned SST) and SST by default (or unplanned SST). SST by default describes the situation where the therapist and the client had not planned to have a single session, but it became SST because the client had either cancelled the next scheduled appointment or did not attend the appointment without cancelling it. As we have seen in Chapter 8, therapists tend to think pessimistically about such unplanned termination. Terms such as 'premature termination', 'non-completion of treatment' or 'dropping out of treatment' have been used to describe such situations. However, we have also seen that when such clients are consulted after the event, a large proportion of them are satisfied with the treatment that they did receive and required no further help. Such people maturely terminated therapy. They concluded that, from their perspective, therapy had been completed and, as such, they had not 'dropped out' of treatment. Rather, they had brought treatment to a satisfactory close. Of course, there are still many people who are neither helped nor happy with the first and only session that they have. And yet the majority are happy.

If SST can be effective even when it is not planned, then planning for it should enhance its therapeutic potency. Here, intentionality is a key facilitative condition for SST. What happens, then, when both parties bring such intentionality to the process?

THERAPIST INTENTIONALITY

Therapist intentionality in SST is marked by the therapist holding and communicating the idea that if the client is ready to work hard so is the therapist in helping the client to solve their problem as quickly as possible, perhaps in the first session. The core ingredients of therapist intentionality are (1) a 'rolling up of one's sleeves' and getting down to work as soon as possible and (2) a keenness to help the client as quickly as possible. The safeguard is that an additional session or sessions will be made available if needed. However, no matter how keen and hard-working the therapist intends to be, this will only yield therapeutic benefit if it is matched by a similar level of client intentionality.

CLIENT INTENTIONALITY

Client intentionality in SST is also marked by the keenness that the client shows in solving their problem as quickly as possible. With such keenness comes two kinds of openness. First, the client is willing to be very open about (1) their problem; (2) their goal; and (3) why they want to achieve a solution as quickly as possible. Vera in Chapter 11 demonstrated such openness, but only when she had a reason to solve the problem quickly. Second, the client is open in the sense of being willing to consider a range of potential solutions and choosing the one that both suits them best and is most likely to bring about a quick solution. Vera chose the only viable solution to the problem in the time frame she allocated to problem solution. Again, the time pressure led her to be open to doing what she had avoided doing when she experienced no such pressure.

In conclusion, much can be achieved in SST if the therapist and the client share the intention to get the job done as quickly as possible.

EXPECT CHANGE

The year 1968 was particularly interesting for publications on the role of expectations in psychology. In a ground-breaking book on teacher expectations in the classroom, Rosenthal & Jacobson (1968) found that children whose teachers expected them to achieve well did, in fact, achieve more than children whose teachers did not expect them to achieve well. This was the case despite no other differences between the two groups of children. Also that year, Jerome Frank, author of a seminal book on psychotherapy entitled *Persuasion and Healing* (1961), who also wrote the foreword to Talmon's (1990) book on SST, published an important article on the role of expectations in psychotherapy (Frank, 1968). Frank's basic point in that article was that therapeutic outcome depends, in part, on the expectations that both the therapist and the client have of the process and what the client gets from it.

Thus, one of the conditions that facilitate the outcome of SST is the set of expectations that the therapist and the client bring to the process. If both participants expect change, then it is more likely to happen than if they don't. If the therapist expects that client change can be achieved from the session, but the client doesn't believe this, then the 'feel' of the work will be of the therapist pulling along a client who will resist the therapist's pace. If the client thinks that they can achieve what they want to from the session and the therapist doesn't, then the 'feel' of the work will be of the client becoming frustrated at being held up by the therapist.

It is also important that both the therapist and the client have realistic expectations from SST. While change does happen, it is rarely what Miller and C' de Baca (2001) call 'quantum change', by which is meant vivid, surprising, benevolent and enduring personal transformation. Much more common is when the client takes a different perspective on the problematic situation or changes their behaviour in some way.

Even if both the therapist and the client hold realistic expectations of what the latter can achieve from SST, if the therapist pushes for change it may not happen. When this happens, the therapist is too focused on the outcome of the session to the detriment of its process.

In conclusion, and taking all of the above factors into consideration, perhaps the best facilitative condition in this respect is as follows. Both the therapist and the client have realistic expectations of what can be achieved from SST and work hard to achieve it by attending to the process by which the client's goal can be achieved rather than be overly focused on the goal itself.

CLARITY

There is a reality TV programme on BBC Television called *The Apprentice* in which Lord Sugar, the British multimillionaire businessman, offers a £250,000 investment to the winner of a 12-week process to partner him in the business proposed by the person. The contestants, a group of aspiring entrepreneurs, compete with one another, taking part in several business-related challenges. What is apparent from watching the programme is the clarity with which Lord Sugar expresses himself to the contestants. They are left in no doubt what the nature of the tasks are and what is expected of them.

One of the tasks that the SST therapist has in the process is to express themself with great clarity. If not, then the client will be confused, and a confused client will not derive much benefit from SST. In this respect, it is important not to overestimate the client's self-awareness. Good SST therapists are not afraid to state the obvious for the sake of clarity. The purpose of therapist clarity in SST is to facilitate client understanding. Given this purpose, clarity is enhanced under the following conditions:

- when the therapist speaks at a rate that facilitates the client's comprehension of the points that they are making;
- when the therapist 'chunks' information so that the client can digest what is being communicated; and
- when the therapist modulates their voice to convey meaning and refrains from talking in a monotonous manner.

Therapist clarity is important throughout the process, but is particularly so in three areas:

DOI: 10.4324/9781003386353-36

1. *When the therapist provides information about the SST process to the client.* Doing so helps the client to know where they stand which helps them to feel secure enough to participate fully in the process. Thus, if only one session is on offer, then this needs to be made clear. However, if more sessions are possible, then this needs to be communicated without taking away from what can be achieved from a single session. Here is an example of what a therapist might say in this context:

> If you and I are prepared to work hard, we might be able to help you achieve what you hope to get from therapy in this session. However, if at the end of the session you think that you need an additional session or sessions, then this is possible as well. Would you be interested in proceeding on this basis?

2. *When the client is planning a change in their behaviour.* In this case, it is important that the person knows what they are going to do and this is facilitated by the therapist's clarity on the issue.

3. *When the therapist periodically summarises the work that the two have done up to that point.* Such summaries help ensure that the therapeutic dyad remains on point and that they have a shared understanding of where they are and where they have got to go. Having said this, many SST therapists prefer clients to make such summaries themselves, particularly towards the end of the session so that therapist and client are clear on what the client is gaining from the session.

34

EFFECTIVE SESSION STRUCTURE

As I discussed in Chapter 13, time is an important factor in SST and how the therapist and the client make use of time often determines the outcome of the single session. It is generally important for the session to have a structure so that certain key tasks can be accomplished. Having said this, I am not suggesting that there is a fixed structure that SST therapists must follow. Rather, I am suggesting that there are several tasks that need to be carried out by both participants in an orderly manner. It is useful to bear in mind, however, that some clients respond well to a highly structured session, while others prefer a more fluid structure which they can modify if appropriate.

THE INGREDIENTS OF EFFECTIVE SESSION STRUCTURE

The following are the hallmarks of a well-structured session. I will discuss some of these points elsewhere in greater depth so I will cover them briefly here to demonstrate how, taken together, they create such a structure.

Viewing the session as complete in itself and agreeing this explicitly

Even if the therapist and the client have agreed that an additional session or sessions are possible, therapy structure is facilitated when both regard the session that they are having as complete in itself. This should also be acknowledged and agreed. However, if it is viewed as the first of a series of sessions, even if this series is brief, the focal structure of the session is compromised which, in turn, tends to dilute the potency of SST.

Planning the session according to the time available

In Chapter 20, I made the point that the length of a single session in SST can vary quite a lot and it is important that the therapist plans the session according to the time available to both parties. This skill comes from experience and it isn't unusual for therapists new to SST to rush towards the end of the session because they have not paced themselves well. In particular, they tend to spend too much time allowing their clients to tell their stories in their own unfettered way at the beginning of the session. However, with supervision and experience, therapists usually learn to encourage their clients to express themselves in a focused way so that they can utilise the time better and carry out a well-structured session.

Creating a focus and keeping to it

SST works best when the client has a specific problem for which they are seeking help. When they have more than one problem, then the therapist helps them to choose the problem on which they wish to focus. Once this is done, the therapist helps the client to maintain this focus.

Being goal-directed

SST works best when both the therapist and the client know where they are heading. Thus, it is important that the therapist helps the person become and stay goal-directed throughout the session. I will discuss this issue more fully in the next chapter.

Creating a solution and, if possible, rehearsing it

By a solution, I mean something that will help the person to address their problem effectively so that they no longer feel the need to seek help. If the therapist can help the client to rehearse this solution in the session in some way, then this will increase the likelihood that the client will implement it in real life.

Summarising periodically

The therapist should ideally summarise the work that they and the client have done in the session and should do this periodically to keep both of them on track. Alternatively, the client may be asked to provide such periodic summaries themselves. At the end of the session, the client should be asked to summarise what they are taking from the session. If the therapist provides the end-of-session summary then they will not know what the client's takeaway is.

Bringing the session to a close

The final part of the session is its end. Apart from the client summary, some agreement should be made between the therapist and the client. Thus, the two may agree:

- to have no further sessions;
- to have no further sessions, but to have a follow-up at a future specified date;
- to wait for the client to digest the session and implement the solution and then request another session if necessary; or
- to book another session.

In conclusion, an effective session structure in SST is characterised by a definite beginning, a clear end and a logical middle section.

35

EFFECTIVE GOAL-SETTING

As I mentioned in Chapter 18, the practice of SST is goal-directed. Also in that chapter I extrapolated from the work of de Shazer (1991), and made the point that effective client goals in SST tend to be:

- salient to the client;
- small rather than large;
- described in specific, behavioural terms;
- achievable within the practical contexts of the client's life; perceived by the client as involving their own contribution; described by the client as involving the 'start of something' and not the 'end of something'; and
- aimed at the presence of new feelings and/or behaviour(s) rather than the absence or cessation of existing feelings and behaviour(s).

When asked for their goals in SST, clients may respond by giving vague or general goals (e.g., 'I want to be happy'), the absence of problematic states ('I don't want to be anxious') or the presence of positive states ('I want to be confident'). When this happens, the therapist needs to respond quickly and effectively. This is done as follows.

1. respect the client's initial goal statement;
2. help the client to be more specific; and
3. ask the client what they would be happy to have achieved at the end of the session that would lead them to think that they could deal with things on their own without further sessions.

 DOI: 10.4324/9781003386353-38

HELPING THE CLIENT TO SET AN ADVERSITY-RELATED GOAL: A PERSONAL APPROACH

Often a client will come to SST facing an adversity. Before that adversity can be effectively addressed, the client needs to be in a good frame of mind to deal with it. As this adversity is negative, it is healthy for the client to have negative feelings about it, but negative feelings that encourage rather than discourage problem-solving. The role of the therapist here is to help the client to specify such an emotion as shown in the following exchange between myself and a client. While there are many approaches to goal-setting in SST, the following dialogue demonstrates my own when the client needs to deal effectively with an adversity.

WINDY: So, you are anxious about giving public presentations in case you say something stupid. Is that correct?

CLIENT: Yes, that's right.

WINDY: Do your feelings of.anxiety about saying something stupid help you to give a good presentation or not?

CLIENT: They don't.

WINDY: So, what is your goal about the prospect of saying something stupid when you give a presentation?

CLIENT: Well, I want to feel confident about giving presentations.

[This is a common client response. Here, the client is setting a positive emotional state about the situation (i.e., giving presentations) rather than a healthy negative feeling goal about the adversity in the situation (i.e., saying something stupid in the presentation).]

WINDY: Will feeling anxious about saying something stupid help you to develop confidence about giving public presentations?

CLIENT: No.

WINDY: So, what if I were to help you to be concerned, but not anxious, about saying something stupid while giving a public presentation? Would that help you to develop such confidence?

CLIENT: Yes it would.

WINDY: And if I helped you to do that in this visit …?

CLIENT: That would be great.

[I have helped the client to set a healthy, but realistic, goal about the adversity which needs to be addressed before the client is in the right frame of mind to develop confidence. When this is done, the client can often develop such confidence on their own as was the case here.]

Spending time over goal-setting with a client is time spent well in SST.

36

THE THERAPIST'S USE OF EXPERTISE RATHER THAN BEING THE EXPERT

I made the point in Chapter 23 that SST is client-centred and client-driven. It is generally accepted in the SST community that the focus in single-session work is on whatever skills, abilities and strengths the client brings to the session that can be used to help the client achieve their goals. However, the therapist needs to have the clinical talent (i.e., abilities and skill) to help the client to do the following:

- identify their skills, abilities and strengths;
- see their relevance to the pursuit of their goals; and
- select ways in which they can implement these skills, abilities and strengths in the service of goal achievement.

Furthermore, the SST therapist needs to be able to do all these promptly and with clarity.

As Hoyt et al. (2018b: 15) eloquently put it, the role of the therapist in SST is to 'use their expertise primarily to help clients better use their own expertise'. This facilitative role of SST therapists is a dominant one in the SST literature as evidenced by the contributions to Hoyt et al. (2018a). I have called such approaches 'constructive' (see Chapter 19). In these approaches, the client is seen to have all that is necessary to solve their problem, and the therapist's basic task is to make them realise this and act on it.

While recognising that SST can be practised in a variety of different ways where therapists draw from a variety of different approaches (see Chapter 21), the prevailing view in the SST community is a little negative towards what I have referred to here as 'active-directive' approaches. For example, in Hoyt et al.'s (2018b: 19) depiction of these 'active-directive' approaches:

> change is primarily brought about by the therapist forming an opinion about what is wrong ('How is the client stuck?') and then proceeding to provide what the therapist discerns to be the needed remedy – be it insight, explanation and instruction, specific skill training, paradoxical behavioral directives to obviate interpersonal problems, etc.

In my view, it is true that SST therapists from these active-directive approaches (such as CBT, REBT, psychodynamic, Gestalt therapy) are more likely than their 'constructive' counterparts to *offer* a view on the client's problems and how they can be addressed. However, the most important word in the preceding sentence is *offer*. The effective, active-directive, SST therapist would ask for the client's viewpoint on their problem and possible solution. If this viewpoint is counterproductive – albeit from the therapist's perspective – the therapist will give reasons for their view and offer an alternative viewpoint for the client's review. If the latter makes sense, then the two proceed from there. If not further discussion and negotiation will ensue. In Hoyt et al.'s view, the active-directive therapist does not involve the client in directing the single session. In my view, they do.

I see SST as a fusion between what the client brings to the process and what the therapist brings to the process. My view is pluralistic on this latter point. Of course, the SST therapist will strive to harness the client's talents and encourage their use to achieve the client's goal. However, the SST therapist should also feel free to share something that the client does not know about or suggest a way forward that might be new to the client. It is both-and rather than either/or. In this way, the therapist can share their expertise rather than be 'the expert' which is a role that may take away power from the client. As Sheldon Kopp (1972) would advise SST therapists, show your clients that while you may have expertise, you are no guru. You are just another human being struggling.

HELPFUL ATTITUDES FOR SST THERAPISTS

Talmon (1990: 134) brought his seminal book on SST to its conclusion by listing what he calls 'a partial checklist of what I consider to be helpful attitudes for the single session therapist'. These appear in Table 37.1 with a few additions. What I have done in that table is to group the attitudes into what appears to be four clusters. I will discuss these four clusters in this chapter.

THE POWER AND INTEGRITY OF THE SESSION

When the focus of SST therapists is on the session itself and how they view it, their attitudes seem to centre on its power and integrity. Eminem asks what you would do with just one shot in the introduction to his song, 'Lose Yourself'. SST therapists would assuredly answer: 'Capture it' – and it is noteworthy in this respect that the first two international conferences on SST and walk-in therapy referred to 'Capturing the Moment'. So, by dint of its singularity, SST has power. However, as the attitudes in this cluster show, it also has integrity. It is complete. In the moment, this is all we have, even though more may be possible later.

SST IN CONTEXT

While the attitudes in the above cluster focus on the session itself, the attitudes in the cluster I have chosen to call 'SST in context' show that it is important to place this approach to therapy in context. As these attitudes make clear, SST is embedded in the client's life in both the short and long term

DOI: 10.4324/9781003386353-40

Table 37.1 Four clusters of helpful attitudes for SST therapists (modified and extended from Talmon, 1990)

The power and integrity of the session
- This is it
- View each and every session as a whole, complete in itself
- All you have is now
- It's all here
- Focus on here and now and future exploration

SST in context
- Therapy starts before the first session and will continue long after it
- Show interest in spontaneous changes outside the session
- Therapy occurs over the person's life cycle. It's not a one-shot deal
- Life is full of surprises
- Life, more than therapy, is a great teacher
- Time, nature and life are great healers

Slow, steady and humble
- Take it one step at a time
- You do not have to rush or re-invent the wheel
- Small change may be sufficient
- You don't have to know everything to be helpful

Optimism
- The power is in the client
- Never estimate your client's strengths
- Expect change. It's already well under way

---

and in the changes that they create in their life outside the session. The SST therapist who fails to see this fails to see that the client's life will present opportunities for further change that the therapist can prepare the client to notice and capitalise on.

SLOW, STEADY AND HUMBLE

When I first heard of SST I thought of a flashy, guru-like therapist bringing about a quantum change in the client. As the attitudes in the cluster that I have called 'slow, steady and humble' attest, nothing can be further from the truth. Rather, they paint the picture of a therapist who is patient, realistic, methodical, humble … and focused!

OPTIMISM

Such well-balanced humility, however, is linked closely with the therapist's optimistic views of SST as shown in the fourth cluster of attitudes that I have termed 'Optimism'.

In summary, SST therapists tend to think of SST as a contextualised, powerful way of working with clients where small but important changes can be set in motion by unflappable, but optimistic, practitioners utilising the strengths of these clients.

38

CHARACTERISTICS OF 'GOOD' SST THERAPISTS

Talmon (1993: 128–129), in a client guide to SST, advised that good SST therapists tend to

- listen, understand and relate well to clients;
- help clients to differentiate between problems that can be changed and problems that can't be changed and to focus on the former;
- identify and amplify useful changes and client strengths; and
- remove, effectively and efficiently, the obstacles to their goals.

In my own approach to SST, known as 'Single-Session Integrated Cognitive Behaviour Therapy (SSI-CBT)', I outlined several characteristics of effective SSI-CBT therapists (Dryden, 2022a). In my view, most of these characteristics are also hallmarks of good SST therapists in general and are as follows. Thus, good SST therapists do the following.

CAN TOLERATE LACK OF INFORMATION ABOUT CLIENTS

As we have seen, a defining feature of SST is focus. Given this, therapists will not have the time to go into relevant matters in detail or ask for as much information as they would in longer-term therapy. As such, good SST therapists need to be able to tolerate not having as much client information as they might prefer to have.

 DOI: 10.4324/9781003386353-41

CAN QUICKLY ENGAGE WITH CLIENTS

In SST what is important is to be able to engage with clients. This is usually done by focusing very early on their problem and/or what they want to get out of SST. However, by eliciting clients' strengths and other variables that will aid them in helping these clients more effectively, SST therapists will engage with clients more efficiently because they will be focusing on their attributes rather than just on their deficits. In addition, rapid engagement is facilitated by SST therapists showing their clients, by their demeanour and behaviour, that they are genuinely interested in helping them as quickly as possible.

CAN BE AN AUTHENTIC CHAMELEON

My friend and colleague, the late Arnold Lazarus (1993), introduced the concept of the therapist as 'authentic chameleon' into the psychotherapy literature, a concept that describes a characteristic of 'good' SST therapists. Here, such therapists can authentically vary their interpersonal style with different clients and can astutely determine which clients would resonate with which style. SST can be practised by therapists whose style is the same across clients, but my view is that these therapists will be less effective than therapists who are flexible in their interpersonal relationships with their clients.

ARE FLEXIBLE AND HAVE A PLURALISTIC OUTLOOK

As I mentioned in Chapter 14, SST can be best regarded as a mindset rather than a specific approach and can, therefore, accommodate different approaches to SST. Therefore, therapists who practise SST will bring their own way of using their approach to the work. However, in my view, good SST therapists are prepared to be flexible and pluralistic in the practice of SST (Cooper & McLeod, 2011). This can be demonstrated in several ways:

- by acknowledging that there is no one right way of practising SST – good SST therapists vary their practice with different clients and are prepared to use methods both within and without their preferred approach when the situation calls for it;

- by bringing a both-and perspective to the work rather than an either/or perspective;
- by drawing on clients' strengths and resources as was discussed in Chapters 27 and 28; and
- by involving clients fully at every stage of the process.

CAN THINK QUICKLY ON THEIR FEET

Some therapists prefer to take their time in therapy and to reflect in a leisurely manner about the process as it unfolds. Such therapists would find the practice of SST quite challenging because it requires the therapist to think quickly on their feet. Therapists who have this cognitive facility and enjoy opportunities to use it are those that tend to make effective SST practitioners. Having said this, some SST therapists, especially those who work with families and are supported by an observing team, will schedule a break for 'thinking time', when they will step away from the therapeutic action, think about the session and consult with colleagues who will help them to formulate an intervention.

CAN HELP THE CLIENT FOCUS QUICKLY

In an important respect, the effective practice of SST depends on therapists helping their clients to find a meaningful focus for the work. If such a focus cannot be found, then the potency of SST as a way of working is significantly diluted. Thus, therapists who can help clients focus and can do so quickly, but without rushing them, tend to do very well in SST (see Chapter 54).

CAN USE METAPHORS, APHORISMS, STORIES AND IMAGERY AND TAILOR THEM TO THE CLIENT

Ideally, the process of SST should have an emotional impact on clients. This may happen in the normal course of the therapeutic conversation, but it may be enhanced if the SST therapist employs a suitable metaphor, a pithy and relevant aphorism, an appropriate story or an image developed either by the client on their own or suggested by the therapist. These methods help encapsulate the main learning point for the client in a highly memorable way and tend to be remembered both for the methods and the learning point well after SST has finished. Therapists who can readily employ such methods may be more suited to the practice of SST than are therapists who rely only on straightforward verbal dialogue.

39

SST: THE DOS

I argued above and will develop the point further in Chapter 42 that the practice of SST is flexible and pluralistic. Nevertheless, I think it is fair to say that there are agreed dos and don'ts in SST. In this chapter, I will outline the dos, and in the following chapter, I will outline the don'ts. These points will be schematic because most of them are amplified elsewhere. However, I have presented them in this form because I wanted to convey the sense that, collectively, there are elements of SST practice to aim for (that I explore in this chapter) and elements to avoid (to be explored in the following chapter). The following points have been gathered from various sources such as Bloom (1992), Talmon (1990), Paul and van Ommeren (2013) and Dryden (2017, 2022a).

- *Engage the client quickly through the work.*
- *Be clear about why we are here, what we can do and what we can't do.*
- *Be prudently active.* Your activity as a therapist should promote client activity rather than render the client passive.
- *Be focused and help the client stay focused.*
- *Keep the focus by interrupting the client when necessary.* Give a prior rationale for doing this and elicit the client's agreement. Interrupt with tact.
- *Elicit the problem from the client's perspective.*[1]
- *Assess the problem.*[2]
- *Elicit the client's goal/preferred future and keep focused on this.*

---

1 This may not apply to solution-focused SST therapists.
2 Again, this may not apply to solution-focused SST therapists.

 DOI: 10.4324/9781003386353-42

- *Ensure that this forward focus is underpinned by a value if possible.* When the client is mindful of their values, they will tend to pursue their goal even when the going gets tough. If an SST-related value is identified, encourage the client to keep this mind when working both in the session and after the session.
- *If relevant, ask the client what they are prepared to sacrifice to achieve the goal/preferred future.*
- *Bridge to the future whenever possible.*
- *Whenever practicable, explain what you are doing.*
- *Encourage the client to be specific as possible but be mindful of opportunities for generalisation.*
- *Identify the client's internal strengths and encourage them to make use of these strengths.*
- *Identify what external resources are available to the client and encourage them to make use of these resources where relevant.*
- *Identify previous attempts to solve the problem.* Capitalise on successful attempts. Distance from unsuccessful attempts.
- *Identify and be mindful of the client's learning style.*
- *Make liberal use of questions.* Give the client time to answer your questions. Ensure that the client answers the questions you ask them.
- *Check out the client's understanding of any substantive points you might make.*
- *Identify and respond to the client's doubts, reservations and objections including those that may be expressed non-verbally.*
- *Look for ways of making an emotional impact.* However, don't push for it as the more you push for such impact, the less likely it is to occur.
- *Try to ensure that the client takes one meaningful point from the session and has a plan to implement this point.*
- *Have the client practise the solution in the session if possible.*
- *Ask the client to summarise to keep the process on track and the momentum going. If the client struggles to do this, provide the summaries yourself.*

- *Just before closing, have the client summarise the session and what they are going to take away from it.* Make explicit any important points that the client has missed, if necessary.
- *Tie up any loose ends.*
- *Discuss the possibility of how the client can access further help, if relevant.*
- *Plan for follow-up.*

40

SST: THE DON'TS

In this chapter, I will discuss some therapeutic activities in which SST therapists tend not to engage. Again, these points have been gathered from Bloom (1992), Talmon (1990), Paul and van Ommeren (2013) and Dryden (2017, 2022a).

- *Don't take an elaborate history.* In the film *Ghost Town*, Ricky Gervais plays a cynical New York dentist who goes to A&E complaining of bowel problems. At intake, he is asked several questions about his history to which he replies 'irrelevant'. This is a good reminder for the SST therapist only to ask questions that are relevant to the client's concerns. The therapist does not have the time or the reason to take an elaborate history.
- *Don't let the client talk in an unfocused, general way.* In general, left to their own devices, clients will talk about their concerns in a general way without focus. Given that time is at a premium in SST, such general, unfocused talk will not help the client to get much out of the single session. Working with specificity and focus is what is needed in SST. The exception to this is if the client states that they want to use the session to explore without structure.
- *Don't spend too much time in non-directive, listening mode.* Therapists are generally taught to give new clients an extended opportunity to talk in their own way at the beginning of therapy and to listen attentively and non-judgmentally. While it is important for clients in SST to be heard, the SST therapist ensures they give their non-judgmental attention to the client while helping them to

focus on their prime concern. They consequently do not spend too much time in a non-directive, listening mode.

- *Don't develop rapport independent of the task of SST.* Following on from the above, critics of SST claim that therapists need more than a session to develop a rapport with clients and that such rapport precedes taking a problem and/or solution focus. SST therapists do not agree, and research shows that SST therapists can and do develop a strong alliance with their clients (Simon et al., 2012).
- *Don't assess where not relevant.* Not all SST therapists engage in problem assessment, but those who do avoid assessing areas that may be interesting to know about but are unnecessary to the focus of SST. In my practice of SST, I usually spend a lot of time in problem assessment mode. In particular, it is important for me to know precisely what adversities my clients struggle with and how they inadvertently maintain their problem. However, this assessment is done in a focused way, with little, if any, unnecessary data-gathering (Dryden, 2017, 2018a, 2022a).
- *Don't carry out an elaborate case conceptualisation.* Case conceptualisation involves the therapist and the client working together to gain an overall picture of the factors that account for the development and maintenance of the client's problems and how they may be linked. While this is a valuable exercise, there is no time in SST for the therapy dyad to engage in it and this is why I say that SST is assessment, not conceptualisation, driven (Dryden, 2017, 2022a). As I said in Chapter 3, this poses a challenge for CBT therapists who find it difficult to intervene without being informed by a case conceptualisation.
- *Don't rush your client.* Just because time is at a premium in SST (Dryden, 2016), it does not follow that SST therapists rush their clients. In fact, those who do are generally ineffective. I often point to the example of Mesut Özil, the ex-Arsenal footballer, who was very effective, but never seemed to be in a rush. Good SST therapists take their time!
- *Don't assume that your client knows what you are doing or why you are doing it.* It is tempting for therapists to

think that if clients give non-verbal signs that they under-stand that they know what their therapists are doing and the reasons for doing it then they do, in fact, understand. Good SST therapists don't make this assumption and will; err on the side of caution in explaining what they do and why they are doing it (see Chapter 33 on 'Clarity').

- *Don't ask multiple questions.* SST therapists tend to ask a lot of questions, but show patience in doing so. They avoid asking clients multiple questions if answers are not quickly forthcoming. As I showed in the previous chapter, good SST therapists give their clients time to think.
- *Don't leave your client hanging.* In ongoing therapy, there is a time for leaving clients hanging at the end of sessions. Creating such tension, at times, encourages clients to think things through on their own to good effect. However, this should ideally not be done in SST where good closure and absence of unfinished business tend to be hallmarks of a productive single session.

A CONDUCIVE ENVIRONMENT FOR SST

Therapy does not take place in a vacuum, and when considering the conditions that facilitate SST it is important to consider the environmental context in which it takes place. So, what are environmental conditions that facilitate SST?

SUPPLY AND DEMAND

When an agency employs therapists and the demand for their therapeutic services can be accommodated then the agency is unlikely to offer SST. It is when supply cannot meet the demand that SST will be considered. Thus, when I was consulted to help a university to redesign their counselling service along SST lines, it was because they had a six-week waiting list for an appointment.

However, it is important to recognise that reducing waiting lists and waiting times are frequently the consequence of introducing SST into a service. They should not be the prime therapeutic reason for its introduction. This should be to provide help at the point of need to many people who want to gain help from a brief contact with an agency.

POSITIVE ORGANISATIONAL FACTORS

Whether or not SST flourishes in a counselling agency depends on several positive organisational factors.

Training

When the agency's counsellors are provided with suitable training in the theory and practice of SST and where these

   DOI: 10.4324/9781003386353-44

counsellors are encouraged to air their doubts, reservations and objections (DROs) about SST, then this facilitates the implementation and development of SST in that agency. It does not flourish when such training is not provided or is provided only in a rudimentary way and where expression of such DROs is not encouraged.

Team's willing attitude and support

When a team of therapists feel that SST has been imposed on them, then they will tend to resent this and, in some way, resist its introduction. Thus, the staff need to be in favour of its introduction. This is more likely to happen when SST is largely compatible with the staff's core counselling beliefs and practices (Weir et al., 2008). Furthermore, Talmon (2018: 150–151) makes the point that SST is more likely to flourish 'where the therapists are working as a team with training and research being an active part of the process' than when they don't.

Research on the implementation of SST in Victoria in Australia showed that not only did such team support enable the implementation of SST, but its implementation also had a positive effect on staff morale (Weir et al., 2008).

Organisational support

While the support of the working team is important in the implementation and maintenance of SST, this form of service delivery would not survive without positive organisational support. This support needs to be administrative, supervisory and consultative.

Supervision

Once a counselling team has been trained in SST, then it is important that the SST work of that team is regularly supervised by a supervisor experienced in the practice and supervision of this form of service delivery. It is not good practice for SST work to be supervised by experienced supervisors of longer-term therapy who have not also had extensive experience of practising SST. The are several reasons for this. First, such supervisors lack the SST mindset that is also important for the practice of SST (see Chapter 14). Second, lacking the experiences of SST, such supervisors will have no feel for the work and will not be able to contribute to the development of their supervisees' SST work from an experiential basis. It would not be expected that a therapist's couple therapy work would be supervised by a supervisor who lacks experience of working with couples. Why, then, should it be any more acceptable for a therapist's SST work to be supervised by a supervisor lacking experience of doing SST?

SST AND THERAPISTS' EARNINGS

SST is more likely to be adopted when therapists' earnings are not based on a fee for time. Therapists working in a private practice setting usually have concerns about their earning potential if they were to include SST in their practice. Talmon (1990) argues that therapists in private practice might consider charging more for SST than for ordinary therapy. SST may be more expensive than ongoing per session, but it is cheaper than ongoing therapy per treatment.

THE PLURALISTIC NATURE OF SST

I have made the point before in this book that SST has a pluralistic nature (see Chapter 1). It is my view that adopting a pluralistic view is conducive to its success.

WHAT IS PLURALISM?

Pluralism can be defined as the philosophical belief that 'any substantial question admits of a variety of plausible but mutually conflicting responses' (Rescher, 1993: 79). It shows a commitment to valuing diversity and suspicion of single, all-embracing 'truths', as I have argued elsewhere (e.g., Dryden, 2018b).

SST-relevant principles of pluralism

The following are several pluralistic principles that are relevant to SST:

- There is no one absolute right way of understanding clients' problems and solutions in SST – different viewpoints are useful for different clients.
- There is no one absolute right way of practising SST – different clients need different things, and therefore SST therapists need to have a broad practice repertoire.
- Disputes and disagreements in the SST field may, in part, be able to be resolved by taking a 'both-and' perspective, rather than an 'either/or' one.
- It is important that SST therapists respect each other's work and recognise the value that it can have.
- SST therapists should ideally acknowledge and celebrate clients' diversity and uniqueness.

DOI: 10.4324/9781003386353-45

- Clients should ideally be involved fully throughout the SST process.
- Clients should ideally be understood in terms of their strengths and resources as well as their areas of struggle.
- SST therapists should ideally have an openness to multiple sources of knowledge on how to practise SST, including research, personal experience, and theory.
- It is important that SST therapists take a critical perspective on their own theory and practice – being willing to look at their own investment in a particular position and having the ability to stand back from it.

EXAMPLES OF PLURALISTIC PRACTICE IN SST

Talmon (2018: 153) provides the following good examples of pluralistic practice in SST. He calls these 'dynamic poles' in SST. He says that he may take what appear to be opposite positions, but they should be regarded as both-and rather than either/or:

- Validating a patient's story via empathic listening and challenging the problematic elements in the same storyline.
- Increasing a sense of hope or a realistic sense of optimism, and helping a person to accept certain parts of the harsh reality.
- Offering neutral (and at times passive, silent) listening in one part of a session, and in another part, presenting active, focused questions.
- Being non-directive at one point of the session, and at other times giving prescriptive-like directions.

To this, I would add the point that for some people what is important is not problem assessment, goal-setting or solution-finding, but being given an opportunity to talk in their own way and at their own speed for a whole hour and have the therapist understand them.

CHARACTERISTICS OF
'GOOD' SST CLIENTS

In Chapter 38, I outlined what I consider to be characteristics of 'good' SST therapists. When these characteristics are present, they increase the possibility that SST will be successful. In this chapter, I will outline the characteristics of 'good' SST clients and argue in the same way that when clients bring these characteristics to SST, they will get more out of the process than when they don't.

MALAN ET AL.'S (1975) STUDY

Malan et al. (1975) studied the therapeutic mechanisms employed by 44 clients who were seen for an initial consultation but who never received treatment at the Tavistock Clinic in London. Their data suggest that clients who get the most from SST are those who:

- demonstrate insight;
- show a capacity for self-analysis;
- can work through feelings with the people involved;
- demonstrate normal maturation and growth;
- have a history of therapeutic relationships, especially marriage;
- can take responsibility for their own lives;
- are able to break a vicious cycle between themselves and their environment;
- can benefit from genuine reassurance; and
- show that they can learn directly from experience.

DOI: 10.4324/9781003386353-46

Talmon (1993), in his client guide to SST, argued that the following characteristics will help clients get the most out of therapy including SST. Thus 'good' SST clients tend to:

- see their problems as a challenge;
- confront their problems head on;
- take responsibility for their problems and potential solutions;
- focus on available solutions which they are prepared to implement immediately;
- appreciate their capacity for resilience, compassion and forgiveness; and
- have an 'if it works, don't fix it' viewpoint.

I have outlined several client characteristics that facilitate the outcome of effective SSI-CBT (Dryden, 2017; 2022a) and, in my view, they will help clients get the most out of SST in general. Thus, 'good' SST clients do the following.

HAVE A REALISTIC VIEW ABOUT WHAT CAN BE ACHIEVED IN SST

When clients have a realistic view of what SST can and can't do, and they are prepared to enter the process with that view, then this aids the process. It is when clients have unrealistically high or low expectations concerning SST that the process is compromised.

ARE READY TO TAKE CARE OF BUSINESS NOW

SST works best when clients are ready to deal with their problems now. This is why it is so important that therapy is on offer for such people when they need it. When both therapists and clients are ready to go at the same time, then the power of SST is used to the full. However, no matter how talented and ready the SST therapist is, if the client is not ready to take care of business, then the process won't yield any meaningful effect.

ARE PREPARED TO BE AS ACTIVELY ENGAGED AS POSSIBLE IN THE PROCESS

The potency of SST is best utilised when the client is an active participant in the process rather than a passive recipient of therapist wisdom.

CAN FOCUS AND CLEARLY AND SPECIFICALLY ARTICULATE THEIR TARGET PROBLEM AND RELATED GOAL

If the client takes away one meaningful point from SST that they can apply in their life and which will make a difference, then the therapist has done their job. However, this can only be achieved if the client is clear about what they want help with, specific about their goal and is able to focus on these points without distraction.

ARE PREPARED TO PUT INTO PRACTICE WHAT THEY LEARN FROM THE SESSION

Learning without application makes SST an interesting experience for the client. For them to truly benefit from the process, they need to act on what they learn.

ARE PREPARED TO ENGAGE IN ACTIVITIES WHERE THEY CAN PRACTISE SOLUTIONS IN THE SESSION

In order to benefit most from such real-life application, the client who is prepared to engage in an in-session rehearsal of such action often derives the most benefit from SST.

CAN RELATE TO METAPHORS, APHORISMS, STORIES AND IMAGERY

What often stays with a client who has been through SST is a meaningful aphorism, metaphor, story or a visual image. Clients who relate to such ways of conveying meaning often get more out of the process than those who don't because they can draw on such meaning when they need to.

HAVE A SENSE OF HUMOUR

As Lemma (2000) has shown, humour can be a powerful therapeutic factor. Therefore, to get the most from SST, it is useful if clients have a good sense of humour and can take themselves seriously, but not too seriously (Ellis, 1977).

THE PROCESS OF SST

As Hoyt (2018) has pointed out single-session therapy has its own process. In my view there are six phases to this process.

PHASE 1: BEFORE THE CLIENT AND THERAPIST AGREE TO WORK TOGETHER IN SST

You might think that the process of SST begins when the person first attends the session, but, in my view, it is important to consider what happens before then and to view this as part of the SST process. As such, I have found it useful to make use of work that emanated from American interpersonal-based social work (e.g., Seabury, Seabury & Garvin, 2011) concerning the various help-seeking roles that a person may occupy before beginning SST. These roles are as follows.

The explorer role

Once the person decides that they want help for a mental health issue, they may explore what forms of help are available to them. When they do so, they are occupying the explorer role. As such, they do not yet contact a therapy agency or specific therapists. They are discovering and weighing up their options, one of which, of course, may be SST.

The enquirer role

When the person is occupying the enquirer role, they contact the agency or therapist with questions about some aspect of the therapeutic process. These enquiries may be practical (e.g., concerning fees or how to schedule appointments) or they may relate to the nature and process of therapy. When people have questions about SST, it is to find out more about it and what kind of help is available if they require further assistance. A person occupying the enquirer role may approach several agencies/therapists with the same questions. It is important that the SST models good practice by getting back to the person quickly to answer their queries which may be made by email, by telephone, by text or in person.

The applicant role

When the person occupies the applicant role, they have made up their mind that they want to become a client (at an agency or with a specific therapist) and they are in effect applying for such help. It is important to note, however, that they are not yet a client.

The client role

The person becomes an SST client when they give their informed consent to proceed. Thus, they understand what SST can offer them, and what it can't, and want to move forward based on this understanding. They also understand and agree to abide by relevant policies such as the agency's or therapist's confidentiality policy. I also think that it is important that the therapist should also give their informed consent to proceed. Rarely, the client may wish to access SST but the therapist has significant doubts and when this happens a full discussion needs to had with the person before a negotiated decision is made concerning whether or how to proceed.

PHASE 2: THE PRE-SESSION PREPARATION PHASE

Once the therapist and client have contracted to work with one another in SST by appointment or once the person has engaged with an open-access SST facility then before the session takes place the person is given an opportunity to prepare for the session, usually by completing a questionnaire designed to help them get the most from the session (see Chapter 49). It is made clear to the client that this is a recommended part of the SST process and that they can choose not to complete it. However, if they do so, then they are encouraged to share it with their therapist so that the latter can prepare for the session as well.

PHASE 3: THE BEGINNING PHASE OF THE SESSION

After the formalities of contracting have been completed, the main task of the SST therapist in the beginning phase of the session is to build a working alliance with the client quickly (see Chapter 51). This involves discovering what type of help the client is looking for (see Chapter 22) and what they want to take away from the session. This enables the client and therapist to co-create a focus for the session which is designed to help the client achieve their session goal.

PHASE 4: THE MIDDLE PHASE OF THE SESSION

Once a focus has been created then the therapist helps the client according to the client's helping preferences. If, as is most common, the client is stuck with an emotional/behavioural problem and wants help with this, the therapist will assist them both to get to the heart of the issue and to identify a solution to this problem.[1] Solutions for change are discussed, selected and rehearsed, drawing on a range of relevant factors, action planning is done and obstacles to change are identified and a way of dealing with them formulated. The basic task of the therapist in this phase is to facilitate change and to introduce novelty where indicated.

PHASE 5: THE ENDING PHASE OF THE SESSION

Once the client has developed a solution, rehearsed it and made plans to put it into action, the therapist knows that they have reached the ending phase of the session. At this point, the therapist encourages the client to summarise the work that they have done and to detail what they are going to take away from

---

1 If the therapist is solution-focused they may concentrate on helping the client develop a solution and focus less on understanding the problem.

the session (known as 'take-aways'). The therapist invites the client to mention anything relevant to the issue that they have not already mentioned and ask any questions related to the work done that they want to ask before the close of the session. The client is then reminded that they can access further help and how this may be done before the session is brought to a close, hopefully with the client's morale restored, at least in part (see Chapter 14).

PHASE 6: POST-SESSION

After the session there may be up to three points of contact:

1. Directly after the session to gauge the client's immediate feedback on the session (see Chapter 86).
2. A few weeks after the session to determine whether or not the client wants to access further help.
3. An agreed date (usually between one and six months) when the client is contacted to provide outcome data (what has been the outcome of the session) and service evaluation data (what the client thought of the service with which they were provided) – see Chapter 87. This is commonly known as 'follow-up'.

Part 4

CRITERIA FOR SST

THE CLIENT CRITERIA QUESTION

Whenever I give presentations on SST, by far the most frequently asked question concerns the indications and contra-indications for SST (see Dryden 2022c). When I first developed my CBT-based approach to SST (Dryden, 2017), I outlined such criteria, but I soon realised that doing so was a mistake for two reasons. First, instead of offering a single session of therapy to someone at their first point of contact, I was developing a single session of assessment to determine who would benefit from a single session of therapy. As such I was not best utilising perhaps the only occasion that I would see the person and be able to offer them help at the point of their need. Second, as I discovered later, the best way to determine who would benefit from SST is to offer them a single session and to determine at the end of the session if they benefited from it. Thus, when I came to write the second edition of my book on my CBT-influenced approach to SST (Dryden, 2022a), I omitted the material on indications and contra-indications.

SST IS OPEN TO ALL

Most SST therapists are against adopting a criteria-based approach to SST. Instead, some take an embedded approach to SST provision while others offer open-access SST hitherto known as 'walk-in' therapy.

The embedded approach to SST provision

An example of the embedded approach is that of Jeff Young (2018: 48–49) whose response to the question concerning who is suitable for SST and who is not is as follows:

We believe the best response to this question is to avoid having to answer it by embedding SST in the service system so that clients can return if they want to. Embedding SST into the service system so that all services the organization normally provides are available following an initial session, conducted as if it may be the last, allows the practitioner and the organization to avoid the 'difficult if not impossible' decision of who is suitable and who is not suitable for a 'one-off' session. For many therapists and some managers, the assumption that clients facing complex problems require 'deep' change which can only occur in long-term work is very strong and entrenched. The SST literature continues to build data to challenge this assumption.

Open-access, walk-in therapy

By its nature, walk-in therapy offers therapy to whoever needs it and uses the service. As such it is best regraded as an open-access therapy. If clients using this service are at risk, risk assessment is carried out by on-duty therapists, but these clients are still offered help within the single-session, walk-in paradigm. Walk-in therapists agree with Young who says that it is rarely possible to predict who will and will not benefit from SST. As such, no pre-session criteria-based assessment is made of clients who come to an open-access, walk-in service. If it turns out that they have come to the wrong place, then they are treated with respect and acceptance and signposted to the right form of help. It should not be forgotten that such people may need to use the walk-in therapy clinic in the future and how they are treated on their first visit will determine whether or not they use the service again.

THERAPIST INDICATIONS AND CONTRA-INDICATIONS FOR SST

Not all therapists are interested in practising SST and, of those who are, not all will make effective SST practitioners. In this chapter, I will consider the therapist indications and contra-indications for SST. I have considered the helpful attitudes that SST therapists need to hold in Chapter 37 and the characteristics of 'good' SST therapists in Chapter 38, but have not, as yet, considered what therapist factors contra-indicate the practice of SST.

THERAPIST INDICATIONS FOR SST

In considering the various lists that appear in the literature concerning what are therapist indications for SST (e.g. Dryden, 2017; Hoyt & Talmon, 2014a; Talmon, 1990, 1993), it seems to me that all can be placed under the headings of flexibility and pluralism.

Effective SST therapists are flexible and pluralistic in outlook and practice

Being flexible as a practitioner in SST basically means two main things. It means:

- that while the therapist may have their practice preferences, they are flexible in the implementation of these practices and will not use favoured interventions when it is clear that these are not proving useful or are not relevant for the client; and

DOI: 10.4324/9781003386353-50

- the therapist varying their style of participation in the process, but in a genuine manner to enable the client to get the most out of SST – Arnold Lazarus (1993) calls this being an 'authentic chameleon'.

Being pluralistic as an SST therapist means being able to hold and embrace seemingly contradictory positions at different times and with different clients. It means:

- having faith in the power and integrity of SST *and* viewing it more broadly within the context of the client's life;
- being open to the possibility that this may be the only session for the client *and* to the possibility that the person may require an additional session or sessions;
- having humility in terms of what one can and can't do *and* being optimistic in expecting change to occur;
- being able to work quickly in developing rapport and helping the client to be and remain focused on a key issue *and* taking one's time and not rushing the process; and
- privileging the client's view of the problem and what might constitute an appropriate solution *and* offering one's own views on these matters when appropriate.

THERAPIST CONTRA-INDICATIONS FOR SST

By contrast, therapist contra-indications for SST seem to fall into two main classes: rigidity and poor skill.

Ineffective SST therapists are rigid in outlook and practice

SST therapists who are ineffective tend to take the process of SST and themselves as SST practitioners too seriously and are rigid in the way see and practise it. Thus, they tend to think that SST must take one session only and regard themselves as a failure if they have not helped the client after the session has finished. With this rigid view in mind, they rush and push the client too hard and thus produce the very resistance that will interfere with client gain.

Thinking that they are the most important variable in promoting client change, they underestimate and underuse their clients' strengths and resilience, thus stripping the process of two important growth-promoting ingredients.

Ineffective SST therapists lack the skill to practise SST well

When therapists are flexible about SST, they can still practise it ineffectively due to poor skill. Thus, ineffective SST therapists fail in several ways. In particular, they fail:

- to develop effective working relationships quickly with clients;
- to be clear in their communications with clients;
- to help clients focus on their core concerns;
- to keep clients on track once a focus has been created;
- to help clients to set workable goals; and
- to identify and use clients' strengths and resources.

If therapists cannot address these skill deficits, then, in my opinion, they should not be SST therapists.

No therapist should be compelled to practise SST

In the same way as no client should be compelled to have SST when they do not wish to make use of this form of service delivery, no therapist should be compelled to practise SST when they do not want to. This has employment issues for some therapists who do not wish to practise SST when their employing agency has introduced SST and requires them to practise it. However, this is an HR issue and as such it falls outside the present book's focus.

SERVICE INDICATIONS AND CONTRA-INDICATIONS FOR SST

As I pointed out in Chapter 41, whether SST will be effective as a service delivery will depend, in large part, on the environment in which it is practised. In this chapter, I will complete my discussion on the indications and contra-indications for SST with a discussion of these as they pertain to the service in which SST is located.

SERVICE INDICATIONS FOR SST

The following are, in my view, good indicators that SST will flourish as a method of service delivery:

- *Service-wide support.* It is important that the majority of workers in a service support SST as a mode of service delivery. Before it is introduced, all stakeholders in the service need to be able to share their enthusiasm and raise their doubts, reservations and objections (DROs) to SST and have these discussed in a respectful manner. Managers, therapists and administrative staff need to be involved in the decision concerning whether or not SST is introduced. If it is introduced, then those therapists who don't wish to be involved should have their wishes respected. In this way, any covert attempts to sabotage SST will be minimised.
- *Proper training.* Before implementing SST provision in an agency, it is important that all key personnel are sufficiently well trained. This should involve both skills development and opportunities to share and discuss doubts, reservations and objections to SST.

DOI: 10.4324/9781003386353-51

- *Ongoing supportive supervision.* While adequate training in SST is necessary before SST is launched within an agency, ongoing supervision of how SST is practised is important to refine skills and protect client welfare. This should be provided by supervisors experienced in the practice of SST and the supervision of SST therapists.
- *Proper administrative support.* Within an organisation or agency, if there is not sufficient administrative back-up to support the SST service then it will soon wither. Thus, in agencies where SST flourishes, administrative staff are active participants in the team and their feedback is crucial to ensure the smooth running of the service.
- *SST integrated in service provision.* It is important that SST is fully integrated into the agency's service provision rather than isolated from it and potentially seen as a 'hived-off' part of what the agency provides run by one or two enthusiastic individuals.
- *Accessible to the public.* It is important that SST service provision is accessible to the public, both in terms of service advertisement and in terms of geographical location. Thus, if people know about it and it is easy to access, then it will tend to be used.
- *Ongoing research and evaluation.* Weir et al. (2008) have made the point that SST services are likely to succeed if they are underpinned by feedback – both client outcome data and service delivery data. If the team is actively involved in these activities, then the service will benefit.
- *Continuing professional development (CPD).* An SST service will be enhanced if therapists are regularly bringing new ideas concerning how to improve service delivery. Also, engaging in CPD activities invigorates therapists and this can only be good for SST service delivery.
- *Therapists should not only practise SST.* One way of keeping fresh as an SST therapist is to practise therapy of differing lengths. In this case, SST is informed by longer-term work and longer-term work is informed by SST. In this case, the agency benefits as a whole from therapists who have variety in their working lives.

- *Links with other agencies where SST is practised.* One way of keeping an SST service delivery fresh, and thereby increase the chances that it will be an ongoing success, is to form links with other agencies who offer SST service provision. This will enable both agencies to share experiences, learn from each other's mistakes and to try out what works for the other agency.

- *Provides training for others.* Once an agency has established an SST service delivery, embedded it in the agency's overall work and run it for a while with success, then it may consider offering training in SST for others. This has the knock-on effect of regularly showing how the service works to those wishing to learn about this method of service delivery. Feedback from eager neophytes can often challenge standard practice in ways that can refresh staff who are perhaps a bit smug that things are working well.

SERVICE CONTRA-INDICATIONS FOR SST

SST as a form of service delivery might fail if the conditions are not right for it to flourish. When the following conditions exist and can't be modified, then they are, in my opinion, service contra-indications for SST.

- *SST is imposed.* Sometimes when an agency is struggling with long-term waiting lists, they panic and impose the introduction of SST into their service delivery without adequately preparing the ground. Imposing SST on therapists who are neither adequately briefed nor trained is to be avoided.

- *Led by a minority of evangelical supporters.* Sometimes the idea of SST is introduced into an agency by one or two highly enthusiastic advocates of SST. When they are given their head and set up the service without preparing the ground by discussing it fully with management, other therapists and administrative staff, then the service will tend to falter because it lacks strong enough supportive foundations.

- *Insufficient training.* If therapists are not properly trained in SST, they are unlikely to offer an effective service, and this will be reflected in client feedback.
- *Insufficient supervision.* Similarly, lack of effective supervision won't lead to the correction of common therapist errors in the practice of SST, and this will again lead to poor client feedback.
- *SST not integrated into the agency.* If SST becomes isolated in the agency, then eventually this will have a negative impact on even the most enthusiastic of SST therapists. After a while, these enthusiasts may leave and not be replaced.
- *No administrative support.* As the proper administrative support of any therapy agency is important, the failure to provide this for the SST arm of an agency usually predicts its demise.
- *The agency's climate does not encourage the expression of doubts, reservations and objections (DROs).* If therapists are not encouraged to voice their concerns about SST, these will remain and be expressed indirectly to the detriment of SST service provision.
- *Not accessible to the public.* If people don't know that SST is on offer in an agency and it is housed in a place that is difficult to access, then the service will not be used.
- *No links with other agencies where SST is practised.* If the agency in which SST is practised has no links with other like-minded agencies, then the SST will exist in splendid isolation and will eventually atrophy with the attendant risk to its continuation.

Part 5

GETTING SST OFF ON THE RIGHT FOOT

RESPOND EFFECTIVELY TO THE PERSON'S VERY FIRST CONTACT

BE RESPONSIVE, ATTENTIVE AND ACCESSIBLE

When a person makes contact for any kind of therapy, it is my view that they merit a prompt response from someone in the therapy service who is accessible and attentive. If it is clear at the outset that the person is actively seeking SST, the therapist should strike while the iron is hot and capitalise on the person's readiness to be seen by offering a time to talk about the SST service and other forms of service delivery that the therapist or therapy service offer.

DISCERN WHAT HELP-SEEKING MODE A PERSON IS IN AND RESPOND ACCORDINGLY

When a person contacts a therapist, they are in one of two modes: enquirer or applicant. When a person is in the enquirer mode, they are seeking the right approach and/or right therapist at a price that they can afford (if in the private sector), but they have not come to any decision about who they wish to consult. If they are in applicant mode, they have decided to see a particular therapist or seek help from a particular agency, and the onus here is on the therapist to judge whether they can offer help to the person. If not, then an appropriate referral should be made. It should be noted that the person only becomes a client when the person has given their informed consent to proceed.

DOI: 10.4324/9781003386353-53   149

OUTLINE SERVICES

It is a good idea sometimes for the therapist (or agency representative) to outline what services are on offer, which would include a thumbnail description of SST. Then the person can decide whether SST is appropriate for them and, if so, whether the therapist (or agency) is most suitable.

EXPLAIN THE PROCESS OF SST

Once the person has made contact, the therapist (or agency representative) should offer a more detailed explanation of the process so that the person is better prepared for the next phase. Utilising an opening gambit offered by Hoyt et al. (1992: 69), the therapist might say: 'Many people who seek therapy find that a single session can help a lot. So, if we are both ready to address your problem, then I'll do my best to help you get what you are looking for from therapy in that one session. If you need further help after that, then that is possible too. Is that something that you would like to pursue?'

HELPING THE CLIENT TO PREPARE FOR THE SESSION

Whether SST is by appointment or by walk-in, it is very useful to invite the client to prepare themself for the session by asking them to complete a pre-session questionnaire. The purpose of this pre-session questionnaire is to help the person get the most from the session that follows. In Table 49.1, I present a pre-session questionnaire that I invite people to compete to help them prepare for their single session with me. In an accompanying email, I make clear the following:

> I have found it useful to ask clients to prepare for their session with me and to that effect, I would be grateful if you would download and complete the attached form. Let me emphasize that this is not mandatory; just something that will help you get the most from our session. If you decide to complete it, I would be grateful if you would share a copy with me by email attachment so I can prepare for our session too.

DOI: 10.4324/9781003386353-54

Table 49.1 Pre-session questionnaire

I invite you to fill in this questionnaire before your session with me. This will help you to prepare for the session so that you can get the most from it. It also helps me to help you as effectively as I can. Please return it by email attachment before our session. Please be brief and concise in your answers.

Name: Date:

1. What is the issue that you want to focus on in the session?
   Be concise. In one or two sentences get to the heart of the problem, if possible.

   ```
   
   
   ```

2. Why is this significant?
   What's at stake? How does this affect your life? What is the future impact if the issue is not resolved?

   ```
   
   
   ```

3. What do you want to get from the session?

   ```
   
   
   ```

4. Specify briefly the relevant background information.
   What do you think I need to know about the issue to help you with it? Summarise in bullet points.

   ```
   
   
   ```

Table 49.1 (Cont.)

5. How have you tried to deal with the issue up to this point?
   What steps, successful or unsuccessful, have you taken so far in addressing the issue?

6. What are the strengths or inner resources that you have as a person that you could draw upon while tackling the issue?
   If you struggle with answering this question, think of what people who really know you and who are on your side would say.

7. Who are the people in your life who can support you as you tackle the issue?
   Name them and say what help each can provide.

8. What help do you hope I can best provide you in the session?
   Please check the main <u>one</u>.

   □ Help me to develop greater understanding of the issue
   □ Just listen while I talk about the issue
   □ Help me to express my feelings about the issue
   □ Help me to solve an emotional or behavioural problem; help me get unstuck
   □ Help me to make a decision
   □ Help me to resolve a dilemma
   □ Other (please specify):

Thank you.
Windy Dryden

Part 6

GETTING THE MOST FROM THE SESSION

AGREE OR REVIEW PARAMETERS

In the SST literature, an important distinction is made between SST by default and SST by design. In the former, the person has had one therapy session, the therapist and the client agree to have a further session or sessions, but the client either cancels this appointment without rescheduling another or does not show for the second session. As we have seen in Chapter 8, such clients are generally regarded as 'drop-outs' from treatment, but a sizeable number of these people are satisfied with the session that they had and decide that they do not need to have further help.

In SST by design, the therapist and client plan, at the outset, to have a single session to see if the therapist can help the client take away from the session what the client hopes to achieve. If so, then the person gets on with their life. If not, the client can access further help. SST by design also occurs in walk-in services, where the person knows that they can walk in and see a therapist and then walk out again. They may walk in again at a later date for another session, but probably with a different therapist.

Whichever approach to SST by design is taken, it is important for the therapist and the client to agree on parameters if the session is their first contact, or to review parameters even if they have already agreed on them at the pre-session contact.

WHAT ARE THE PARAMETERS?

By now it should be clear that there are few universally agreed principles and practices in the field of SST. However, there are areas of consensus. One such area is that it is important for both the client and the therapist to be clear on the nature of their contract. What is said next will vary, as will be shown below.

ONE SESSION WITH THE POTENTIAL TO HAVE MORE

As I have already discussed, there are some SST therapists, albeit few in number, who only offer one session. If this is the case, the therapist should make this explicit at the outset and get the client's agreement. In addition, if there is to be a follow-up session or contact, this needs to be made and put in the diary.

However, it seems to me from the literature on SST (e.g., Hoyt & Talmon, 2014a; Hoyt et al., 2018a) that the prevailing view is that the therapist conveys a message to indicate that one session may be sufficient, but more is available if needed. For example, a therapist may say something like, 'We have agreed to meet today, and if we both really focus we can help you to head in a direction that is right for you, and, if so, you may decide at the end that this is all that is needed. If not, further help is available. Shall we move forward on that basis?'

EXPECTATIONS

Some SST therapists prefer to spell out what might be called 'realistic expectations' for SST. These state that change can be achieved in a short period of time and it is possible that such change can be initiated by the client in the session with the therapist's help and that the client can continue this process on their own later. If a client has several problems, it is put to them that the therapist will help them to focus and work towards the solution of one of these, whichever will benefit them the most.

UNIQUE FEATURES

If there are any features that are unique to the therapist's practice of SST, then the therapist should make them clear at the outset and seek the client's agreement. For example, in my own practice of SST, I ask for permission to record the session. I state that part of the SST package that I offer involves me sending the client a digital voice recording of the session and a written transcript of the recording for the client's later review. I make clear that while these are primarily for the benefit of the client, they also help me to reflect on my work and improve my service delivery (Dryden, 2017, 2022a).

51

BE MINDFUL OF THE WORKING ALLIANCE IN SST

Research shows that clients who benefit from SST report that they had a better working alliance with their therapists than those who did not benefit (Simon et al., 2012). It is very important, therefore, that the SST therapist needs to pay attention to the working alliance between them and their client. In what follows I will use my reformulation of Bordin's (1979) tripartite model of the working alliance (Dryden, 2006, 2011). This posits that there are four components of the alliance: bonds, views, goals and tasks.

1. The therapist needs to build a good *bond* between them and their client and do so as quickly as possible. In my view, the best way that the therapist can do this is to demonstrate to the client that they genuinely want to help the person as quickly as possible but to do so without rushing the client.
2. It is important that the therapist and the client share the same *view* concerning the nature and purpose of SST. In particular, if more sessions are possible, then this needs to be made explicit by the therapist and understood and agreed to by the client before the two embark on the session.
3. It is important for the therapist and the client to have shared and realistic *goals* concerning what can be achieved from SST. In my experience, SST is most valuable helping clients to get unstuck so that they can get on with the business of living. Thus, shared goals that represent un-stuckness are particularly valuable.
4. It is important that the client can make sense of any *tasks* that the therapist suggests that they use and can see the

 DOI: 10.4324/9781003386353-57

relevance of doing them to achieving their goal. Given the nature of SST, it is important that any suggested task is simple to understand and implement, even though doing so may not be easy.

Many therapists are wary of SST because they think that they will not be able to form a strong enough working alliance with their clients for them to do any useful work in the session with them. I hope the points I have made above and Simon et al.'s (2012) research suggest otherwise.

52

BEGIN THE SESSION

If the client has completed a pre-session questionnaire (see Table 49.1), then the therapist can refer to this during the session. If they have not returned the form or have not been sent one, then the therapist can proceed as follows. First the therapist should ask the client what their understanding is concerning the session that they have come for. If the client understands that the purpose of the session is to help them take away what they have come for and if they need more help than they can have it, then they can proceed with the session. If the client is unsure of the session's purpose or if they think that they are coming for a different service, then the therapist needs to make clear the nature of SST and invite the client to proceed on that basis. If the client does not want to proceed, then the two need to agree on a way forward which may involve a referral to a different form of therapy delivery.

Assuming that the therapist and the client decide to proceed, how can the therapist initiate the process? Normally, the therapist does this by being active, focused and asking pertinent questions, as illustrated by Hoyt et al. (2018b).

When the client has a problem for which they are looking for help – which is the most frequent request in SST – the therapist adopts a problem-focused approach. As such they might begin by asking the client:

- What do you call the problem? What name do you have for it?
- If we were only going to meet once, what problem would you want to focus on solving at this point in time? (Haley, 1989)

DOI: 10.4324/9781003386353-58

When exploring variation in the problem, the therapist might ask:

- When is the problem not a problem?
- When (and how) does the problem influence you, and when (and how) do you influence it? (White, 1989)

When taking a solution-focused approach, the therapist might ask:

- What needs to happen here today so that when you leave, you can feel this visit was worthwhile?
- What are you willing to change today? (Goulding & Goulding, 1979)
- On a scale of 1 to 10, where is the problem now? Where would it need be for you to decide that you didn't need to continue coming here?
- What are your best hopes for today's meeting? (Iveson, George & Ratner, 2014)
- What's your idea or theory about what will bring about change? How would your life be better with these changes?

Solution-focused therapists often take a 'micro' approach to change that is compatible with SST. Questions that such therapists might ask clients at the outset are:

- If we work hard and well together, what will be the first small indications that we are going in the right direction?
- Suppose tonight, while you're sleeping, a miracle happens, and the problem that led you here is resolved. When you awaken tomorrow, how will you first notice the miracle has happened? What will be the first sign that things are better? And the next? And the next? (de Shazer, 1988)

A strengths-based therapist would focus on the client's strengths and capabilities as a way of initiating the SST process. For example:

- Given all that you have been through, how have you managed to cope as well as you have?

In the next chapter, I discuss effective problem-focused SST.

FOCUS ON A PROBLEM THAT CAN BE SOLVED, NOT ONE THAT CAN'T BE SOLVED

Since SST is a very focused intervention, it is important that both the therapist and the client spend their time together wisely and this is best done by helping the client to focus on a problem that can be solved rather than on one that can't be solved. A problem that can be solved is one that involves the person dealing with what is in their control and being prepared to deal with it now. A problem that can't be solved, from the perspective of SST is, by contrast, one that is outside the client's control or one that is within their control but which they are not ready to tackle now for one reason or another.

HELPING CLIENTS TO FOCUS ON WHAT THEY CAN CONTROL RATHER THAN ON WHAT THEY CAN'T CONTROL

Often clients come to therapy complaining about adversities. These adversities may represent aversive interpersonal behaviour from others or negative life events. It is important to help clients understand what they are in control of and what they are not in control of here. They are not in control of how others behave, nor are they in control of events or situations that obstruct them from their goals. What they are in control of is their interpretations, beliefs and attitudes towards these adversities and how they act towards them. The SST therapist can help them enormously by encouraging them to make this shift.

An elderly woman needed two days' complete rest and quiet and booked into a very exclusive hotel suite for this purpose, having been assured by the hotel that she would get what she paid for. As she was laying down on her bed, dozing, she was awoken by loud piano music coming from the suite next door. Outraged, she went down to complain to the hotel manager. Skilled in handling delicate situations, the manager thought for a moment and then asked the woman if she had heard of the man who was playing the piano in the suite next to hers. He was, in fact, an internationally renowned concert pianist who was in town for a single concert which had sold out months before. The woman confirmed that she had heard of the man. 'Madam,' said the hotel manager, 'do you know how fortunate you are? You are being given a private concert by the one of the world's greatest concert pianists!' The woman's anger disappeared in an instant, and she quickly excused herself, saying that she did not want to miss any more of her private concert. While not a single-session therapist, the hotel manager demonstrated all the hallmarks of one. He immediately focused on the woman's problem, thought quickly on his feet and reframed the problem from that which was outside the woman's control (i.e., 'the noise coming from next door which was disturbing my rest') to that which was within her control (her choice was whether or not to avail herself of and enjoy the 'private' concert). In doing so, the manager also appealed to one of the woman's key 'drivers' – her vanity!

FOCUSING ON WHAT THE CLIENT IS PREPARED TO DEAL WITH NOW

A client may come to therapy with several problems and even may select a problem to begin with. However, from an SST perspective, this selected problem may not be the best problem to target since the person may not be prepared to get down to business to deal with as quickly as possible, that is *now*. Given this, when the client mentions a number of problems, the SST therapist may ask something like:

- Which one problem would you wish to solve as quickly as possible and which you are prepared to give your all to address?

HELPING THE CLIENT TO GET UNSTUCK

I see SST as particularly suited to problems with which the client feels stuck. The client is often stuck because they are doing things repeatedly, which they think will help them, but which in fact account for the stuckness. The therapist's role in such cases is to encourage the client to see things from a different perspective and/or help them consider acting differently. I say that SST is particularly useful for 'stuck' problems because it helps transform the client from someone who 'feels' at a loss concerning how to get unstuck to someone who feels encouraged to try things that they have not previously considered. All the client needs is someone who can provide a broader perspective, make a suggestion or two and then get out of the client's way after the client has become unstuck.

Malcolm sought therapy because he was anxious about sweating in public. He had tried many ways to stop sweating, all of which maintained the problem rather than solved it. I suggested that his problem with sweating was his relationship with it. I wondered what would happen if he regarded sweating to be like a misbehaving child who craved attention, positive or negative. Malcolm recognised that what such a child disliked was lack of attention. When they eventually learn that they are not going to get it, they stop misbehaving. Malcolm found this helpful and resolved to stop trying to stop sweating and get on with talking to people even while he sweated. At follow-up, Malcolm reported that the session had helped him to focus away from sweating, which he now regarded as a nuisance rather than a threat. He had maintained his gains three months later.

CREATE AND MAINTAIN
A WORKING FOCUS

Given that time is at a premium in SST (Dryden, 2016), it is important that the therapist helps the client create a focus and to keep to it once it has been co-created. I have argued (such as in Chapter 22) that at different times in the SST process (for example, when the client wants to address a specific emotional/ behavioural problem) the therapist may adopt a problem focus and a solution focus. Normally, in SST, if the therapist adopts a problem focus, they will adopt a complementary solution focus.

Once this general focus has been initiated, then the therapist and the client need to establish what I call a 'working focus'. This represents the work that the therapist and the client do to address the client's problem and to help them achieve their solution. Let me give an example: Leon came to see me for help with his public speaking anxiety. He was anxious about revealing his ignorance to his audience. We agreed that this was his problem and that he was keen to address it immediately as he had a public speaking engagement in two days' time. We, therefore, agreed to use this as a concrete example of the problem. Since, Leon was unsure of his goal, I gave him a rationale for setting a goal of being concerned, but not anxious, about revealing his ignorance when he gave the presentation in two days' time, which he accepted. This was our working focus. From that point, my task was to keep him to that focus. This meant that every time he strayed from that specific example, I gently brought him back to it.

 DOI: 10.4324/9781003386353-60

POLITE, RESPECTFUL INTERRUPTION

Most clients will be able to keep to the agreed working focus when the therapist helps them to do so. However, some clients find it more difficult to maintain their focus, and the therapist needs to interrupt them politely, respectfully and sometimes firmly. In my experience, when clients stray from the agreed working focus, they do so in two ways. First, they give a lot of detail about the situation in which their problem occurred, too much for the purposes of SST, and, second, they easily go from the necessary specifics of the working focus and the agreed concrete example of their problem to the unnecessary generalities of the target problem and other problems that they may have.

On the latter point, I encourage clients to imagine that they are playing the murder mystery game known as 'Cluedo' (or 'Clue' in North America) when we are working in a focused way in SST. The purpose of Cluedo is to find the specific identity of the murderer, in which specific room the murder was committed and with which specific murder weapon. The purpose of SST is for therapists and clients to look for specific ways in which clients can help themselves deal with specific examples of their specific problems and thus reach their specific goals.

Gain the client's permission to interrupt

When it seems that the client is likely to struggle to keep to the agreed working focus – and this becomes apparent almost immediately with some clients – then it is valuable for the therapist to give a rationale to interrupt the client and to obtain the client's permission to do so. I usually say something like, 'To get the most from our session it is important for us both to stay focused on your goal. Sometimes people find it hard to stay focused and if that happens with us, may I have your permission to interrupt you and bring you back to the focus?' Clients who have a problem with staying focused generally recognise this and are relieved when the therapist offers to interrupt them and thus readily give their permission.

When the therapist has a problem with interrupting clients

Many therapists have been trained to facilitate their client's self-exploration and have been warned against interrupting the client's 'flow'. While taking this approach may be helpful in many therapeutic circumstances, it is generally not useful in SST where the emphasis is on zeroing in on one issue rather than opening the conversation up in a broad sense.[1] While understanding the need for focused work in SST, some therapists resist the theory and practice of interrupting their clients because they think that it is untherapeutic and/or rude to do so. On the first point, my response is that it is untherapeutic in SST to allow the client to wander from issue to issue in the limited time available and not to interrupt the client when they do this. On the second point, my response is that it is possible to interrupt the client with tact, respect and politeness, and from a different perspective it is rude (meaning 'unhelpful') not to do so. I would go so far as to say that if a therapist has an enduring reluctance to interrupting clients, it may be that they are not suited to single-session work.

ENSURING THAT CLIENTS ANSWER IMPORTANT QUESTIONS

Many years ago, a Portuguese friend and colleague fell out with his PhD supervisor, and I was asked by his university to take over the supervision of his doctoral thesis, which I agreed to do. In Portugal, the PhD viva is conducted in public and is attended by scores of people. Just before the viva began the head of department took me aside and said that it was widely known that I was the candidate's friend and colleague and it was important that I did not show any positive bias towards him in the viva. 'Be firm with him if necessary, but show your independence', I was advised. There were six examiners including myself and when it came to my turn to ask questions,

---

1 The exception to this is when the client wants to use the session in talking about whatever they wish to talk about without a focus.

things progressed smoothly. Then I asked the candidate a tricky question to which he gave a lengthy answer, but one which was not in direct response to my question. When he had finished, I paused, looked directly at him and said, 'Mr Oliveira,[2] that was a very full and complete answer to a question that I did not ask you. Now, can you answer the question that I did ask you?!' to which the audience literally gasped. In making this intervention, I did what I was asked to do: I was firm with the candidate and thus showed my independence.

I have not told this story because I recommend the manner in which I intervened at the viva. Far from it! I have told the story to demonstrate the importance of checking whether or not the client has answered an important question in SST. If not, the therapist needs to point this out in a gentle, respectful manner and encourage the client to answer the question. Having said this, if the client keeps moving away from the question, it is best for the therapist not to pursue matters and to ask about a related matter. Flexibility is key here as elsewhere in the SST process. In order to sharpen one's skills at identifying instances of people not answering questions put to them, I usually recommend that therapists listen to the *Today* programme on BBC Radio 4, especially when the presenters interview politicians.

2 Not the candidate's real name.

HELP CLIENTS DEAL WITH ADVERSITY, IF POSSIBLE

Clients often come to therapy because they have emotional problems. These tend to be anxiety, depression, guilt, shame, anger, hurt, jealousy and envy. People experience these emotional problems when they face a range of adversities, and the emotion gives a clue concerning the nature of the adversity. In my view, it is important for SST therapists to know the adversity themes that accompany the eight major emotional problems for which people seek help. This is particularly the case for those SST therapists who take a problem-focused approach as well as a solution-focused approach to the work. I have listed the adversity-related themes for each of the eight emotions in Table 55.1.

WHEN TO TAKE AN ADVERSITY FOCUS IN SST

Adopting an adversity focus is a feature of my approach to SST known as 'Single-Session Integrated Cognitive Behaviour Therapy (SSI-CBT)' (see Dryden, 2017, 2022a). Extrapolating this focus to SST in general, in my view, adopting an adversity focus is particularly important:

- *When the client's main strategy is to avoid the adversity or withdraw from it the moment it occurs, or they think it is about to occur.*
- *When the client reacts to the adversity with disturbed feelings and/or unconstructive behaviour when facing the adversity.*

   DOI: 10.4324/9781003386353-61

- *When the client is stuck and needs a different approach to the adversity in order to get unstuck.* This is best done when the client is encouraged to face the adversity rather than avoid it or reframe it so that they can process it and think creatively about how to deal effectively with it.
- *When the client keeps responding unhealthily to the adversity, even when they correct their distorted inferences.* For example, Lorna was anxious about being criticised. Previous therapy had focused on helping Lorna to see that her inference that she would be criticised was distorted and needed to be corrected. Although this strategy was useful to her in the short term, she kept on predicting criticism about which she made herself anxious. SST was focused on helping her to assume temporarily that she would be criticised and to deal with this as a fact. This helped her to process being criticised in a healthy way and also encouraged her to be more objective about the possibility of being criticised.
- *When reframing the problem does not work at all or when it may work, but only for a short time.* In the latter case, the client needs to face the adversity in order to deal effectively with it. Thus, in Chapter 53, I mentioned the case of the elderly woman who was helped to reframe an interruption to her rest as an opportunity to have a private recital from an internally renowned pianist. If this reframe had not worked, then the woman would have the choice to deal with the disruption (the adversity in question) with disturbance or without disturbance.
- *When the client's main adversity is their response to their response to adversity.* Sometimes, the client's main problem is not their initial disturbed response to an adversity, but their disturbed response to this disturbed response. In Rational Emotive Behaviour Therapy (REBT), this is known as meta-disturbance (Dryden, 2021b). The emotion of 'shame' is a common 'secondary' meta-disturbance that, if effectively addressed, leads to the person being able to live better with their primary disturbance.

Table 55.1 Emotional problems and related adversities (actual or inferred)

Emotion	Adversity (actual or inferred)
• Anxiety	• Threat
• Depression	• Loss • Failure • Unfair plight to self or others
• Guilt	• Violation of moral code • Failure to abide by moral code • Hurting another
• Shame	• Falling short of ideal • Revelation of negative information about self • Others look down on or shun self
• Problematic anger	• Frustration or goal obstruction • Others' bad behaviour • Transgression of personal rule • Disrespect from others • Threat to self-esteem
• Hurt	• Undeserved bad treatment from others • Other is less invested in relationship than is self
• Problematic jealousy	• Another poses a threat to one's relationship • Uncertainty in relation to the above threat
• Problematic envy	• Another has what one prizes but does not have

NEGOTIATE A GOAL

In the field of SST, the words 'problem', 'solution' and 'goal' are frequently employed without precise attempts to differentiate between them. In using these terms in this chapter, I will utilise definitions provided by the *Oxford English Dictionary*.

DEFINITIONS OF 'PROBLEM', 'SOLUTION', 'GOAL'

- Problem: 'A matter or situation regarded as unwelcome or harmful and needing to be dealt with and overcome.'
- Solution: 'A means of solving a problem or dealing with a difficult situation.'
- Goal: 'The object of a person's ambition or effort, an aim or desired result.'

SST WITH PROBLEMS, SOLUTIONS AND GOALS

From this, we can see that some SST therapists are prepared to work with problems (unwelcome matters), goals (desired results in tackling problems) and solutions (means of achieving goals), while others are prepared to just work with goals and solutions. Given this, I see solution-focused therapy as only meaningful if it focuses on solutions and goals. If it just focuses on solutions – which are means – then it will be therapy that focuses on means without ends. In the same vein, I see goal-oriented therapy as involving both goals and solutions. If it just focuses on goals, then it will be therapy which specifies a destination without any discussion of the means to get there.

DOI: 10.4324/9781003386353-62

FOCUS ON GOALS

A 'goal' is, thus, an endpoint towards which the client is prepared to strive. In SST, the client does not end therapy once they have achieved their goal. They end it when they know what they are aiming for and have been helped by the therapist to see that they can get there on their own.

'SMART' GOALS

There have been several different ways of conceptualising therapeutic goals. Perhaps the most well known – 'SMART' goals – was created by Doran (1981) to help managers write goals and objectives. While there have been different versions of the 'SMART' acronym, the version that I think is most applicable to SST is as follows:

- 'S' = **Specific.** Specific goals should be clear enough to help the client see what they are aiming for. This will vary from client to client.
- 'M' = **Motivating.** While 'M' usually stands for 'measurable', my view is that 'motivating' is more useful for SST, particularly if it makes clear what the reasons are for change.
- 'A' = **Achievable.** If the client cannot achieve a goal, it has no place in SST.
- 'R' = **Relevant.** If a goal is not relevant to the client's life, then it is unlikely that they will work to achieve it.
- 'T' = **Time-bound.** It is important that the goal can be achieved in a specified period of time, but, as mentioned above, what is most important is that within the time constraints of SST the client can see where they are heading and has the confidence that they can get there after therapy has ended.

'WHAT WOULD YOU LIKE TO ACCOMPLISH TODAY?'

Moshe Talmon (1993: 140) suggests that the SST therapist asks the client this question to orient the client, at the outset, that therapy is a goal-oriented endeavour and to create the possibility that therapy might be concluded if the person accomplishes what they have set out to accomplish at the end of the session.

BEHAVIOURAL GOALS

In Chapter 55, I made the point that whenever possible, SST clients should be helped to face and deal with adversity rather than be helped to bypass it. When doing so, what type of goals should be set with clients? In my view, there are two types of goals that are important to consider here: behavioural goals and emotional goals. I will deal with behavioural goals here and emotional goals in the next section.

When highlighting behavioural goals, the therapist and the client work together to formulate behaviours that are most likely to change the adversity if it can be changed. Here, it important to remember the point that I made in Chapter 53: help the client focus on what is within their control. For this reason, the SST should help the client to understand the difference between influence and change when discussing how to deal with adversities that refer to the behaviours of others. The client's behaviour can only influence the behaviour of another person and not change it directly. Given this, the therapist and the client should set behavioural goals that are most likely to influence the other person based on a joint understanding of what that person is most likely to respond to favourably.

HEALTHY NEGATIVE EMOTIONS AS ADVERSITY-RELATED GOALS

There are two scenarios when emotional goals should be set in SST. The first is when the person's emotional response to the adversity is problematic and will interfere with them carrying out their agreed behavioural goal. The second is when the adversity is unlikely to change and thus the task of the client is to put up with the adversity without disturbance, particularly when they cannot get away from the adversity.

In my approach to SST – Single-Session Integrated CBT (Dryden, 2017, 2022a) – I draw upon a distinction that is made in Rational Emotive Behaviour Therapy (REBT), namely between unhealthy negative emotions and healthy negative emotions (Dryden, 2021b). As the term makes clear, 'unhealthy negative emotions' (UNEs) are emotional responses to adversities (such as those listed in Table 55.1) that are negative in tone and unconstructive in effect. Common examples of UNEs are anxiety, depression, guilt, shame, hurt and the problematic forms of anger, jealousy and envy. By contrast, 'healthy negative emotions' (HNEs) are emotional responses to the same adversities (as listed in Table 55.1) that are also negative in tone, but constructive in effect. Common examples of HNEs, which should be viewed as healthy alternatives to the above-listed UNEs, are concern, sadness, remorse, disappointment, sorrow, and the non-problematic forms of anger, jealousy and envy.

It is important to note from the above position that emotional goals in response to adversities are negative in tone. According to this view, it is not healthy to feel positive or neutral about something negative (i.e., an adversity). It is healthy to feel negative about something negative!

From the perspective of REBT, the way to help clients achieve their emotional goals in the face of adversity is by helping them to change their rigid and extreme attitudes towards the adversity to flexible and non-extreme attitudes. However, from an SST perspective, the important issue is that the therapist helps the client change processes that the client thinks will enable them to achieve such emotional goals.

UNDERSTAND HOW CLIENTS UNWITTINGLY MAINTAIN THEIR PROBLEMS AND USE THIS UNDERSTANDING TO HELP THEM SOLVE THESE PROBLEMS

One of the reasons why people have problems is because they unwittingly maintain them. I say 'unwittingly' here because from the perspective of the client they are trying to solve the problem, not perpetuate it. For SST therapists who are problem-focused, identifying these problem maintenance factors helps both the therapist and the client to understand what the latter needs to change.

COMMON PROBLEM MAINTENANCE FACTORS AND THEIR HEALTHY ALTERNATIVES

Here is a range of problem maintenance factors and their healthy alternatives. The latter are only suggestive, for what really counts is what the client decides is for them a healthy alternative to a problem maintenance factor.

Avoiding issues–facing issues

When a client has a problem, they may experience an urge to avoid that problem. They often do so before encountering the problem, or they may withdraw from the situation once the problem has begun to be experienced. The healthy alternative to avoiding issues is to face them. Such facing can be done in a 'full, intense' way or in a way that I have called 'challenging, but not overwhelming' (Dryden, 1985).

Facing issues in a full, intense way. An example of full, intense facing of issues is the 'one-session therapy' of simple phobias (OST) where the person agrees to face their phobic object over a period of up to three hours (Davis III, Ollendick & Öst, 2012) which generally leads to the extinction of the phobic response. The important ingredients here are that: (1) the person is given a rationale for the treatment which they accept and to which they commit in a long session; and (2) it is worth it to the person to go through what is a painful process.

'Challenging, but not overwhelming'. Here, the person agrees to face their adversity in a way that is challenging, but not overwhelming for them. Throughout the process, this is defined by the client. In SST, the therapist introduces the concept and, if the client wishes to use it, they both plan how the client will implement the concept in their life as soon after the session as is practicable. The therapist encourages the client to take the concept and use it going forward into the future.

Encouraging the client to picture themself facing their issue in their mind's eye is something that the SST therapist can suggest that the client can do in the session as a prelude to doing so in their own life.

Avoiding discomfort–bearing discomfort

We increasingly live in a world dominated by our sense of comfort. The reason people give for not wanting to do something that is in their best interests is 'I'm not comfortable' and they expect this to be understood and accepted, certainly not challenged. However, change involves discomfort. As I often say, 'If it ain't strange, it ain't change'. Thus, a legitimate target for change in SST is 'avoidance of discomfort' when it maintains the person's problem. A 'bearing discomfort' stance has the following features:

- bearing discomfort is a struggle;
- bearing discomfort is possible;

- bearing discomfort will be done if the person sees that it is in their best interests to do so;
- bearing discomfort will be done if the person thinks that they are worth bearing it for;
- the person is willing to bear discomfort;
- the person commits to bearing discomfort; and
- he person takes appropriate action.

In helping the client to develop what I have termed an attitude of 'bearability' (Dryden, 2021b), it is useful for them to put such an attitude into their own words and for them to imagine bearing discomfort as clearly as possible using imagery, again as a prelude to doing so in their own life.

Finding distress unbearable–bearing distress

It is increasingly appreciated that people's reaction to their own distress can serve to maintain their problems and is thus a legitimate target for change (Leyro, Zvolensky & Bernstein, 2010). The three most common components of distress unbearability are: (1) finding the emotional, cognitive, imaginal and/or urge to act components of the distress unbearable; (2) fear of losing self-control; and (3) self-referential meaning (e.g., 'I am weak for feeling this way').

The SST therapist can help the client address such issues and help them recognise that: (1) they can bear their experience; (2) they can control this experience once they stop trying to eliminate it; and (3) they can develop the same compassionate view of themselves for experiencing the distress as they demonstrate to their loved ones. These messages can be reinforced by the appropriate use of chairwork in the session (see Chapter 75).

Rigid thinking–flexible thinking

When a client thinks rigidly, they have fixed ideas about how things have to be. This rigidity may apply to the adversity, their disturbed feelings about the adversity, other people or themselves. These rigid ideas serve to maintain their problem.

Helping the client to think flexibly involves helping them realise that their preferences indicate what is important to them and that they have a choice whether to keep these preferences flexible by acknowledging that they don't have to have them met or make them rigid. The therapist helps the client with their choice by encouraging them to think what type of thinking is most healthy for them and will help them solve their problem.

Not testing inferences–being prepared to test inferences behaviourally

Clients often maintain their problems by not testing the inferences that they make about the adversity and by acting according to their untested inferences. For example, a person may think that people whom they have just met will think them boring. As such, they don't engage in conversation with the people. It is important that the person is encouraged to test out their inferences behaviourally by, in this case, engaging the others in conversation and see what happens. In an SST context, the client can only test this out in imagination, but if they also do this in reality after the session, they can benefit from such behavioural experiments (Bennett-Levy et al., 2014).

Silent assent–assertive boundary setting

Often when clients complain about being treated badly by others, it is because they have done nothing in response and can be said to be silently assenting to such behaviour. As Hauck (2001) has noted, when a person is treated badly by others and does not protest about such behaviour, then the other people will continue to treat the person badly. The antidote to silent assent is assertive boundary setting, which the client can practise in the session by role-playing with the therapist.

Reinforcing others' bad behaviour—reinforcing others' good behaviour

Similarly, people unwittingly help to maintain bad behaviour in others by unwittingly rewarding such behaviour. In addition to asserting themself with the other, it is important that the client reinforces good behaviour when the other exhibits it.

WHAT TO CHANGE, I: INDIVIDUAL-FOCUSED CHANGE

The purpose of SST, like other forms of therapy, is to help the client effect change. Personally, I think that SST best helps clients get unstuck and get on with their lives, and reach a point where they would not seek therapy. As I will discuss later in this chapter, change can be brought about by modification-based strategies or by acceptance-based strategies, as shown in Reinhold Niebuhr's Serenity Prayer:

> God grant me the serenity
> to accept the things I cannot change;
> courage to change the things I can;
> and wisdom to know the difference.

In this chapter, I will discuss the issue of individual-focused change, where the therapist helps people to solve their particular problem by making a change within themselves. In the following chapter, I will discuss the issue of environment-focused change, where the therapist helps the person to solve their particular problem by making a change in their environment. While the two strategies are not mutually exclusive in that a person may find it easier to make an internal change after making an external change, I will discuss them separately.

THE 'BASIC I.D.' FRAMEWORK

In thinking about the question 'what can the person change in themselves in SST?', I have found it instructive to use the 'BASIC I.D.' framework originated by Arnold Lazarus (1981):

　　　DOI: 10.4324/9781003386353-64

B = Behaviour
A = Affect
S = Sensation
I = Imagery
C = Cognition
I = Interpersonal relationships
D = Drugs and biological functioning

When working with individuals in SST, therapists mainly work directly with clients to produce change in behaviour, sensation, imagery and cognition. As Lazarus (1981) notes, it is not possible to change a person's affect directly; rather, affect change occurs when change occurs in one or more of the other modalities. In SST, it is also not possible to change an individual client's interpersonal relationships (in the 'I.' modality) directly; rather change here is effected largely by encouraging the person to change their behaviour towards the other person and observing the impact of that change. Finally, most SST therapists are not qualified to deal with queries about the client's current or possible medication needs (in the 'D.' modality) and will refer the client to the appropriate professional.

In conclusion, in answer to the question of what the targets are for change in SST, my answer is behaviour, sensation, imagery and cognition, and, when effective, changes in these modalities will produce a constructive change in affect.

COGNITIVE CHANGE

Change in the cognitive modality tends to be inferential or attitudinal. Here, I define an inference as 'a hunch about reality that goes beyond the data at hand and which may be correct or incorrect'. I use Colman's (2015) definition of attitude as 'an enduring pattern of evaluative responses towards a person, object, or issue'.

Attitudinal change

Imagine that a client is furious with their mother for being intrusive when she asks the client, 'What's on your agenda today?'

Helping the client to make an attitude change involves the therapist encouraging the client (a) to assume temporarily that her mother is being intrusive and from there (b) to identify their fury-creating attitude towards such intrusiveness. Once this attitude has been identified, the client can be helped to change it in order to deal more constructively with this adversity.

Inferential change

Inferential change involves the client standing back and examining the evidence for and against the inference they have made and possible alternative inferences. After reviewing the evidence, the client is encouraged to opt for the inference that best fits the evidence. In the above example, the client concluded that her mother was not being intrusive when asking her what was on her agenda. Rather, it was her mother's way of asking about her day.

Normally, in SST, the therapist does not have the time to help the client make both an attitudinal change and an inferential change, so the two have to decide which change will best solve the client's problem.

BEHAVIOURAL CHANGE

In SST, the therapist can encourage the client to make a change in behaviour and offer the person an opportunity to rehearse this in the session, but, if this is the only session that the person attends, then the therapist will not know whether or not the person implemented this change in their life or, if they did, what was the outcome of such behavioural change.[1] There are a number of ways in which the SST therapist can help their client in the realm of behavioural change.

Urge to act

The therapist can help the client distinguish between an urge to act and overt behaviour. This is particularly important for

---

1 The SST therapist who conducts a follow-up session will discover this, but only much later (see Chapter 87).

the clients whose problem is impulsive in nature. Helping such a client to slow down the process between the urge to act and deciding whether or not to act on that urge is the focus of the intervention here. After this has been done, the therapist can help the client to use imagery to rehearse the experience of having the urge and not acting on it.

Behavioural change to test inferences

In Chapter 57, I briefly discussed the use of behavioural experiments to help clients test their distorted inferences, and this approach is best used when a change in attitude towards a negative event is not likely, possible or desired by the client.

Behavioural change to consolidate attitude change

When encouraging the client to change a specific attitude which is implicated in the person's problem, it is useful for the person to act in ways that will consolidate this attitude. Given the nature of SST, the client should be encouraged to select behaviour that they can practise regularly in the service of attitude change.

Influencing others

I have mentioned several times in this book that if a client has a problem with another person, one way of encouraging that person to change is for the client to change their behaviour towards them first. This may be tried out in role-play with the therapist first to assess the likely impact of the new behaviour on the other person.

Skills development

When the client's problem is due to or exacerbated by a behavioural skills deficit, then the therapist may help them by helping them acquire or develop the relevant skill.

Act in accord with values

Practitioners of Acceptance and Commitment Therapy (ACT) contend that rather than get embroiled in the business of modifying troublesome cognitions and emotions, a client is best served by being encouraged to accept their presence while acting in ways that promote the person's values (e.g., Flaxman, Blackledge & Bond, 2011).

SENSATION CHANGE

Sensation change involves encouraging the client to focus on helpful sensations as ways of bridging to more constructive use of other modalities. For example, I once helped an SST client change their anxiety-creating cognitions after first accessing a sensation of warmth.

IMAGERY CHANGE

Quite often clients are negatively affected by troublesome mental images, which they can learn to modify to more constructive images. These can then be rehearsed, particularly before behavioural change is implemented. Imagery techniques are often combined with sensation techniques (e.g., where a client is asked to identify and picture a relaxing scene and to focus at the same time on sensations of relaxation).

MODIFICATION-BASED CHANGE AND ACCEPTANCE-BASED CHANGE

In the field of cognitive behavioural therapy (CBT), strategies to change troublesome thoughts and feelings, for example, involve either helping the client to modify the cognitions that underpin their feelings or to accept the presence of these thoughts and feelings while initiating value-based action. SST therapists can draw upon both approaches to change and consult their clients concerning which approach they consider to be most helpful to them (Dryden, 2021b).

Having discussed the issue of individual-focused change, in the next chapter I will discuss the issue of environment-focused change.

WHAT TO CHANGE, II: ENVIRONMENT-FOCUSED CHANGE

In the previous chapter, I discussed the issue of change by discussing the areas in which the individual can change themself to solve their problem, if emotional/behavioural problem-solving help is the reason for which they are seeking help. However, there are times when the person is better served when the therapist helps them to consider making a change in their environment to solve their problem. In discussing environmental change with an SST client, I encourage them to think of themself as a plant. I point out that different plants thrive in certain environments and wither in others. I ask them to consider in which environments they thrive and in which environments they wither. Armed with this information, I ask my client to consider the environment in which they experience their problem and whether they need to change this environment to solve their problem or whether they need to remain in this environment and change an aspect of themself.

There are, of course, situations where it is clear that the client does need to make an environmental change (e.g., when the client is being abused in some way), and equally there are situations in which the client cannot change their environment (e.g., when the client has to stay in a bad job for financial reasons). However, in most other situations the client can solve their problem either by making an internal change or by changing their environment.

In this situation, the therapist and the client need to decide together whether to pursue an individual-focused change or an environment-focused change. As I said earlier, both forms of change may be possible, but the consequences of each form

 DOI: 10.4324/9781003386353-65

may be very different. Certainly, the content of the single session will be very different depending upon which form of change is selected by the client and the therapist.

Let me provide an example. Robin sought therapy for work-related anxiety. He had been headhunted for a very well-paid job in a large organisation because of his high-level programming skills. However, his new work environment was closely managed, and his boss was intolerant of programming mistakes. Robin's therapist asked him whether he was thriving or withering in his new work environment. Robin was clear – he was withering. He reported that he thrived in an environment typified by his last job. In that position, the firm he worked in was small and he was given a lot of autonomy, and programming mistakes were accepted.

Robin's therapist outlined that they could go one of two ways. First, the therapist could help Robin deal better in his current position. Here his anxiety would be addressed, but even if this was achieved, he would still be working in an environment in which he did not thrive. This approach to Robin's problem would be an example of what I call here individual-focused change. Second, the therapist could help Robin recognise that no matter what he changed about himself, he would not be happy in his present job and that he needed to seek a work environment in which he thrived, where he was given autonomy and where mistakes are seen as part and parcel of developing innovative computer programs. Robin was clear. He opted for environment-focused change.

FOCUS ON AND USE PIVOT CHORDS

Rosenbaum, Hoyt and Talmon (1990) note that an important task for the therapist is to demonstrate that they understand their client from the client's frame of reference. However, in addition, the therapist needs to offer the client a new perspective from which they can solve their problem. The concept of the 'pivot chord' is useful for SST therapists in implementing these two tasks.

Rosenbaum et al. (1990: 180) note that, in music, 'the pivot chord is an ambiguous chord that contains notes common to more than one key and so can imply several different "directions" to the music and facilitate the transition from one key to another'. They go on to say that, 'an important task of the SST therapist is to construe the client's difficulty in such a way that it can function as a pivot chord for change. The therapist can be helpful by putting the symptom into a larger pattern in which the problem contains the seeds of new directions for the client'.

Steenbarger (2003) discusses Tom, a financial trader, who came for help with his problem with work-related anxiety. He said that he was fearful of getting a stroke. When discussing his problems, he mentioned, in passing, that he had a dog called 'Nipper'. To stop both of them being overwhelmed by Tom's increasingly agitated account of his anxiety, Steenbarger asked Tom about his dog and found that the only thing that calmed him down was having Nipper on his lap and stroking her belly. Steenbarger asked Tom to imagine this in the session, and, as he did so, he was able to feel calm and warm. At this point, Steenbarger (2003: 37) introduced the pivot chord:

DOI: 10.4324/9781003386353-66

STEENBARGER: When you wake up with your anxiety, how would you like to *really* experience a stroke? [Tom responded with shock.]

TOM: What?

STEENBARGER: A Nipper stroke. When you are stroking Nipper, you're making that puppy feel loved and wanted, and that feels good to you. Suppose you could stroke yourself the way you stroke Nipper?

Tom liked the idea of 'giving himself a stroke' and used this as a cue to dealing with his stress rather than becoming anxious about his own feelings of anxiety. Steenbarger (2003: 38) concludes thus: 'The "stroke" metaphor, delivered at a time of emotional upheaval and following a shift to a warmer feeling, was the pivot chord that made the shift possible.' Thus, giving himself a stroke became both what Tom was anxious about and what helped him with his anxiety. The therapist introduced ambiguity into the client's frame of reference and helped him to reframe the concept of giving himself a stroke by using the concept of the pivot chord.

AGREE MARKERS FOR CHANGE

The question is often asked at training workshops, 'Is SST effective?' Dryden (2020), Hoyt and Talmon (2014b), Hoyt et al. (2018b) and Hymmen, Stalker and Cait (2013) have reviewed a great deal of evidence on the efficacy of SST. While it is important for a client to know that SST has a strong research base, what is more important to the person is the question, 'Will SST be effective for me?'

To answer this latter question, the client and their SST therapist need to identify markers for change. There are two different, but related, markers here: outcome markers and progress markers. From a working alliance perspective (see Chapter 51), it is important that the therapist and the client agree explicitly concerning the nature of these markers.

OUTCOME MARKERS

As the name makes clear, an outcome marker represents a clear indication that the person's outcome goals have been met. Here are some questions to encourage the client to think about outcome markers:

- 'What would convince you that you have accomplished what you wanted from therapy?' (Talmon, 1993: 140–141)
- 'What would your life look like when you don't need therapy anymore?' (Talmon, 1993: 148)
- 'If you solved your problem, what would be different about your life?'

The more specific these markers, the better, as specific markers give a clear indication that the person's goals have or have not

DOI: 10.4324/9781003386353-67

been reached. However, such is the nature of SST, both the therapist and the client will not know the outcome of the intervention until after the client has implemented it in their own life. Also, the therapist may never know if outcome markers have been met unless they conduct a follow-up. So, in short, agreed outcome markers indicate the hoped-for end-point of SST. They point to where the client wants to end up and show whether or not this has been achieved.

PROGRESS MARKERS

Imagine that a client is travelling from London to Glasgow by train and that there are several intermediate stations. London is akin to the client's problem, Glasgow is their desired outcome, and the intermediate stations constitute the progress they are making towards their desired outcome.

Given this, it is important for both the client and the therapist to be clear about and agree the client's progress markers. Here are some questions to encourage the client to think about progress markers:

- 'How would you know things are starting to improve even just a little?' (Talmon, 1993: 143)
- 'What would tell you that you were making progress towards your goals?'
- 'Given that you are stuck, what would be the first indication that you were getting unstuck? … and the next?'

Again, given the nature of SST, the therapist will not learn of the client's achievement of their progress markers. What is important is for the therapist to encourage the client to remember these progress markers and to suggest that they set up a system to use them. It is useful to note that for some clients the setting of an initial progress marker is sufficient and they would be overwhelmed if a series of linked markers are set, while for other clients having a clear idea of such a series is motivating. As with other issues, which approach should be used needs to be discussed with the client.

NOTICE AND
ENCOURAGE CHANGE

In the previous chapter, I introduced the concept of progress markers. These are identifiable points that indicate to the client that progress is being made towards their outcome goal. I also made the point in the previous chapter that as the therapist will probably not be around to witness the client's achievement of these progress markers, as these will occur after SST has ended, the therapist needs to discuss with the client how they can best notice these changes and how they can use their achievement to encourage further change. In addition to the client noticing change in their mind and being encouraged by it, the change-oriented focus mentioned above can be maintained by the following.

KEEPING A 'NOTICING CHANGE' LOG

The therapist can suggest that the client keeps a 'noticing change' log in which the client notes change with respect to their problem and goal, where and when it occurred, and what they did to effect the change.

ELICITING THE SUPPORT OF OTHERS

In Chapter 28, I discussed the importance of the therapist helping the client to identify people in their life who can help and support them to get the most out of SST. In the present context, this means that the client might ask another person to give them feedback when they notice that the client has demonstrated a relevant change. In doing so, this person would also provide encouragement and support to the client as they apply what they have learned from the single session.

     DOI: 10.4324/9781003386353-68

FOCUS ON THE SECOND
RESPONSE NOT THE FIRST

When a person faces an adversity, and they respond in the first instance problematically, one way of helping them in SST is to encourage them to see that their initial response is not the problem. Rather, what constitutes the problem, and potential solution, is their subsequent response to this first response.

Let me illustrate this by first considering how to work with a client who has a problem with failure and comes to therapy when she fails her driving test. Her initial problematic response was the cognition, 'I'm a failure'. As outlined in Table 63.1 the problem is not the client's initial response that they are a failure. The problem is how they respond to that initial response. Thus, I have outlined four problematic responses and two constructive responses to the cognition, 'I'm a failure'. In working with the client, the therapist might take their subsequent problematic response to the cognition, outline the other five options and encourage the person to choose the option that they think will provide the best solution to their problem with failure.

The same approach could be used with another client who has a problem with dealing with an urge to act in a self-defeating manner in specific situations. Again, the problem is not the urge itself, which is their initial response to the situation in question; rather, it is their subsequent response to this urge. Additionally, their solution is also to be found in their subsequent response. Table 63.2 outlines one problematic response and two constructive responses to the urge. As before,

DOI: 10.4324/9781003386353-69

Table 63.1 The person's subsequent responses to their first response are often more important than the first response itself, I: Problematic cognitions (e.g., 'I'm a failure')

First response	Subsequent responses	Impact on well-being
'I'm a failure'	Notice the thought, accept that the thought is present and then take constructive action	Constructive
'I'm a failure'	Examine the thought and then act on a new healthy thought	Constructive
'I'm a failure'	Accept as true	Unconstructive
'I'm a failure'	Shame-based self-criticism	Unconstructive
'I'm a failure'	Question thought until eliminated; self-criticism when this fails	Unconstructive
'I'm a failure'	Distraction	Unconstructive
'I'm a failure'	Thought suppression	Unconstructive

Adversity = Failing a driving test

in working with the client, the therapist would take the client's subsequent problematic response to the urge, outline the other two options and encourage the person to choose the option that they think will provide the best solution to their problem.

Table 63.2 The person's subsequent responses to their first response are often more important than the first response itself, II: Problematic urges

First response	Subsequent response	Impact on well-being
Urge to engage in self-defeating behaviour	Act on the urge	Unconstructive
Urge to engage in self-defeating behaviour	Notice the urge, accept its presence and then act according to goals and values	Constructive
Urge to engage in self-defeating behaviour	Develop healthy cognitions about the urge and then act according to goals and values	Constructive

Adversity = Exposure to situation in which the urge is likely to be experienced

LOOK FOR EXCEPTIONS
TO THE PROBLEM

Ratner, George and Iveson (2012) note that the fallibility of human beings means that not only do humans have problems but also that they do not 'do' their problems perfectly. There are 'exceptions' to the person's problem if looked for hard enough. This is a core assumption of solution-focused therapy: 'It is impossible to behave with total consistency and however stuck in a problem pattern, there will always be exceptions, times when we do something other than the problem, something that with nurturing has the potential to become a solution' (Ratner et al., 2012: 106).

The task of the SST therapist is, therefore, to help the client find exceptions to the problem which can help towards the development of the solution. As an example, take Talmon's (1993) discussion of Pat, who came to therapy for help to lose weight. She was living at home, and her mother regularly harassed her about her weight. Her therapist discovered that despite Pat's ongoing struggle to lose weight, there was a time when she considered that her weight was just right over an extended period of time. This was when she was in college and more active. Rather than focusing on her weight, the therapist's strategy was to encourage Pat to translate the 'exception' (staying at a weight that was right for her while being away from home at college) into the 'rule'. To this end, Pat joined a graduate programme that allowed her to live on campus away from home and took dancing and singing lessons which were activities that she liked but had not engaged in since leaving college. Pat's therapy only lasted a single session, but she was

 DOI: 10.4324/9781003386353-70

encouraged to use a solution that she previously employed and this was achieved without a deliberate focus on the problem.

This case shows that developing exceptions was done within an environment-focused change paradigm (see Chapter 59). If Pat was not able to leave home and go to college, then the therapist would have had to help her search for exceptions to her problem while living with her mother or help her to deal with her mother in other ways.

LOOK FOR INSTANCES OF THE GOAL ALREADY HAPPENING

In the development of solution-focused therapy, there was a move away from identifying and working with the client's 'exceptions' to the problem to identifying and amplifying instances of the solution (or the goal) already happening (Ratner et al., 2012). Take the case of Rita. She was scared of being criticised at work, and her goal was to be able to handle criticism better from her boss. When asked by the therapist what would she think, feel and do if she were handling being criticised better, she replied thus: 'I would think that while his criticism might be valid, it did not make me a failure. I would be feeling uncomfortable, but not anxious and I would stick up for myself if I thought he was unfair in his criticism, and thank him if I thought it was fair'.

Having elicited Rita's goal, the therapist asked her if there were any instances in her life in which she was achieving her goal in the face of criticism. Rita thought for a moment and then replied, 'Yes, I do that a lot with my friends. I think that I handle criticism well when my friends criticise me'. But, she added, 'they don't have control over my career'. The therapist then asked Rita whether her boss had control over her career or influence over it. Rita again reflected on the question. 'I see what you mean', she said, 'I have been assuming that my career was in his hands, but it really isn't. Yes, he has influence, but I have control, and even if he tries to keep me down if I stand up for myself, then I can do something about it'.

Rita did not think that she needed any more sessions because she believed that she could achieve her goal, which she did as she reported at three-month follow-up.

 DOI: 10.4324/9781003386353-71

Rita's case shows a number of things in my view:

- People often do enact instances of their goal.
- They are often unaware of this fact but can gain access to it when asked to by the therapist.
- Even if they are aware that they are already meeting their goal, albeit in a different area of their life, they often need help to generalise from one area to the next.[1]
- In relating the instance, the client often reveals additional information that helps account for the problem which needs to be addressed if the goal is to be realised. Thus, Rita thought that her boss had control over her career and that this prevented her from realising her goal. When the therapist helped her to see that this was not the case, this barrier to solving her problem was effectively dealt with.

---

1 This example does not show this point, but I have generally found this to be the case. Here, Rita saw immediately that she could generalise her desired behaviour from one area to the salient area.

ENCOURAGE THE CLIENT TO DO MORE OF WHAT WORKS OR MIGHT WORK AND LESS OF WHAT DOESN'T WORK

SST therapists vary concerning the stance that they take towards their clients' problems. If they are solution-focused, they will focus on the client's problem only to help the person to identify and work towards a solution, However, if they are problem-focused as well as solution-focused they will spend some time assessing the client's problem. One of the purposes of doing so is to help themselves and the client to understand what the latter has previously done to try and solve the problem. This assessment of previous solution attempts is important in that it helps both the therapist and the client understand what the client has done to try to help themself that has proven helpful in some way and what has not proven helpful.

In an influential paper from the Mental Research Institute (MRI) Brief Therapy Center in Palo Alto, California, Weakland et al. (1974) stressed that it is what a client and significant others in their life do to help solve the client's problem that unwittingly serves to maintain it. From this, it follows that the therapist not only needs to know what the client has done to try to solve the problem but also what these significant others have done. If these others are present in SST,[1] they can speak for themselves on this point, but if they are not, then the client

---

1 As I pointed out in the Preface, this book largely focuses on SST with individuals.

    DOI: 10.4324/9781003386353-72

will have to report on what these others have done in the service of solving their problem.

THERAPIST QUESTIONS

In what follows, I provide two lists of possible questions that the therapist can ask the client. The first list concerns what the client themself has done (or could do) to try to solve the problem. The second list concerns what other people have done (or could do) to help the client solve the problem.

Therapist questions concerning the problem-solving attempts of the client

- 'What have you done to solve the problem?' For every response given the therapist can ask: 'What was the outcome of this problem-solving attempt?'
- 'What have you done to solve the problem that was helpful in any way? What was helpful about it? Are you willing to do more of this?'
- 'What have you done to solve the problem that was not helpful? What was unhelpful about it? Are you willing to stop doing this or to do less of it?'
- 'Is there anything that you haven't tried yet that you think might be helpful. What is it? How do you think it might help? Are you willing to try it?'

Therapist questions concerning the problem-solving attempts of significant others

- 'What have other people in your life done to help you solve the problem?' For every response given the therapist can ask: 'What was the outcome of this problem-solving attempt?'
- 'What have others done to help you solve the problem that was constructive? What was constructive about it? Are you willing to ask them to do more of this?'
- 'What have others done to help you solve the problem that was not unconstructive? What was unconstructive about

it? Are you willing to ask them to stop doing this or to do less of it?'
- 'Is there anything that others haven't tried yet that you think might be helpful to you? What is it? How do you think it might help? Are you willing to ask them to do it?'

All the above information helps the therapist and the client to plan a solution to the person's problem, as will be discussed in Chapter 78.

MAKE AN EMOTIONAL IMPACT

In layperson's terms, it is important to strike a balance in SST between head and heart. Too much head and the client comes away from the session with some good theoretical ideas, but without the emotional resonance to promote change. Too much heart and the risk is that the client may have an emotionally cathartic experience, but without any clear idea about what to apply from the session to their own life. In this respect, the goal of the SST therapist is to strive to create a therapeutic environment in which the session has a productive emotional impact on the client; productive in the sense that it both engages their heart and head which can work together to facilitate later change. Before I discuss some ways in which the therapist can increase the session's emotional impact on the client, let me issue a caveat. The therapist should not go into the session intending to provoke the client's emotions. Rather, they should go gently and look for ways to help the client connect their feelings with what they are discussing so that they can integrate their thoughts and emotions while searching for a solution.

FIND AND USE SOMETHING THAT REALLY RESONATES WITH YOUR CLIENT WHILE HELPING THEM

It is difficult for the therapist to know what is going to resonate with the client when helping them address their problem and/or search for a solution. The following points are worth keeping in mind.

Use language that is meaningful to the client

The SST therapist is advised to listen carefully to the language that the client uses in the session. If they use certain words or phrases frequently, then this may be one indication that such language is meaningful to them, particularly if it is accompanied by affect. Also, the therapist may find that the client responds emotionally to certain words or phrases that they may use. In both cases, the therapist should endeavour to use such language with the client, but not overuse it. In the latter case, the client may think that the therapist is 'clever' or 'disingenuous', which are to be avoided, if possible.

Utilise relevant imagery

The same applies to any recurrent imagery that the client may use. Such imagery may indicate the client's preferred sensory modalities (e.g., visual, auditory, olfactory or sensory) and the therapist may encourage emotional engagement by talking the client's language when working with such imagery.

Utilise the visual medium as well as the verbal medium

SST is largely a talking therapy, and, as such, there is a lot of verbal communication between the client and the therapist. However, to enhance the impact of SST, it is useful sometimes to present visual representations of verbal concepts, especially for those clients whose learning is enhanced by the visual medium. In Figure 67.1, I present the 'Big I–Little i' technique which shows that the 'Big I', which represents a person, is comprised of myriad aspects represented by little i's. It shows that a person cannot be defined by any of their parts. I use it to help the client to promote self-acceptance.

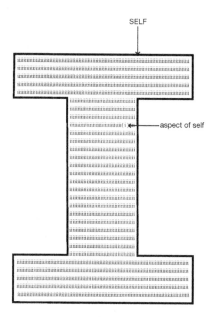

Figure 67.1 The 'Big I–Little i' technique

REFER TO YOUR CLIENT'S CORE VALUES TO PROMOTE CHANGE

In my view, it is important for the SST therapist to discover their client's core values during the session. The purpose of this is so that the therapist can use these to help the client to connect their goals and goal-directed activities to their values. A client will probably strive more persistently towards a goal when it is underpinned by a core value than when it is not.

In the following six chapters, I discuss a number of ways in which the SST therapist can help increase the impact of the session to facilitate the chances of the client getting the most out of the session.

UTILISE THE CLIENT'S INTERNAL STRENGTHS AND EXTERNAL RESOURCES

In Chapters 27 and 28, I made the point that two major assumptions of SST are that it is strengths-based and resources-based. In the first case, the SST therapist is oriented to helping the client to identify their strengths, meaning positive internal aspects of themselves that they can bring to the single session and use to help them solve their problem. In the second case, the SST therapist also helps the client to identify external resources that may also help them to solve their problem.

If the client has completed a pre-session preparation form, then they may have had the opportunity to identify strengths and resources that could be used *in general* to aid the SST process. If this is the case, then the therapist can make use of this information in the session to encourage the person to select *specific* strengths and *specific* resources when considering different ways of solving their specific problem for which they have sought help. For this purpose, it is important for the therapist to consult the pre-session form which they should have to hand.

The best time to discuss the possible use of strengths and resources in the session is when the therapist and the client have agreed to target a particular problem and have set a goal. In exploring possible solutions, the therapist can take each possible solution and ask:

1. 'Which of your *strengths* can you use when implementing this possible solution?' The therapist may have to remind

 DOI: 10.4324/9781003386353-74

the client of the strengths that they identified on the pre-session preparation form if necessary. It is important to realise that the client may need to use different strengths with different potential solutions, although they may have one or more strengths that may be generally applicable.

2. 'Which of the *external resources* that you have access to can you make use of while implementing this possible solution?' Again, a particular resource may be more relevant than others when considering potential solutions. When it comes to utilising other people for support and help, for example, it may be the case that certain people have more relevant expertise than others and this needs to be considered by the client when thinking about whom to ask for help and support with different potential solutions.

If the client has not completed a pre-session form, then the therapist will have to devote some time to help the client identify strengths and resources and how they may be used in the solution selection process.

69

IDENTIFY AND UTILISE THE CLIENT'S ROLE MODEL

When sending clients a pre-session form to complete, some SST therapists may ask the client about people whom they know personally or by reputation who might serve as a role model. This may help in two ways in SST: as a person to emulate and as someone who might support the client. If this is not done before the session, it can be done during the session.

A ROLE MODEL TO EMULATE

First, while considering possible solutions to their problem, the client may select a role model whom they think has the skills or qualities to employ a potential solution successfully to achieve the goal that the client has set. The therapist first asks the client to specify what these skills and qualities are and to say whether they can emulate these. If the person thinks that they can, then the therapist would encourage the client to imagine emulating the role model but doing so in their own way. If they can do so successfully, then this tends to increase the chance that they will select the potential solution as their chosen solution.

Sharoff (2002: 115–116) has outlined a number of steps that the SST therapist can use to help the person emulate a role model in the service of solving their problem:

1. Identify the model.
2. Overcome resistance to being like the model.
3. Show similarities between the model and the patient.
4. Encourage curiosity about the model's outstanding skills and how they operate.

DOI: 10.4324/9781003386353-75

5. Identify the model's skills and how they operate.
6. Form a contract with the patient to work on developing those skills.
7. Educate the patient about how to perform the needed skills.

THE THERAPIST AS ROLE MODEL

In Chapter 24, I mentioned therapist self-disclosure when discussing therapist openness. If the therapist has experienced a similar problem to the client but has overcome it, then the therapist might disclose this and detail what they did. However, my advice is that the therapist only does this after explaining about therapist self-disclosure and seeking the client's consent to proceed. When the therapist has made the disclosure, then they can discuss its applicability and value with the client before the client decides to take what they have found helpful about what the therapist disclosed. Even if the client has not found the therapist's disclosure useful, sometimes hearing it stimulates the client to think of their own problem-solving strategy.

A SUPPORTIVE ROLE MODEL

While a role model whom a client chooses to emulate is often a well-known figure, usually not known personally to the client, a supportive model is usually someone known to the client and is someone admired by the client who is perceived to 'have the client's back', meaning someone for whom the client's welfare is paramount. This is often a family member such as a parent, grandparent or sibling. The client might be encouraged to ask the person directly for support or may imagine the person supporting them in their mind's eye.

If a client has both types of role model 'in their corner', then this is often a powerful and positive force for change.

70

UTILISE TOPOPHILIA IN SST

In my experience, competent SST therapists are mindful of different ways that they can make SST more effective for their clients and will try out effective strategies that have their origin both inside and outside therapy. An example of the latter is research that has reviewed the impact that meaningful places have on our well-being as humans (National Trust, 2017). As the report notes, 'the poet, W.H. Auden coined the word "Topophilia" in 1948 to describe the way people experience a strong sense of place; often becoming mixed with their sense of identity and an underlying sense of belonging' (National Trust, 2017: 3).

This research, which used both an online survey of 2,000 people and a fMRI study of 20 people, showed that people's responses to special places were much higher in the amygdala (an area in the brain that is central to emotional processing) than was their response to meaningful objects like special photographs and wedding rings. Thus, significant places are likely to have greater emotional importance for us than what we deem to be personally important objects.

This finding can be used in several ways in SST. First, the therapist can help the client to describe what is for them a place associated with positive growth and ask them to imagine this place at the outset as a way of helping the client to go into the session with a *general* sense of well-being. Second, having ascertained the client's special place, the therapist can ask the client to imagine this place at *specific* points in the session, for example, (1) when they are setting a therapeutic goal; (2) when they are searching for the best solution to their problem; and (3) while picturing themself implementing the solution. Third,

DOI: 10.4324/9781003386353-76

the therapist can suggest that the person physically visit the place, if possible. One specific purpose of such a visit might be for the client to renew their commitment to problem-solving in an environment likely to motivate and mobilise them.

THE USE OF STORIES
AND PARABLES

It is sometimes helpful for the SST therapist to make use of a pertinent story or parable which presents a point to the client in a way that may be meaningful and memorable to them and is relevant to their problem and/or potential solutions. Let me provide three examples of stories/parables that I have told clients in SST.

THE STORY OF THE CHINESE FARMER[1]

I use the following with clients who have problems in seeing beyond the immediate consequences of adversities and who could benefit from taking a longer-term view on events and clients who see things in black and white and could benefit from taking a more pluralistic view of the world.

> Once upon a time, there was a Chinese farmer, whose horse ran away. And all the neighbours came around that evening to commiserate, 'So sorry to hear your horse has run away. That's too bad.' And the farmer said, 'Maybe.'
>
> The next day the horse came back, bringing seven wild horses with it, and all the neighbours came around in the evening and said, 'Oh, isn't that lucky. What a great turn of events. You've now got eight horses.' And the farmer said, 'Maybe.'
>
> The next day his son tried to tame one of these horses and was riding it and was thrown and broke his leg. And all the neighbours came around that evening and said, 'Oh, dear that's too bad.' And the farmer said, 'Maybe.'

1 As told by Alan Watts: www.youtube.com/watch?v=byQrdnq7_H0.

 DOI: 10.4324/9781003386353-77

The following day the conscription officers came around looking for people to recruit for the army and they rejected his son because he had a broken leg. And all the neighbours came around that evening and said, 'Isn't that great.' And the farmer said, 'Maybe.'

If they don't get the point, I read them what Alan Watts says at the end of the YouTube video of him relating this story.

The whole process of nature is an integrated process of immense complexity, and it is really impossible to tell whether anything that happens in it is good or bad because you never know what will be the consequences of a misfortune and you never know what will be the consequences of good fortune.

'YOU HAVE TO GET ITS ATTENTION FIRST' (MINUCHIN & FISHMAN, 1981)

I tell the following story to clients who claim that people don't listen to them and whose problems are rooted in their failure to be heard.

A farmer had a donkey that did everything that it was asked. When told to work, the donkey worked. When told to stop, the donkey stopped. And when told to eat, the donkey ate. One day the farmer sold the donkey to his neighbour. He told his neighbour that all he had to say to the donkey was 'Come on donkey, sweet, sweet donkey, let's go to work, for example' and the donkey would obey his order. After settling the donkey into his new shed for a few days, the new owner excitedly went into the shed and said, 'Come on donkey, sweet, sweet donkey, let's go to work'. But the donkey did not move. The same happened the next morning and the next. Vexed, the new owner went to the farmer to get his money back. The farmer was puzzled and said that he would come over the next morning to investigate. The next morning the farmer came into the donkey shed with his neighbour, looked around, picked up a two by four plank of wood, whacked the donkey on its nose with it and said, 'Come on donkey, sweet, sweet donkey, let's go to work', and the donkey started work. Amazed the new owner enquired as to the farmer's method. 'I'm awfully sorry', said the farmer, 'I forgot to tell you one important thing. You have to get its attention first!'

THE WISE RABBI STORY

I use the following story when people are facing an adversity that they cannot change. I use it to show them that they can withstand what they believe they cannot tolerate and that things frequently seem worse than they actually are.

Many years ago, a religious Jewish couple were having difficulties arising from living in a one-room dwelling with two screaming children. They both believed that they couldn't stand their situation and were disturbed as a result. Being Orthodox Jews, they sought advice from their local rabbi, a wise old man who was well respected for his sage advice. After listening to the couple's story, he advised them to invite both sets of parents to live with them and to return in a month's time to report their progress. The couple was perplexed by this advice but, being dutiful Jews, carried out the rabbi's advice to the letter.

One month later they returned to the rabbi even more distressed than before. 'We're getting to the end of our tether, rabbi. Things have gone from bad to worse. Both sets of parents are arguing, and the children are screaming even louder than before.' The rabbi listened carefully before pronouncing the following words: 'I want you to go home and collect all your geese and chickens from the farmyard and have them live with you, your children, and your respective parents, and come and see me again in a month's time.'

If the couple were perplexed before, they were dumbfounded now but, as dutiful Jews, again they followed the rabbi's advice to the letter.

One month later they returned, at their wits' end. 'We're at the breaking point, rabbi,' they said. 'The animals are creating pandemonium, our parents have almost come to blows, and the children's screams can be heard at the other end of the village. We're desperate, rabbi. Please, please, please help us!'

The rabbi again listened patiently and quietly, and then said, 'I want you to go home, put the geese and chickens back into the farmyard, send both sets of parents home and come and see me in a month's time.'

One month later, the couple returned, looking cheerful and happy. 'Things are so much better, rabbi. You have no idea. It's so peaceful. The kids are still screaming, but that is bearable now. You've helped us so much, rabbi. Thank you.'

As with all stories and parables, it is important for the SST therapist to check at the end of any story told what the client has learned from it. Failure to do this might mean that the client takes away a mistaken or irrelevant message. If they have grasped the point of the story or parable, then the SST therapist can then discuss with them how they can apply the relevant principle to help them solve their problem.

72

USE HUMOUR

While SST is a serious business, it does not always have to be practised in a serious way. The use of humour in therapy has often been discussed and has its proponents and its critics (Lemma, 2000). One of its proponents was Albert Ellis, the founder of Rational Emotive Behaviour Therapy. Ellis (1977) argued that one way of viewing psychological problems was that they were the result of a person taking themself, others and/or life *too* seriously and that, consequently, the therapist could help the person by encouraging them to adopt a humorous perspective. They can best do this by using humour in the single session, if they have a sense of humour, which, sadly, not all therapists do, in my experience. In addition, the client may not have a sense of humour or, if they do, they might think that humour has no place in therapy. Given all this, the therapist needs to tread carefully when thinking about using humour in SST.

My approach here is to ask the client directly whether they think that humour has a place in therapy and whether they would value me offering a humorous perspective on their problem if I did so sensitively. If I do so, the impact of my humorous intervention is usually immediately apparent.

Swaminath (2006) has argued that the use of therapist humour can be of potential help to the client in the following ways:

- It creates a more relaxed atmosphere and helps break down barriers.
- It can convey the message that the therapist is humane.
- It can build trust and empathy if used appropriately.

DOI: 10.4324/9781003386353-78

- It can help the client to relax and talk more freely.
- It can convey messages succinctly and effectively.
- It encourages communication on sensitive matters.
- It can be a source of insight into conflict.

In addition, therapist humour can best help the client, in my view, by promoting constructive cognitive change within an emotionally aroused context (Dryden, 2017, 2022a).

73

USE PARADOX

When the therapist encourages the client to use paradox in SST, they do so by prescribing the very symptom the client wants to resolve. As discussed in Chapter 57, clients often perpetuate their problems by their attempts to address them. For example, consider a client who has problems sleeping. All their efforts are designed to get to sleep with the consequence that the person stays awake. When the SST therapist suggests the use of paradox, they encourage the client to tackle their problem by trying to stay awake and resist the inclination to fall asleep. If the person does this, they are approaching the problem in a different, albeit counterintuitive way, but this is often successful.

Another use of a paradoxical technique is one known as *reductio ad absurdum*. Here the person is encouraged to exaggerate the problem, often in an extreme way. Take, for example, a client who has a fear of sweating. They deal with it in an intuitive way by trying a variety of ways of hiding the problem from others. Such ways might include wearing dark clothing, standing near an open window, carrying a portable fan and avoiding eating spicy foods. However, given the paradoxical nature of anxiety, as I pointed out above with the example of the person with a sleep problem, the person who has an anxiety problem about sweating maintains the problem by trying to hide it and using the above strategies which are in the service of this goal. Using the paradoxical *reductio ad absurdum* technique, the therapist encourages the client to sweat more rather than less and to see if they can't drown other people with their sweat. In trying to sweat rather than not to sweat and in trying to make it obvious rather than to hide it, the emphasis

 DOI: 10.4324/9781003386353-79

is changed radically, which often results in a diminution of the problem because the person gains control of it (Fay, 1978).

As Foreman (1990) has argued, it is important to obtain the consent of clients before such techniques are employed and, thus, the therapist needs to make clear the rationale for their use. In this way, the therapist is practising SST ethically.

74

USE THE 'FRIEND TECHNIQUE'

One of the phenomena that is characteristic of many clients is that they treat and regard themselves differently from how they treat and regard others for the same things. Thus, a possible solution for such clients is that they become consistent in their attitude towards themselves and toward others in ways that benefit themselves. One way in which the SST therapist can facilitate this process is by using the 'friend technique'.

THE 'FRIEND TECHNIQUE'

The purpose of the 'friend technique' is to help the client to see that they have a more tolerant and compassionate attitude towards a good friend than they have towards themself. From there the therapist can encourage the client to adopt this same tolerant and compassionate attitude towards themself. It is the SST version of 'how to be your own best friend' and is best employed with self-devaluation issues. An example follows:

THERAPIST: So, because you lost your job you feel depressed, and that is linked to your attitude that you are a failure and that this leads to your depression. Is that right?

CLIENT: Yes.

THERAPIST: Now I'm going to help you examine this attitude. What's the name of your best friend?

CLIENT: Sarah.

THERAPIST: Now let's suppose that Sarah came to you and told you that she had lost a job that she valued. Would you say to her 'Get out of my house — you're a failure'?

CLIENT: No, of course not.

THERAPIST: Would you think of her as a failure?

 DOI: 10.4324/9781003386353-80

[This is an important step to include in case the client would think of her friend as a failure even though she wouldn't actually say this.]

CLIENT: No.

THERAPIST: How would you think of her in the event of her losing her job?

CLIENT: Well, it wouldn't change my view of her. Even if she made a bad error, she'd still be the same Sarah.

THERAPIST: The same fallible Sarah?

CLIENT: Of course.

THERAPIST: So, let me get this straight. Sarah loses her job, and she's the same fallible Sarah. You lose your job, and you are a failure. Is that right?

CLIENT: I see what you're saying.

THERAPIST: I guess you have three choices. First, view yourself as fallible if you lose your job. Second, start viewing Sarah and other people as failures if they lose their jobs. Or third, have one rule for you and another for others. Which choice do you want to make?

CLIENT: The first.

THERAPIST: OK, so let me help you do that, and we can discuss any obstacles that might come up. OK?

CLIENT: OK.

There are several variants to the 'friend technique'. For example, the therapist could have asked the client if they would teach a child that they would be a failure if they lost a job in later life and then outline the same three choices if they said no. Parenthetically, very few clients say 'Yes, I would tell my friend (or the child) that they would be a failure if they lost a job', but, if they do, it is an indication that the therapist and the client would probably require more than one session to understand and deal with the factors involved in the client's negative attitude!

75

THE USE OF CHAIRWORK IN SST

One of the ways to bring SST alive for a client and to increase the likelihood that the person can integrate intellectual and emotional learning from the process is for the therapist to suggest chairwork to the client.[1] Kellogg (2007: 8) says that:

> chairwork is a psychotherapeutic technique that typically involves the use of two chairs that face one another. The patient sits in one chair and has a dialogue with an imagined family member or other person sitting in the opposite chair; alternatively, the patient moves back and forth between the two chairs and speaks from different aspects of him- or herself.

Kellogg (2007) notes that there are five core ways in which chairwork can be used in therapy, four of which are particularly useful in SST.[2]

EXTERNAL DIALOGUES

In an external dialogue, the client is encouraged to talk to someone to whom they have something to say, and they are suffering from not saying it. The client may not be able to speak to the other person because that person may be dead or unavailable to have a conversation with. The therapist offers the client the opportunity to talk directly to the person and say what needs to be said, switching chairs when it makes sense to and responding to self from the position of the other person.

1 I recommend Pugh (2019) or Kellogg (2015) for a comprehensive discussion of how to use chairwork in psychotherapy. Pugh (2021) has developed an approach to SST based on chairwork.
2 The fifth is working with dreams.

 DOI: 10.4324/9781003386353-81

SST therapists differ concerning how much to guide the process and tentatively give voice to what the client is leaving unsaid. But they all tend to agree on the importance of helping the client to 'gain closure' or 'end unfinished business' should the client consider that doing so may help to solve their problem.

INTERNAL DIALOGUES

When the SST therapist suggests the use of internal dialogue chairwork, it is to address the client's problem which is characterised by a conflict within the person. Here the focus is on conflicts within the individual. Young, Klosko and Weishaar (2003) suggest that it can be useful for the client to give a name to the different parts of 'self' once identified (e.g., 'critical Ralph' and 'compassionate Ralph'). Working with so-called 'inner critics' is very common in SST, and the therapist can help the client to address the punitive aspects of such a 'self-part' by encouraging the client in the 'healthy' chair to respond to the demanding and extreme nature of such a voice and to promote flexibility and non-extremity. Another way of dealing with inner critics, suggested by Kellogg (2007), is to encourage the client in the 'self-as-wounded' chair to relate their suffering and pain to the 'self-as-critic' occupying the other chair.

An important part of this work is to help the person develop a healthy alternative to the inner critic and to address doubts, reservations and objections to doing so.

CORRECTIVE DIALOGUES

If the SST therapist and their client discover that the latter's problem is underpinned by a maladaptive attitude, for example, then this can be verbalised by the client in one chair. The therapist and the client may first work to develop a healthy alternative to this attitude, and then the client can go back and forth between the two chairs – debating the two attitudes. Alternatively, the client can work to develop an alternative to the maladaptive attitude while engaging in chairwork. This work can become quite emotional and helps to counter the issue of clients saying that they understand the new attitude intellectually but do not really feel them emotionally (Goldfried, 1988).

ROLE-PLAYING

The final way in which chairwork can be used in SST is in skills development (e.g., assertion) with the client learning to assert themselves in a role-play situation. The other person can be put in one chair, and the client can practise asserting themselves with that person with either the client (switching chairs) or the therapist adopting the role of the other person. The therapist might model healthy assertion if the client struggles to be assertive in the role-play. Also, the therapist may increase the level of difficulty while playing the other to encourage the person to gain confidence in their developing assertion skills.

CONVERT MEANING INTO A USEFUL AND MEMORABLE PHRASE

One of the challenges for the SST therapist is to help the client take away something meaningful from the process that will help the client solve their problem. Quite often this solution-oriented factor is something that reflects a change in meaning for the client. It may be a reframing of the problem-related situation, a change in inference or interpretation or an attitude change (see Chapter 58). The more the person can remember this point going forward, the more likely it will be that they will be able to apply it in problem-related situations to achieve their goal. The SST therapist who is able to help the person convert the relevant change in meaning into a short, memorable phrase that the person can use in situ will, in fact, be encouraging the person to get the most from the process. These phrases can serve as personal maxims for the client.

A PERSONAL EXAMPLE

Let me provide a personal example of what I mean.

In Chapter 4, I discussed how I helped myself overcome my anxiety about stammering by listening to Michael Bentine talk on the radio on how he helped himself deal with the same problem. He mentioned that what he did was learned to take the horror out of stammering and to talk to others as often as possible. I converted his meaning into my own pithy maxim, 'If I stammer, I stammer – too bad'. Later, I learned the importance of disidentifying from my stammer and converted this into the following: 'I may stammer at times, but I am not *a* stammerer'.

DOI: 10.4324/9781003386353-82   229

AN SST EXAMPLE

Let me now provide an example of converting meaning into a useful and memorable phrase from SST. I was working with Brian, who sought my help for anger towards his wife. She wanted them both to have ballroom dancing lessons, which he refused to do, and he tried all manner of things to try to get his wife to give up this idea. The more he tried, the worse his marital and anger problems became. He reluctantly agreed that as he could not change his wife, he would try and influence her instead, by modifying his own behaviour. He liked the analogy that by trying to change his wife, he was maintaining his problem by digging himself into an ever-growing hole. Once he gave up this behaviour, we reviewed his options, one of which was to go dancing with his wife. He was more amenable to this idea once he stopped insisting that she stopped insisting that he had to go. I heard later that he did go dancing with his wife, hated it, but she stopped asking him because he showed willing. He told me that he took from therapy a phrase which he used then and still uses, a phrase that encapsulated what he learned from me. The phrase was, 'Stop digging, start dancing!'

EDUCATE WHEN CLIENTS APPEAR TO LACK INFORMATION OR HAVE FAULTY INFORMATION

Many SST therapists see their major role as helping clients solve their problems by reconnecting them with their pre-existing strengths and encouraging them to apply these to problematic situations. Such therapists hold that they don't have the time to help their clients develop skills that are not already in their repertoire. Other SST therapists do think that they have time to do this. However, there are situations where a person's problem is neither due to failure to apply pre-existing skills nor to the absence of important skills. It is due either to lack of information which, if they had it, would lead them to solve their problem or misinformation which, if corrected, would again lead to problem resolution.

In such circumstance, the SST therapist can help the person by providing them with the missing information or by correcting the misinformation.

TWO EXAMPLES

In this section, I will give two examples of missing information and faulty information and how to deal with them.

The first example refers to the fact that a lot of clients believe that it is possible to eliminate negative experiences such as painful emotions, problematic thoughts and behavioural urges. Given this, they try their best to eliminate the troublesome experience which only results in its maintenance. How does this happen? The more the client experiences the unwanted feeling, thought or urge, the more they try to eliminate it, and the more they try to eliminate it, it remains or increases. In this way, a problem-maintaining vicious circle is developed.

Here the SST therapist would help the person by correcting their information and explaining that it is not possible to eliminate experience and that it is better to accept its presence in what is popularly known as a mindful way. The therapist might then demonstrate this by asking the client to imagine a white polar bear and then eliminate all thought of the polar bear. The person will discover that paradoxically they will still have the bear in mind (see also Chapter 73). The therapist might then explain and teach the client the rudiments of mindful acceptance and have them practise it with the polar bear.

The second example concerns a couple who came to therapy because they were struggling to deal with their decision not to have children because the woman had HIV. They thought that it was inevitable that if they did have a child, s/he would be born with the virus. The woman was having treatment for HIV and had an undetectable viral load. The therapist informed them that they were incorrect and although there was still a chance that the virus could be passed from mother to child, 99.5% of children born to HIV positive mothers are born free of it. The couple were amazed and decided there and then to try for a family and they had no need for further sessions of therapy.

78

AGREE ON THE SOLUTION

There comes a point in the session when the therapist and the client need to agree on a solution to the client's problem if this is the type of help that the client is seeking (see Chapter 22). As discussed in Chapter 55, for the purposes of this book, a problem is a matter or situation regarded as unwelcome by or harmful to the client, and that needs to be dealt with or overcome. Whether or not the therapist decides to work with the client's problem, it is important for them both to know what they are aiming for – that is, what the client's goal is with respect to their problem.[1] This may be a state which marks the client getting unstuck from the problem and on the way to solving it or it may be a state whereby the client is problem-free. More technically, the goal represents the object of the client's ambition or effort, an aim or desired result. It is in the nature of SST that the therapist will not know if the client has achieved their problem-related goal until a follow-up session is conducted, if one is (see Chapter 87).

The solution is a means of solving the problem or dealing with a difficult situation. It enables the person to reach their goal. As shown in the diagram in Chapter 56, the solution is the bridge between problem and goal. Before I discuss what types of solutions may be selected in SST, I want to make the point that what is important is that the therapist and the client agree on what solution the client will implement. This is an important aspect of the working alliance that I discussed in Chapter 51.

---

1 It is important to distinguish here between what the client wants to achieve from the session (i.e., their session goal) and what they want to achieve with respect to the problem (i.e., their problem-related goal).

TYPES OF SOLUTIONS IN SST

Although there is no set structure to SST, it is possible to consider that there are different phases of the session. In the early part of the single session, the therapist and the client are concerned with creating a focus and understanding what the client wants to achieve from therapy. In the middle part of the session, the two consider possible solutions (if the client has a problem that they wish to address) and at some point choose one that the person can concentrate on. In the final part of the session, the client rehearses the solution, if possible, makes a plan to implement the solution and says goodbye. The type of solution that the client chooses tends to mirror the focus of the session as discussed in Chapters 58 and 59. Here the main solution categories are as follows.

Environmental solutions

If the client's problem stems from them being in an aversive environment that can be changed, it makes sense for them to change it. For example, Linda was working in an environment that was highly critical and called upon people to make quick decisions. Linda did not thrive in such an environment. Rather, she realised that she needed to be in a work environment in which she was encouraged and in which she was given time to think matters through before making decisions. It was apparent in the session that Linda could not change herself to fit into her present job, so she resolved to change jobs.

Behavioural solutions

Behavioural solutions are best selected when the client's problem is due to deficits in their behaviour, or their behaviour is bringing about unintended negative effects related to their problem.

Cognitive solutions

Cognitive solutions are those that involve the client changing some aspect of their thinking about salient aspects of the problem. There are different types of cognitive solution:

Attitudinal change. Such change involves the client adopting a different viewpoint towards the adversity about which they have a problem. The change in viewpoint is designed to help them get unstuck and change the adversity if it can be changed or adjust it constructively if it can't be changed. As cognition and emotions are closely linked, attitude change is also designed to promote a constructive emotional response to the adversity.

Inferential change. As discussed in Chapter 58, an inference is a hunch about reality which may be accurate or inaccurate. When the client has a problem, it may be because they have made a distorted inference about the situation. The inferential change solution involves them standing back, examining the evidence and realising that their inference was inaccurate and a more benign inferential change better accounts for the data. When such an inferential change is made, the person solves their problem.

Reframe. A reframe involves the therapist helping the client to put their problem in a new frame so that it is no longer a problem for them. An example of this type of change is briefly discussed in Chapter 53.

Cognitive behavioural solutions

Cognitive behavioural therapy (CBT) is based on the idea that when the person makes a cognitive change, whenever possible, they should make a complementary behavioural change so that the two types of change work together and reinforce one another. If such a solution can be found and implemented by the client, it provides a powerful means for achieving their goal.

79

ENCOURAGE THE CLIENT TO PRACTISE THE SOLUTION IN THE SESSION, IF POSSIBLE

Once the client and the therapist have agreed on a solution,[1] then, if possible, the therapist should encourage the client to practise the solution in the session. There are reasons for this:

1   Such practice gives the client an early experience of what it is like to implement the solution and helps them determine whether or not they think they can make the solution work.
2   Such practice gives both the therapist and the client an indication of any aspect of the solution that needs to be modified based on the client's experience of rehearsing it and on the therapist's observation of that rehearsal.

FORMS OF PRACTICE

The client can practise the solution in the session in several ways.

Mental rehearsal

Mental rehearsal involves the client picturing themselves implementing the solution in their mind's eye.

Mental rehearsal of a behavioural solution. When the client imagines themselves putting their chosen behavioural solution

---

1   Again, I am assuming in this chapter that the client has nominated a problem that they wish to address.

 DOI: 10.4324/9781003386353-85

into practice, it is best if they do so realistically rather than perfectly because a perfect performance is unlikely in real life and failure to live up to the ideal standard may discourage the person from persisting with the behavioural solution. If the client struggles to picture themself implementing their behavioural solution, they can be encouraged to imagine one of their role models doing so, again realistically and not perfectly. Then they can imitate the role model but in their own style.

Mental rehearsal of a cognitive solution. Such rehearsal is more difficult, but possible, especially when the therapist encourages the client to get into the mindset of the solution and, if appropriate, to use a pithy maxim that is a short, powerful reminder of the mindset (see Chapter 76).

Mental rehearsal of a cognitive-behavioural solution. When the client can imagine themself acting constructively while holding a chosen healthy mindset, then this combination is particularly powerful in facilitating change, as mentioned in the previous chapter.

Behavioural rehearsal

Behavioural rehearsal involves the client practising the behavioural solution in the session. When this involves the client acting in a different way towards another person, the client can do so while imaging the presence of the other or the therapist might play the role of the other.

As noted above, doing this can enable both the client and the therapist to reflect on the client's behaviour and make appropriate modifications which are then incorporated in a reprise of the behavioural rehearsal. Working in this way, the client ends up with a clearer, more refined form of the behavioural solution.

As with mental rehearsal of a cognitive-behavioural solution (see above), when the client is practising this solution in the session, the therapist can first encourage the client to get into the appropriate mindset before they rehearse the requisite behaviour and to maintain the mindset throughout the practice of the solution.

When behavioural rehearsal (and cognitive-behavioural rehearsal) does not involve another person, the therapist can use their creativity in suggesting how the client can practise the solution in the session. For example, I once saw a person for a single session that was focused on his procrastinating behaviour. It transpired that what he found particularly difficult was to move from being comfortable to being temporarily uncomfortable. He was waiting for the motivation to do so, hence his procrastinating. Cognitively, we developed the solution that he did not need to be motivated to start work and, behaviourally, he needed to practise moving from a comfortable state to an uncomfortable one. He practised this in the session by sitting very comfortably in my consulting room and then standing up while rehearsing his cognitive solution. He did this several times, and at the end of his rehearsal, he felt more confident that he would be able to use this cognitive-behavioural solution to solve his procrastination problem.

Another example of non-interpersonal cognitive-behavioural rehearsal comes from the work of Reinecke et al. (2013). They gave clients who had panic disorder a cognitive-behavioural rationale which helped them to understand the factors that maintain panic disorder and what they need to do to address it effectively and then offered the clients an immediate opportunity to rehearse the solution in the session, by practising it in a locked room. Such rehearsal proved to be a key ingredient of the effectiveness of the single session.

Chairwork

As discussed in Chapter 75, chairwork involves the client addressing their problem while using chairs to facilitate dialogue between self and others or between different parts of self. As such, chairwork gives the client an opportunity to rehearse their chosen solution where it involves such dialogue. I refer the reader to Chapter 75 for an extended discussion of the use of chairwork in SST (see also Pugh, 2021).

HAVE THE CLIENT
SUMMARISE THE PROCESS

As the therapist and the client approach the end of their time together, the therapist needs to think about bringing the session to a conclusion. There needs to be a link between what has gone and what is yet to come which shows that the session is part of a process of change that started even before the therapist and the client met and will continue after the session has ended.

At this point, many therapists will summarise the session for the client (Talmon, 1990, 1993). My practice, however, is to invite the client to summarise the session first. I have two reasons for doing so. First, I want the client to be as active in the session as possible and having them summarise the session is in keeping with this principle. Second, the client will more likely take forward their own summary than one provided by me. However, I do reserve the right to add to the client's summary if I consider that they have omitted something important.

COMPONENTS OF THE SUMMARY

Ideally, the following should be covered in a good summary (Talmon, 1990, 1993).

- A statement of the client's problem and the problem-related goal. The therapist should show empathy for the client's difficulty with this problem and optimism that the goal can be achieved.

- A review of the work that was done on the problem and/or towards the goal.
- A clear statement of the solution (and associated learning) and the strengths that the client can bring to effecting it as well as any resources they can make use of.

TAKE-AWAYS

In Chapter 79, I discussed the importance of the client practising their agreed solution in the session before taking it away
with them. Take-aways refer to anything of substance that the
client 'takes away' with them that helps them to implement the
solution that they co-created with their therapist.

Wherever possible, it is useful for a client to have a written
note of their take-away. This raises the question of who should
provide the written note. Some SST therapists tend to provide
written notes of salient points and give them to their clients at
the end of the session. This is particularly valuable for clients
who would appreciate having something to take away with
them in the therapist's own hand. Other therapists favour
the client making such written notes for themselves since
doing so increases the client's sense of ownership of the point
represented by the note. Therapists informed by pluralism
would tend to ask the client which approach they would favour.
Perhaps the most important ingredient here is clarity (see
Chapter 33). I mentioned in Chapter 51 that clients are more
likely to carry out therapy tasks when it is clear to them what
they have agreed to do than when it is not clear (Kazantzis,
Whittington & Dattilio, 2010).

WHAT CONSTITUTES A PHYSICAL TAKE-AWAY?

There are many documents that constitute take-aways in SST
and I refer the interested reader to Cooper and 'Ariane' (2018)
for a review from the perspective of narrative therapy. In the
practice of SST, therapists have tended to make use of the
following physical 'take-aways':

- A written note of the agreed solution.
- A written note of the first step to be taken that implements the solution.
- Any diagrams that are created or referred to in the course of the session (e.g., Figure 67.1).
- A written account of any stories or parables told by the therapist, if available (see Chapter 71).
- A written account of any aphorisms or sayings developed by the client or co-created by the therapy pair to encapsulate a change of meaning for the client.
- Visual representations of meaning change which can be downloaded from the internet and put on the client's smartphone.
- In my practice of 'Single-Session Integrated CBT' (Dryden, 2017, 2022a), I routinely offer my clients a digital voice recording and transcript of the session for later review.

In Chapter 10, I made the point that in SST often 'less is more' and therefore the SST therapist should guard against providing too many physical take-aways from the session to safeguard the session's impact.

ACTION PLANNING AND IMPLEMENTATION

Putting into practice what one learns from therapy sessions is the sine qua non of therapeutic change. Typically, in ongoing therapy, particularly in therapies that come under the CBT umbrella, this is done by the negotiation, implementation and reviewing of specific homework assignments. At the end of the session in SST, the therapist does not know for certain if the client will return (even if they say they will) and thus implementation of learning has to be approached in a different way. This is done by the negotiation of an action plan and a discussion of how this is to be implemented.

ACTION PLAN

An action plan, therefore, is based on the learning from the session that the client is going to take away from the session and that needs to be implemented. Unlike specific homework assignments an action plan details in a more general way what the client is going to implement. It specifies when the person is going to implement the general course of action, where and how frequently. Perhaps the main point in developing an action plan with a client is that the person can integrate this plan into their life with relative ease. Otherwise, they will not be able to sustain its implementation.

IMPLEMENTATION

While what the client *first* decides to do to implement their learning is important, what perhaps is more important is

DOI: 10.4324/9781003386353-88

realising that they need to commit themself to ongoing implementation.

What follows is an example from my own practice of what I call 'Single-Session Integrated CBT' (Dryden, 2022a: 196). Having discussed when, where and how often a client will implement their action plan, such implementation should ideally reflect some of the following principles,[1] expressed here directly to the client:

- Use a brief and memorable version of your healthy thinking.
- Your behaviour should be consistent with the healthy thinking that you wish to develop.
- You should have your healthy thinking in your mind before acting on this thinking.
- Practise thinking healthily and acting constructively while facing the adversity listed in your nominated problem.
- As you face your adversity, you may find yourself slipping back into your old pattern of unhealthy thinking. This is normal, so respond to it with your healthy thinking when this happens.
- You will experience discomfort during this whole process of change. Expect this and bear it. Remind yourself that it is in your long-term interests to do so.
- If necessary, rehearse what you plan to think and do in your mind's eye before doing so in real life.
- Recognize that you may be tempted to keep yourself safe while facing your adversity. It is best not to act on this urge. If you do so, you won't help yourself in the long term.
- Commit yourself to regular practice of your healthy thinking and the behaviour that supports it.
- If you keep practising, your feelings will eventually change.

---

1 Please note that different principles will be relevant for different clients. If necessary, I might provide this as a handout for the client for future reference.

• Look for ways of generalizing your learning from the adversity listed in your nominated problem to other related adversities.

DEALING WITH IMPLEMENTATION OBSTACLES

If appropriate and if there is time, it is important for the therapist and client to discuss what obstacles might exist which would serve to prevent the client from implementing their action plan. When such obstacles are identified the therapist should encourage the client to draw on their past experiences in addressing such obstacles successfully and to use their strengths if they have had no such past experiences. The more the client can be helped to prepare to deal with these implementation obstacles in advance, the better.

END THE SESSION, I: GENERAL POINTS

After the client has provided a summary of the session, indicated what they are going to take away from the session and has agreed an action plan, the therapist should end the session. This involves a covering several points.

DEALING WITH LOOSE ENDS

It is important that the client leaves the session with a sense of completeness about the process. Thus, the SST therapist should provide the client with an opportunity to air last-minute issues by asking something like: 'If, when you get home, you realise that you wished you could have asked me something or told me something, what might that be?' It is important that the therapist responds to what the client raises until the latter is satisfied with the response.

TOWARDS THE FUTURE

It is important that the client leaves the session with a sense of hope and commitment to implementing what they have learned and, to this end, the therapist should ask them how they feel about doing so. This gives the client a second, albeit different, way of raising any unfinished business. If the client responds with optimism, then it is important that the therapist reinforces this. However, if they express any lingering doubts and reservations they may have about putting into practice the learning that they have derived from the process, then these should be dealt with.

 DOI: 10.4324/9781003386353-89

FURTHER HELP, FEEDBACK AND FOLLOW-UP

There are three tasks for the therapist to carry out before bringing the session to a close. These are (1) to discuss the issue of further help, if needed, and how this can be accessed (see Chapter 84); (2) getting immediate feedback from the client (see Chapter 86); and (3) arranging for a follow-up (see Chapter 87).

84

END THE SESSION, II: ACCESSING FURTHER HELP

Unless it has been agreed at the outset that no further therapy is available for the client, the therapist should remind the client that such help is available to the client if required.

WHEN THE THERAPIST IS IN PRIVATE PRACTICE

If the therapist is in private practice, then they have relatively free rein over the options that are available to the client. Before I outline these options, I do wish to stress that it is important for the therapist to present them as equally viable options and that the client's task is to select the one that best suits them. While a therapist may favour one option over the others, such favouritism should not be expressed. The options concerning accessing further help are:

- *To leave things for the time being and contact the therapist if further help is required in the future.*
- *To take time to reflect on what they have learned from the session, to digest it, to take action and to let time pass before deciding whether to seek further help from the therapist.* This help will be determined by what the therapist offers. Thus, it may be another single session, a block of sessions, ongoing therapy or a specialist service (if offered by the therapist).
- *To decide to schedule further help at the end of the session.* Again, this might be another single session, a block of sessions, ongoing therapy, or specialist help.

 DOI: 10.4324/9781003386353-90

Two points are worthy of note here. First, if the therapist does not offer the required specialist help, then a suitable referral is made. Second, any waiting times to access further help should be disclosed.

THE AGENCY'S POLICY

It is obvious that if a therapist is working in an agency rather than in private practice, then that therapist is mandated to implement any policy that the agency has with respect to the issue of the client accessing further help. For example, in some agencies, it is made clear that the agency will contact the client two to three weeks after the session to see how things are going and to inquire whether or not the client wants further help. If not, they are reminded that they can always come back to the agency should they require further help in the future.

Some university counselling services in the UK have a 'one-at-a-time' mode of SST delivery. This means that the client can only access one counselling session at a time, with a set period (usually two weeks) between sessions. Ostensibly, no limit is placed on how many sessions a student can have as long as these are accessed one at a time with a two-week gap between sessions. However, some agencies undertake a review once a client has had a set number of sessions.

OPEN-ACCESS SST

In agencies that provide open-access services (also known as walk-in services), a client can walk back in as many times as they wish (although the vast majority don't). It may be that the client who keeps returning for open-access single sessions is better served by a different mode of service delivery and this is discussed with the client. However, if, after the discussion, the client still wishes to attend single open-access sessions, their wish is respected.

85

AFTER THE SESSION, I: REFLECTION, THE RECORDING AND THE TRANSCRIPT

There is a lot to get through in a single session. Given this, it is important for the therapist to suggest to the client that they give themself some time to reflect on the session.

CREATE TIME FOR REFLECTION

It is for this reason that I suggest to my clients that they refrain from re-entering their busy world too quickly and spend about 30 minutes by themselves reflecting on the session, what they have learned and how they are going to put such learning into practice. Some clients may wish to reflect in writing and others in thought.

THE RECORDING AND TRANSCRIPT IN SST: AIDS TO REFLECTION

One of the features of my approach to SST is that I will, with the client's permission, make a digital recording of the session which I will send to them soon after the session finishes. Also, if they wish to have it, I will provide them with a written transcript of the session (Dryden, 2017, 2022a).[1] These both aid the client's reflection process after the session and serve to remind the client of what they have learned. Sometimes, the recording and/or the transcript enable the client to focus on aspects of the

---

1 I provide the recording free of charge but as I pay to have the session transcribed, I pass this cost on to the client if they want the transcript of our session.

DOI: 10.4324/9781003386353-91

process that seemed more important on review than they did at the time and both contain accurate references to the summary that the client provided themself. Some clients have said at follow-up that the transcript gave them an opportunity to copy their summary verbatim which they carried around with them for later review.

Given the vagaries of the human memory, both the recording and the transcript provide an accurate reminder of what was covered in the session and are valuable in this respect. Different clients value these media differently. Some value both, while others value one over the other, partly dependent on their learning style. Clients who find the written word more instructive value the transcript, while others who learn better aurally by listening will listen to the recording on an mp3 player, smartphone or tablet. Clients who don't like listening to the sound of their own voice definitely prefer the transcript.

AFTER THE SESSION, II:
CLIENT FEEDBACK

As I have mentioned several times in this book, once a person has had a single session of therapy, it is not known whether they will return for another session. Indeed, we know that, as the modal number of sessions[1] that clients have in public and charitable agencies is one, there is a good chance that they will not return for a second session. Given this, if we want to get a sense of what a client has thought of the session, we need to ask them at the end of the session or very soon after the session has ended. My practice is to send the client an email inviting them to complete and return an attached feedback form that I call the Counselling Session Rating Scale (CSRS) – see Table 86.1. I have adapted this from the Session Rating Scale (SRS) devised by Miller, Duncan and Johnson (2002).

I use this form differently to its original purpose. The SRS form is generally used in ongoing therapy and helps to structure a discussion between therapist and client when the client has indicated potential difficulties in the therapy as evidenced by low scale scores. The subsequent discussion helps the therapist and client to get back on track with the client. My use of the CSRS is across clients and helps me to gauge my strengths and weaknesses as an SST therapist from the client's perspective. Ideally, the form needs to be sent by and returned to someone other than the therapist. When the therapist sends

1 Please recall that the mode represents the most frequently occurring number in a series.

 DOI: 10.4324/9781003386353-92

Table 86.1 Counselling Session Rating Scale

Name: Date:

It is very important for me to monitor my counselling work. So, please rate the session you recently had with me by <u>underlining</u> the number that best fits your experience on the following scales.

The pre-session questionnaire was not useful in helping me to prepare for the session	0 1 2 3 4 5 6 7 8 9 10	The pre-session questionnaire was useful in helping me to prepare for the session
I did not feel heard, understood or respected by Windy Dryden in the session	0 1 2 3 4 5 6 7 8 9 10	I did feel heard, understood and respected by Windy Dryden in the session
Windy Dryden and I did not discuss what I I wanted to discuss in the session	0 1 2 3 4 5 6 7 8 9 10	Windy Dryden and I did discuss what I wanted to discuss in the session
Windy Dryden's approach was not a good fit for me	0 1 2 3 4 5 6 7 8 9 10	Windy Dryden's approach was a good fit for me
Overall, I did not get what I wanted from my session with Windy Dryden	0 1 2 3 4 5 6 7 8 9 10	Overall, I did get what I wanted from from my session with Windy Dryden
If I wanted another counselling session, I would not choose Windy Dryden as my counsellor	0 1 2 3 4 5 6 7 8 9 10	If I wanted another counselling session, I would choose Windy Dryden as my counsellor

(*continued*)

Table 86.1 (Cont.)

Finally, if there was anything that was particularly useful or anything I could have done to have improved the session for you, please let me know in the box below:

```
┌─────────────────────────────────────────────────────────────────┐
│                                                                   │
│                                                                   │
│                                                                   │
└─────────────────────────────────────────────────────────────────┘
```

Thank you for your feedback.

---

the form out and the client is expected to return it to the therapist, then any clients unhappy with the session are unlikely to do so.

87

FOLLOW-UP: OUTCOME AND SERVICE EVALUATION

The follow-up session normally takes place about three months after the single session although here as elsewhere it is preferable for this date to be negotiated with the client. Of course, therapy agencies may specify a date for follow-up that all therapists working in that agency are expected to follow. While some people in the single-session community think that a follow-up session violates the purity of SST, most think that a follow-up session is an important part of single-session work.

WHY FOLLOW-UP?

A follow-up session:

1. Gives an opportunity for the client to give feedback on what they have achieved in the time between the session and the follow-up session and how they have achieved it. Clients generally say that they welcome this the opportunity to do this.
2. Offers the client a further opportunity to request more help if needed. Most agencies that offer SST make clear that clients can access further help when needed so this particular offer at follow-up needs to be viewed in this context.
3. Provides the therapist with outcome evaluation data (i.e., how the client has done). This will help the therapist improve their delivery of SST.
4. Furnishes the service in which the therapist works with evaluation data (what the client thought of the help

provided). Such data will help the organisation to improve the service offered.

MY APPROACH TO FOLLOW-UP

In my private practice with SST clients, at the end of the session I offer the person the opportunity to make a definite appointment with me to have a follow-up phone call which lasts between 20 and 30 minutes. My preference is to schedule the follow-up session three months after the single session[1] to enable any changes the client has made to mature and be incorporated into their life. However, here as elsewhere, I will negotiate the length of the period between the session itself and the follow-up session with the client.

I emphasise to the client the importance of them choosing a time when they can talk without interruption and can give their full attention to the phone call. I have developed a protocol for the follow-up session which can be found in Table 87.1.

HOW TO FOLLOW-UP

While I have detailed my own approach to follow-up, it is carried out within a private practice setting. Agencies probably do not have the time or personnel to carry out routine follow-up by telephone. As such, the most common form of follow-up will be by questionnaire, most probably emailed to the client by attachment after a set period with an explanatory message inviting completion and return. Such a form will probably have items designed to assess client outcome and service evaluation. Some agencies also use objective measures such as the GAD-7 and the PHQ-9 which they give clients pre- and post-SST to have a more objective record of client outcome. Generally speaking, the longer the gap between session and follow-up, the longer the form (if there is only one sent out) and the greater the number of forms sent to the client, the less will

---

1   Of course, if the person requests further help at the end of the session, they will be able to access it. I am writing here about times when the person does *not* request further help.

Table 87.1 Follow-up telephone evaluation protocol

1. I remind the client of the purpose of the follow-up call and establish that they have the time to talk now freely and in confidence for approximately 20–30 minutes without interruption.
2. I remind the client of their problem, issue, obstacle or complaint and establish the accuracy of my statement. I allow the client to modify this statement.
3. Would you say that the issue [re-state as described by the client] is about the same or has changed? If changed, I encourage them to use the following five-point scale:

    (1) - - - - - - (2)- - - - - - - - (3)- - - - - (4)- - - - - -(5)
    Much worse   About the same   Much improved
4. What do you think made the change (for better or worse) possible? If the issue is the same, what makes it stay the same?
5. If people around you give you the feedback that you have changed, how do they think you have changed?
6. Besides the specific issue of … [state the problem], have there been other areas of your life that have changed (for better or worse). If so, what?
7. Now please let me ask you a few questions about the therapy that you received. What do you recall from that session?
8. What was particularly helpful or unhelpful?
9. What use did you make of the session recording and/or transcript?
10. How satisfied are you with the therapy that you received? List a five-point scale as follows:

    (1) - - - - - - - (2) - - - - - - (3) - - - - - - (4) - - - - - - - - (5)
    Dissatisfied   Moderately   Extremely
11. Did you find the single session to be sufficient? If not, would you wish to resume therapy? If so, would you like to see another therapist?
12. If you had any recommendations for improvement in the service that you received, what would they be?
13. Is there anything else I have not specifically asked you that you would like me to know?

Thank you for your time and participation. You can contact me again if you need more therapeutic help.

be the chances that the client will complete and return the material. Also, the greater the difficulty the client experiences in completing the forms, the less will be the chances that they will do so.

WHO CONDUCTS THE FOLLOW-UP

When Talmon (1990) was faced with the realisation that 200 of his clients only came for one session, he made the decision to contact them all by telephone to get feedback on the session. The results of this follow-up were very favourable (see Chapter 2) and this spurred Talmon and his colleagues at Kaiser Permanente to develop what they called planned SST. In retrospect, it may be argued that when a therapist contacts a client out of the blue for feedback, then the client is likely to give a positive response to questions asked. Consequently, the best person to conduct a follow-up session to gather outcome and service evaluation data would be someone other than the therapist who delivered the single session. This might be an assistant psychologist working in an agency or it might be a colleague of the therapist when an arrangement has been agreed that follow-up calls will be made to each other's clients and that any feedback that is given to the therapist is anonymised.

The issue of follow-up in SST is one that would repay greater future consideration.

88

EXAMPLE OF AN SST STRUCTURE

Some years ago, I was invited by the Student Services Department at a UK university to help them replace their existing model of service delivery in their counselling service with one based on SST. The existing system, in which students were offered no more than six sessions, had led to a very long waiting list (6–7 weeks) to see a counsellor and led to dissatisfaction both among students seeking help and counsellors offering help. The new service was advertised to students stressing that it offers single counselling sessions for one hour booked on a session-by-session basis.

I conducted a one-day training session for the counselling service's counsellors who practised a variety of different therapeutic approaches and, together with the head of counselling, I devised the following structure which would serve as a guide for the practice of SST for these counsellors. In this chapter, I will present this structure which serves as an example of how a single session may be offered. It is important to remember that it was created to be used in a particular setting – a student counselling service at a British university.

INTRODUCTION

- Explain the service and the amount of time you will spend together with the student.
- Explain the basics of confidentiality and refer to the counselling service's booklet or policy statement online if the student requires more detailed information.

DOI: 10.4324/9781003386353-94

ASK 'WHAT IS THE SINGLE MOST IMPORTANT CONCERN THAT YOU HAVE RIGHT NOW?'[1]

- Explore the most important type of help needed.
- Prioritise needs. Keep the most immediate and critical needs a priority, yet still be mindful of other needs.
- Assess risk (e.g., immediate risk of suicide/self-harm or harm to others).

MENTION THAT PEOPLE USUALLY TRY TO RESOLVE A PROBLEM THEMSELVES: THEN ASK, 'WHAT THINGS HAVE YOU TRIED?'

- What have you tried that has helped? Encourage them to use these strategies.
- What have you tried that has not helped? Discourage future use.

ASK, 'WHAT INNER STRENGTHS AND RESILIENCY FACTORS DO YOU HAVE THAT IT WOULD IT BE USEFUL FOR US TO KNOW ABOUT THAT MIGHT HELP YOU DEAL WITH THE PROBLEM?'

- Educate the client about key strengths and resiliency factors, such as strong family relationships and friendships, positive outlook, spiritual convictions, sense of hope, feelings of personal control, creativity, persistence and humour.
- Explain the role of inner strengths and resiliency factors as crucial components of the process of moving forward.

---

1 There are, of course, alternative ways of beginning the session. Some counsellors prefer the more general, 'How can I help you today?' while yet others prefer a more goal-directed opening (e.g., 'What you like to take away for our session today that would make having the session worthwhile to you?').

ASK, 'WHAT EXTERNAL RESOURCES CAN YOU MAKE USE OF IN DEALING WITH YOUR PRIORITISED CONCERN?'

- Identify relevant people and organisations.
- Link to resources in Counselling Booklet as appropriate.

ASK, 'WHAT WOULD BE THE SMALLEST CHANGE NEEDED TO SHOW YOU THAT THINGS ARE HEADING IN THE RIGHT DIRECTION?'

- Help the person to plan to bring about this change as soon after the session as possible.

DO THE WORK

- Focus on what you normally focus.[2]
- Actively look for possibilities for change.
- Practise the change in the session.
- Negotiate a take-home task.

ELICIT AND ANSWER ANY QUESTIONS BEFORE BRINGING THE SESSION TO A CLOSE

- What question(s) do you wish you had asked me when you got home today?

IF THE STUDENT EXPRESSES A WISH TO BOOK A FURTHER SESSION, THEN LET THEM KNOW THIS IS POSSIBLE WITH YOURSELF OR ANOTHER COUNSELLOR AND REFER THEM BACK TO RECEPTION

Initial data from the single-session based service showed that students valued the flexibility of the new system, the fact

---

2 As the counselling service was staffed by counsellors from a wide variety of therapeutic orientations, it was important to stress that counsellors could apply the approach that they usually adopt to an SST structure.

that they could be seen quickly and book an appointment at a time suitable to them. Also, at the service's busiest point of the academic term, the waiting list was only five days compared to a wait of 6–7 weeks at a comparative point in the previous year.

Part 7

WALK-IN THERAPY[1]

1 At the time of writing (the end of 2022), a debate has arisen concerning whether the term 'walk-in' therapy is the most appropriate given the situation that some clients are not able to walk in to such a service. As such, the term 'open access' is being proposed as one that is more inclusive and therefore more suitable. However, given that no definitive decision has been taken on this issue in the SST community, I will employ the term 'walk-in' in this book.

DOI: 10.4324/9781003386353-95

TWO PATHWAYS TO HELP

In the United Kingdom, there is a National Health Service which provides psychological services which are free to the population and are funded mainly from general taxation and National Insurance contributions. When someone wishes to seek psychological help for anxiety or depression, for example, Table 89.1 outlines an example of the pathway that they have to take to access that help.

Compare this with the process operating when the person decides to seek help from a walk-in service (see Table 89.2).

Walk-in services are not generally available in the UK, but a comparison between the two pathways would prove a strong argument for their implementation, particularly as the UK government is committed to improving access to psychological therapies for the UK population.

DOI: 10.4324/9781003386353-96

Table 89.1 Pathway 1: What happens once a person decides to seek psychological help from the National Health Service in the UK for a problem with anxiety or depression[a]

- The person contacts an NHS Talking Therapies service for anxiety and depression that provides talking therapies.[b] A receptionist organises an assessment by telephone with a PWP (psychological well-being practitioner)

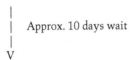
Approx. 10 days wait

- The person is assessed on the telephone by a PWP. If appropriate, a referral is made for psychological help, and the type of help will depend on the assessed severity of the problem

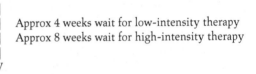
Approx 4 weeks wait for low-intensity therapy
Approx 8 weeks wait for high-intensity therapy

- The person attends their first session. For high-intensity therapy they will be seen by a highly trained therapist. For low-intensity therapy they may be offered: (1) one-to-one therapy conducted by an appropriately trained therapist; (2) attendance at a psychoeducation group; or (3) referral to a self-guided, online computer-based programme.

Note: a. The pathway steps and waiting times listed may vary from region to region in the UK. b. The person may first contact their GP for help and, if so, they may wait up to seven days for an appointment, sometimes longer.

Table 89.2 Pathway 2: What happens once a person decides to seek psychological help from a walk-in centre for a problem with anxiety or depression (from Slive & Bobele, 2018)

• The client decides to seek help from a mental-health professional

• The client arrives at the walk-in service and is asked to complete a brief one- to two-page intake form

• The session begins, usually less than an hour after arrival

---

THE NATURE OF WALK-IN THERAPY

Slive et al. (2008: 6) describe the nature of walk-in therapy thus:

> Developed … as a result of community demands for greater accessibility to mental health services, walk-in therapy enables clients to meet with a mental health professional at their moment of choosing. There is no red tape, no triage, no intake process, no wait list, and no wait. There is no formal assessment, no formal diagnostic process, just one hour of therapy focused on clients' stated wants … Also, with walk-in therapy there are no missed appointments or cancellations, thereby increasing efficiency.

This definition shows by implication the uniqueness of walk-in therapy and its difference from other forms of SST. In walk-in therapy, there is no appointment whereas in other forms of SST an appointment is usually required.

Since Slive et al. (2008) produced the above definition, the field of SST has developed, and the role of a follow-up session has been carefully considered. Some see the follow-up session as part of SST (Dryden, 2017, 2022a; Talmon, 1990) while others don't (Hymmen, Stalker & Cait, 2013). Given that, Slive and Bobele's (2018: 28) recent definition of walk-in therapy is clarifying:

> By *walk-in*, we are referring to an experience where the client walks into the clinic without an appointment, is seen by a therapist as soon as possible, and receives a complete single-session of therapy, at that moment. We have not built in routine follow-up, whether in person or by phone, in this model. Briefly, the model that plans to have a second contact (even if it is called a follow-up) is different from our mindset that the present encounter may be the only one the therapist and client may have. Of course, we

 DOI: 10.4324/9781003386353-97

follow-up in exceptional cases such as when harm to the client or others is possible.

While there is no mention of pre-session paperwork in either of the definitions listed above, in practice people who use a walk-in therapy service are asked to complete a short form before the session mainly for risk assessment purposes.

Jeff Young (2018: 50) notes that given the no-appointment, no-assessment nature of walk-in therapy, 'the same service is provided to people walking in with simple or complex problems'. However, he also stresses that the person can always return for another session so that ongoing therapy may be a possibility, but in a 'one-at-a-time' manner and not necessarily with the same therapist (see Chapter 92).

THE CASE FOR WALK-IN THERAPY

In this chapter, I will outline the case for walk-in therapy services. In Chapter 89, I outlined two pathways to receiving psychological services. The pathway to receiving such help via walk-in services clearly makes the case for walk-in therapy.

INCREASED ACCESSIBILITY FOR CLIENTS

Walk-in therapy removes obstacles to seeking help and thus the frustration that people often feel in trying to get state-funded psychological help is removed because accessibility is increased and made easy. A person can have a therapeutic session just at the right moment for them.

REDUCTION IN WAITING LISTS

It is generally the case that walk-in therapy where an appointment is not needed, as well as SST by appointment, have the effect of reducing waiting lists (Slive & Bobele, 2014).

COST-EFFICIENT

Walk-in therapy services are cost-efficient. The fact that no appointment is needed removes the waste associated with late cancellation or 'no-shows'. Also, the costs associated with 'overtreatment' are reduced.

BENEFITS FOR CLIENTS

Slive and Bobele (2014: 78) have reviewed the literature on walk-in therapy and note that it has the following benefits:

DOI: 10.4324/9781003386353-98

- Clients report improvements comparable with multisession therapy.
- These improvements are often sustained months after the session.
- Clients report high levels of satisfaction with walk-in therapy services. In particular, being able to see a mental health professional at a time of their own choosing often features as a positive feature in client feedback.
- Many clients report that a single walk-in session is sufficient and no further help is requested.

THERAPIST SATISFACTION

Therapists tend to find providing walk-in therapy highly rewarding since their clients tend to be very motivated. They are motivated because they are coming for help at the very point when they need to be helped rather than weeks or months after that point as a result of going through a lengthy assessment and referral process and being placed on a long waiting list. In addition, a therapist's working time is not being wasted by clients cancelling or not keeping appointments, which are two sources of frustration and dissatisfaction for therapists.

FOSTER AN ALLIANCE WITH THE SERVICE RATHER THAN WITH A SPECIFIC THERAPIST

In the field of psychotherapy, it is generally viewed that the working alliance between the therapist and the client is an important ingredient for client change. Indeed, I have made a similar point with respect to SST (see Chapter 51). For example, Simon et al. (2012) found that of clients who did not return for the second session of psychotherapy in their large sample some had the most favourable outcome in the sample and others had the least favourable outcome. The difference was in the quality of the working alliance between the therapist and the client. The former group had the best alliance with their therapist while the second group had the worst. This finding shows people who doubt that it is possible to form a working alliance with clients in SST are mistaken. It is possible, and it has a positive effect.

In walk-in therapy, when a person comes for one session and does not return for another, then it is possible that the person has got what they want from the session and that a good working alliance has contributed to this. However, that person may return for a second walk-in session. It may be that the person did not get what they want the first time and are trying again. Or they may have got what they wanted and are 'walking-in' for help with another problem. It is in the nature of a walk-in service that a person does not know whom they see for help and, if they do return, they may not see the same person twice. This may not trouble the person because in their mind they do not have a working alliance with a specific

 DOI: 10.4324/9781003386353-99

therapist. Rather, they have a working alliance with the walk-in centre. For them a particular practitioner is not looking after their well-being – a helping community is.

Given this last point, it may be in the walk-in service's longer-term interests to foster an alliance between the person and the service. This may be done in how the service portrays itself to clients in advertising (see Chapter 93). It may be done through in-service training where all personnel in a walk-in centre, both therapists and administrators, think in terms of a client–service alliance and talk with one another in such terms. As such, therapists do not talk or think of 'my' clients but of 'our' clients or the 'service's' clients. If this is achieved, then the therapeutic value of the service is maximised from the perspective of clients, since they are not dependent on a particular therapist being at work. They can see any therapist safe in the knowledge that the person has their interest at heart and are determined to help them when they 'drop-in'.

The fact that clients may choose to see a different therapist rather than returning to see the same one was noted by the counsellors at the Arts University Bournemouth, which runs a 'one-at-a-time' counselling service. This was initially disconcerting for counsellors educated to believe in the centrality of the therapeutic relationship. As they noted in the follow-up session that I conducted with them, SST and walk-in therapy challenge several ideas held dear by counsellors and therapists.

93

HOW WALK-IN SERVICES ARE ADVERTISED

One can learn about how a therapy centre conceptualises its walk-in service and what it wants to convey to clients about this service by considering how it advertises the service on its website. Here are two examples, the first from Canada and the second from the UK.

THE WALK-IN COUNSELLING CLINIC (WWW. WALKINCOUNSELLING.COM)

This counselling agency serves various regions in Ottawa, Canada. It advertises its walk-in services thus:
Do you need someone to talk to?

1. What We Offer
   - Support for Life's Challenges
   - Free Counselling Services
   - No Appointment Necessary
   - Trained Professional Counsellors

No referral is required for the Walk-In Counselling Clinic. You will be assisted, with no appointment, on a first-come, first-served basis during our Walk-In Counselling Clinic hours. The Walk-In Counselling Clinic is open to Ontario residents within the greater Champlain region.

The Walk-in Counselling Clinic offers counselling services in English, French, Arabic, Spanish, Somali, Cantonese and Mandarin at a variety of different locations. Clinic hours

DOI: 10.4324/9781003386353-100

are available at different locations throughout the week, including evenings and weekends.[1]

2. Who This Service Is For

The Walk-In Counselling Clinic provides immediate counselling services to individuals, couples and families. The walk-in sessions are free to all members of the community with no restrictions based on age or location/address and no need for an appointment.

Focusing on your strengths, we offer professional counselling services to assist with a wide variety of issues that may include, but are not limited to:

- Depression, anxiety, relationship issues, mental health concerns, alcohol or drug use, personal or job-related stress, anger management, trauma, family conflict/transitions, separation and loss, parenting, sexuality/intimacy, gender identity and gender expression, intimate partner violence or domestic violence, sexual abuse, adjusting to life in Canada, self-esteem/self-image, other life challenges/concerns.

3. What To Expect

The Walk-In Counselling Clinic offers confidential, single-session counselling services on a first-come, first-served basis. When clients arrive at one of our clinic locations, we aim to have them seen as quickly as possible.

Counselling sessions are approximately 1.5 hours in length. Though clients are sometimes referred to other services, in many cases a single concentrated visit is all that is required.

The focus of the session is determined by each client's unique needs. Whether coping with a stressful situation, enquiring about services, or looking for an understanding and non-judgmental ear, our counsellors are trained to help clients address what is most important to them.

---

1 There follows a list of ten locations that offer services on various days between Tuesday and Sunday. Some offer on-site and virtual services, while others offer only video or telephone services.

> Our experienced counsellors help clients identify issues, recognize and build on their own strengths and abilities, and where appropriate help them develop strategies to address their concerns.

I think that this is an excellent example of a clear and succinct description of what this walk-in clinic offers, who it serves and what its clients can expect. My only criticism is that on the website it is not clear to clients how many times they can use the service.

THE CARAVAN DROP-IN AND COUNSELLING SERVICE[2], ST. JAMES, PICCADILLY, LONDON (WWW.THECARAVAN.ORG.UK)

'The Caravan Drop In' is a service provided by the CCPE (Centre for Counselling and Psychotherapy Education) operating out of a caravan that has been provided by St. James's Church, Piccadilly, London. The Caravan has been a feature of St. James's courtyard since 1982. Counselling is offered by volunteers undergoing accredited professional training. Most are training with the CCPE. Its service is advertised online thus:

The Service
The drop-in offers a core service of listening and emotional support, which can – by arrangement – evolve into counselling. The service is available daily on a drop-in basis. Volunteers work at the same time each week. If they are already with someone, they will tell you when they will be free or when the next volunteer's slot begins.

For some people, just a little human warmth and a chat can hit the spot. Others may wish to talk more deeply about what is troubling them. The sessions are 20 to 50 minutes long, at the discretion of the volunteer.

Clients are free to continue using the drop-in, seeing whoever is on duty at the time. Or they may choose to see a particular

---

2   Since the COVID-19 pandemic, the Caravan now offers a telephone service, again available daily.

volunteer again. A client who has been seeing a volunteer regularly can apply for a counselling relationship with that volunteer, entailing agreements as to the focus and commitment to the sessions.

The volunteers adhere to the BACP Code of Ethics and Practice in all aspects of the work, including confidentiality.

This service terms itself both as a 'drop-in' and a counselling service, and on its website, it is clear that the one can evolve into the other. Clients are given permission to continue to use the drop-in, and those who do are given a choice to see whoever is on duty or to see a particular counsellor again. When the latter happens, and the two see one another regularly, it has evolved into counselling, and the client can 'apply' to have that officially recognised as counselling with agreements concerning focus and commitment.

It is interesting to note there are no statements concerning the sufficiency of the drop-in for people and the website appears to convey that both the drop-in and counselling aspects of the service are equally valued internally and this is conveyed externally.

94

A GUIDELINE FOR WALK-IN SESSION STRUCTURE INFLUENCED BY BRIEF NARRATIVE THERAPY

In Chapter 88, I put forward and discussed an SST session structure that was designed for use in a 'one-at-a-time' counselling service for students. This was a 'by appointment' service and not a walk-in service, although the structure could be adapted for use in walk-in services. However, in this part of the book, I thought that it was important for me to present and discuss a session structure that was designed specifically for use in a walk-in service. To that end, I present a guideline for a session structure developed by Karen Young for use in Ontario's walk-in clinics in Canada. As she says:

> This guideline is meant to be used in a flexible, fluid way as the counselor responds with genuine curiosity and is artful in their practice. The guideline is informed by narrative therapy practices and is referred to as Brief Narrative Therapy.
>
> (K. Young, 2018: 64)

While the guideline was developed for use by a team rather than by an individual therapist, in keeping with the flexibility advocated by Young and with the focus on individual therapy taken in this book, I will show how it can be used by an individual therapist working with a single client.

 DOI: 10.4324/9781003386353-101

A GUIDELINE FOR WALK-IN SESSION STRUCTURE INFLUENCED BY BRIEF NARRATIVE THERAPY

Pre-session preparation

The client is asked to complete a pre-session questionnaire. This asks for the client's consent and focuses on their strengths, skills and values, and the responses help the therapist develop some questions that may be asked during the session.

Beginning the session

The therapist outlines the context of the session and explains the risks and benefits to the client, and any documentation is explained.

Setting the agenda

Here the therapist works with the client to identify what is to be the focus of the session and what the client wants to get out of their conversation.

Discover strengths

Here the client is invited to focus on exploring their strengths, skills, abilities, knowledge, values, commitments and preferences. This is done early in the session by asking, for example, 'Before we talk more about 'the problem', would it be OK with you if I ask some questions to find out about you away from this problem so that we both can discover what you can bring to the process that may be helpful to you?' Here, the therapist will also refer to the client's responses on the pre-session questionnaire.

Exploring the problem

Here the therapist and the client work together to develop an understanding of the problem from the client's perspective and, in doing so, work towards a different way of seeing and understanding the problem. To do this, a brief narrative therapist may employ the method of externalising conversations, where the problem is talked about as a separate thing from the person. The therapist might use chairwork to help facilitate a fresh perspective as long as they introduce it in a client-friendly way and the person agrees to engage in this work.

Develop details of knowledge, skills, values and preferences

The therapist explores the above factors with the client with the purpose of constructing a portfolio of helpful client factors that can be used by the client to address the problem. What the client is currently doing to address their problem effectively is particularly noted.

Review and expand what was useful

The therapist and the client discuss together what stood out for them from the above conversation and why this stood out to the client. If a formal list is constructed, it is generated together.

Co-develop next steps

The therapist and the client summarise potentially helpful new ideas or understandings that might help, and specifically how to use these new understandings or ideas, and how they might be implemented. Emphasis is placed on the client planning for any next steps and reasons for change are elicited from the client. The client and the therapist counsellor co-create a plan going forward.

Wrap up

The therapist and the client summarise the work and the therapist may offer last-minute reflections on the impact of the work on them. Any documents constructed during the session are given to the client who then is asked to complete a session evaluation form.

Part 8

OTHER FORMS OF SST

THERAPY DEMONSTRATIONS

In this part of the book, I will discuss a variety of different forms of SST. In this chapter, I will focus on the use of therapy demonstrations. A therapy demonstration is a single session of therapy which is usually practised in the context of a wider therapy training workshop. This workshop may focus on single-session therapy, a particular therapy approach (e.g., person-centred therapy), on a way of working with clients (e.g., the use of chairwork in therapy), on a client issue, concern or problem (e.g., substance abuse) or some combination thereof (e.g., the use of chairwork with clients who have problems with procrastination). While the workshop leader will present material verbally (usually with the aid of a PowerPoint presentation), these days, the audience expects that the person will also 'practise what they preach' and will do a demonstration or series of demonstrations during the workshop. The purpose of a therapy demonstration is to show the workshop attendees a model of good practice which they can then try out for themselves in a peer counselling context (practising the approach with one another) as they seek to learn and develop relevant skills.

While the workshop leader may do what might be called 'micro demonstrations' where, in each, they demonstrate a skill with an attendee briefly, I will concentrate on full-length therapy demonstrations which approximate the single-session experience in that it has a beginning, a middle and an end and aims to help a 'volunteer client' with a genuine problem for which they would like some help and which they do not mind discussing in front of an audience. I shall not be discussing role-play demonstrations where a workshop attendee is asked to play the role of a client with the workshop leader being in the role of the therapist. While these may be valuable, they are not real and therefore do not approximate the SST experience where a client seeks help for a genuine problem.

There is not much literature on 'therapy demonstrations' in workshop settings. Barber (1990) wrote on his own work, conducting such demonstrations using hypnotherapy and I have written about my work in this area (Dryden, 2018a, 2021c). While these demonstrations share similar characteristics with SST with clients, they differ from these in a number of ways.

1. The main purpose of these demonstrations is for the workshop leader/therapist to demonstrate a therapeutic way of working to the watching audience. This person thus has an educational role which a therapist conducting SST with clients does not have. Having said this, the workshop therapist has a duty of care to the volunteer, and this welfare role supersedes their educational role. In clinical demonstrations as well as in SST with clients, the well-being of people comes first.

2. In general, a therapy demonstration is a 'one-off' form of SST where it is made clear that further work with the therapist is not on offer. In SST with clients, as we have seen, further help is available from the therapist, if requested by the client.

3. Periodically, during a demonstration session, the therapist may stop and explain their 'clinical thinking' to the audience. If the therapist is particularly adept, they may give the group a 'running commentary' to explain this thinking and the interventions that stem from it.

4. There will be a question-and-answer period where members of the training group/audience will ask questions of both the therapist and the client. This generally does not happen in clinical SST.

Having stressed the differences between therapy demonstrations and SST with clients, let me close by making the point that they both share the power that working in a focused way can generate in what may be the only time that the therapist and the client see one another.

FILMED TRAINING TAPES

In 1964, Everett Shostrom, a Californian psychologist and noted therapist, filmed three founders of different schools of therapy working with the same 30-year-old woman who was called 'Gloria'. The therapists were: Carl Rogers (founder of what is now known as Person Centred Therapy), Albert Ellis (founder of what is now known as Rational Emotive Behaviour Therapy) and Fritz Perls (founder of what is still called Gestalt Therapy). The films were released in 1965 under the heading, 'Three Approaches to Psychotherapy', but have come to be known as 'The Gloria Films'.

The purpose of this series, the two series which followed ('Three Approaches to Psychotherapy II and III') and the very many others that have been released since was primarily educational. It is one thing reading about an approach to therapy. It is another thing seeing how it is done by someone deemed to be a high-level practitioner of that approach.

It is clear that filmed training tapes are a special form of SST. In most cases, the therapist and the client have not met before and will probably not meet again. While filmed training tapes are examples of SST they differ from SST with clients in the following ways:

1. The purpose of filmed training tapes is two-fold: educational and therapeutic. They aim to provide information to trainees in the field of psychotherapy as well as to provide therapeutic help to the client who has volunteered and given their informed consent to participate in a project which is likely to have wide exposure. By contrast, the exclusive purpose of SST with clients is therapeutic.

2. Following the film, the therapist and sometimes the client is interviewed by a third person who is usually a trained therapist and has some role in the production of the film(s). In SST with clients, the therapist may discuss their work with clients in supervision, but this will be within a confidential setting.

3. In the mid-1960s when the 'Gloria' films were produced, access to these films was limited to a professional audience (trained and trainee therapists). Now, these films can be seen in their entirety on YouTube and thus while filmed training tapes are public events, SST with clients are largely private events.

While there has been little research on the outcome of the SST that is done in filmed training tapes on clients, we do know anecdotally that it can have lasting effects. Gloria's daughter, Pamela Burry (2008), wrote a book on her mother's experience of being a client in the films and what happened next.

As can be seen from the films, Gloria forms a positive attachment to Rogers in the session. Daniels (2012: 112) says:

> it is known that some months after the filming, Gloria attended a conference held by Rogers ... and at his invitation, Gloria joined him and his wife, Helen, for lunch as Rogers wanted to know how Gloria was getting on. At the end of the lunch Gloria asked the couple whether they would object if, in her thinking, she regarded them as her 'parents in spirit'. Rogers and Helen agreed to this request saying that they would be pleased and honoured to have that status in her life. Over the fifteen years to follow, until Gloria's death, there was a great deal of correspondence between Rogers and Gloria.

Gloria regarded this as a positive impact on her life although Daniels (2012) argues to the contrary.

In her book, Burry (2008) writes that her mother had enduring negative feelings about her session with Perls throughout her life, despite her saying that if she could choose, she would want to continue therapy with Perls.[1]

---

1 Howard Rosenthal states that Ellis told him that Shostrom manipulated Gloria into saying that (www.psychotherapy.net/blog/title/the-gloria-films-candid-answers-to-questions-therapists-ask-most).

One disturbing incident happened directly after the filming between Perls and Gloria. Perls approached Gloria who later reported, 'He made a motion to me with his hands as if to say, "Hold your hand in a cup-like form, palm up". Unconsciously I followed his request – not really knowing what he meant. He flicked his cigarette ashes in my hand. Insignificant? Could be – if one doesn't mind being mistaken for an ashtray'.[2]

As can be seen from the above, SST can be for better or for worse!

2 Cited in Daniels (2012: 118).

SECOND OPINIONS

Second opinions are much more common in medicine than they are in psychotherapy. However, the following are times in therapy when a client (and their current therapist, if relevant) would benefit from another view.

- When the client is unsure whether or not the therapeutic approach of their current therapist is right for them.
- When the client is unsure whether or not their current therapist is right for them.
- When therapy is stuck, and nothing the therapist has tried has helped it become unstuck.

Sometimes the client will initiate the process of finding someone to offer a second opinion and sometimes it is at the therapist's behest. In the former case, it is best if the client has the permission of their current therapist to do this and, if they haven't, then it is the 'second opinion' therapist's call if they are going to see the person. In the latter case, the 'second opinion' therapist (SOT) needs to establish, at the outset, whether the client will give them permission to have contact with the referring therapist and, if so, what kind of contact the client will sanction.

When effective, a single-session second opinion achieves the following:

- It helps the client decide whether they wish to engage with the therapeutic approach of their current therapist. If so, the client returns to their current therapist. If not, the SOT clarifies with them what they are hoping to achieve from therapy and how they think they may be best helped to

 DOI: 10.4324/9781003386353-105

get there. From this, the SOT offers a view concerning with which therapeutic approach the client is likely to engage best.

- It helps the client decide whether their current therapist is right for them. If so, the client returns to them. If not, the SOT helps the client to identify the qualities and characteristics needed by their ideal therapist and suggests someone who demonstrates these qualities and characteristics for consultation.
- It helps the client get unstuck with their current therapist.

GETTING UNSTUCK: WHO SHOULD BE INVOLVED?

In attempting to help the client get unstuck in their current therapy, the SOT needs to consider whether they are going to see the client and their current therapist together or separately. If the former route is taken, then we have a form of conjoint therapy with two persons. If the latter route is taken, there are two possibilities. The SOT will see the client first, then speak to the current therapist to give feedback. Alternatively, when the client first makes contact, it is suggested to them that the current therapist might speak to the SOT first before the client is seen and then afterwards when feedback is again given to the therapist. When the current therapist is involved, in my experience the contact will probably be by telephone rather than face-to-face.

The purpose of the SOT giving the current therapist feedback is to help the current therapist to deepen their understanding of the client and the reason for the stuckness and to modify their behaviour towards the client, which hopefully breaks the stuckness.

GETTING UNSTUCK: AN EXAMPLE

One of my therapist colleagues asked me to have a one-off consultation with Sarah, whom he had seen for about six months. They were currently at an impasse in therapy, and the agreed plan among the three of us was that I would give the current therapist relevant feedback at the end of second opinion session.

The current therapist, Mike, asked me to see Sarah on her own and Sarah concurred.

Sarah made contact by telephone. After giving me an update on the current state of play in her therapy, Sarah confirmed that she felt 'stuck' in therapy. Based on that I devised the following questions that I was planning to ask Sarah in our single-session consultation. I sent her a list of these questions before seeing her and asked her to use the list to prepare for our session. Alternatively, I told her to ignore the list and prepare for the second opinion session in her own way, if she preferred. She chose the former route. The list of questions I asked Sarah was as follows:

1. What problems did you first seek help for?
2. What progress have you made on each problem?
3. What have you found most helpful about therapy with Mike?
4. What have you found least helpful about therapy with him?
5. Are there issues that you need to bring up in therapy but don't? If so, what are they and why don't you bring them up?
6. What are your current therapeutic goals? What progress are you making towards them?
7. Are there areas in which you feel you and Mike are not on the same page? If so, what are they?
8. To what extent can you give Mike honest feedback about therapy?
9. To what extent are you ambivalent about change? Are there problems that you feel scared to let go of?
10. Who in your life is therapeutic and untherapeutic?
11. When Mike suggested meeting with me, what was your initial reaction? Has that reaction changed?

In our single, face-to-face, second opinion session, I took Sarah through these questions and on the basis of her responses, I gave Mike this feedback on the phone:

Sarah mentioned that she likes you, feels comfortable with you and generally has a good relationship with you. However, recently she feels that you are getting irritated with her for not improving as fast as she did originally. This has led her not to discuss things with you that bother her that she thinks you might not want to hear. This is in contrast with her grandfather to whom she can tell anything. My view is that this is the main reason for the stuckness.

Mike admitted that he had been feeling a little irritated with Sarah of late and this irritation was about her need for his approval as he could now see. He resolved to take this issue to supervision.[1]

Later, I learned that Mike had discussed this issue with his supervisor and changed his behaviour towards Sarah, who subsequently felt able to discuss the stuckness with Mike and the other issues that she had taken off the therapeutic agenda, which had led to the stuckness.

I regard offering a second opinion to be a specialised form of SST because the SOT will only have one face-to-face meeting with the client (or the therapist–client dyad if they attend together).[2]

---

1 A second opinion is not supervision. The SOT's role is to offer feedback and not engage with the therapist in a lengthy discussion of the case. It is also not therapy with the client, although the client might find it therapeutic to be offered the opportunity to reflect on their therapy and get a fresh perspective from the SOT.
2 As shown above, the SOT will either speak to the current therapist once (to give feedback) or twice (to be briefed and then to give feedback).

Part 9

SST COMMON ERRORS, COMMON CONCERNS AND FREQUENTLY ASKED QUESTIONS

COMMON ERRORS MADE IN SST

In my experience, SST is easy to practise poorly and people new to it often make several common errors. Hoyt & Cannistrà (2021) have written an important article detailing such common errors and I list them here with a brief commentary on each.

INSIST THAT THERAPY BE ONLY SESSION

One of the hallmarks of the single-session mindset is flexibility. This error, especially when the therapist tells the client that they will only have one session, is both rigid and betrays the nature of SST – that the therapist and client will work together to help the client take away from the session what they have come for and, if not, more help is available. The effect of this error is to unduly pressurise both the therapist and the client to no good effect.

DISBELIEVE THAT THERAPY COULD ONLY BE ONE SESSION

It is difficult to envisage a single-session therapist who holds this view but, when they do, they end up attempting to convert SST into longer-term therapy. This is evidenced by the therapist offering the client further sessions as a matter of course, despite the research that shows that the modal number of sessions that clients have in public and charitable therapy agencies is one. The therapist may disbelieve that therapy could only be one session, but many clients beg to differ.

THINK THAT SST IS NOT APPLICABLE FOR COMPLEX OR DIFFICULT PROBLEMS

One of the lessons that have emerged from work done in open-access (walk-in) SST services is that people with complex and difficult problems can be helped as much as those with simpler problems (Riemer et al., 2018). Also, people with complex and difficult problems appreciate the SST focus on what they are particularly concerned about when they seek help rather than the more conventional therapy focus on the totality of their complex situation where their preoccupations are bypassed.

LOWER HOPEFUL EXPECTATIONS

As I have previously mentioned, Jerome Frank (1961) made the important point that what unites clients seeking therapeutic help is their sense of demoralisation. One of the goals of SST is to help clients to restore their morale. When the therapist lowers the client's hopeful expectations, then they are doing the clients a disservice. However, this does not mean that the therapist should foster unrealistically high expectations in the client from SST. This too would be an error.

NOT HELPING THE CLIENT TO CLARIFY A SPECIFIC GOAL FOR THE SESSION

While clients come to SST for help with a number of issues, both specific and general, it is an error not to ask them what they want to achieve by the end of the session. The more specific their goal is, the more they and the therapist can collaborate on helping the client to achieve their session goal. Failing to do so gives the session a directionless feel and may impede the client from getting the most from the session.

DON'T ASK THE PERSON WHAT THEY THINK IS A GOOD WAY TO ADDRESS THE PROBLEM

Many therapists have an idea about how a client's problem can be best tackled. While there is nothing wrong with this per se, in SST it is important to consult the client concerning their ideas about how to tackle the issue. Not doing so, goes against the SST principle that therapy is client-centred and client-led. However, it would also be an error for a therapist not to share their view on this matter, particularly when the client's ideas may unwittingly serve to maintain the problem rather than solving it. Co-creating a way of addressing the problem is often the best way forward.

CONTINUE WITH THE SESSION WHEN THE WORK HAS BEEN DONE

In SST we use time creatively and flexibly. Thus, I tell my clients that my SST sessions are *up to* 50 minutes in length. Thus, if the client and I have finished our work, say, after 40 minutes then it is time to end the session. Indeed, to continue with the session just because it is 'supposed' to last for 50 minutes might well be a mistake, since the client may bring up another issue that we don't have time to deal with and as a result we will end the session on a low rather than on a high. So, to continue with a session after a conclusion has been reached is a definite error in SST.

AVOID SMALL STEPS

'A journey of a thousand miles begins with a single step' is a common saying that originated from a Chinese proverb. The quotation is from Chapter 64 of the Dao De Jing ascribed to the Chinese philosopher Laozi, as detailed in Wikipedia.[1] This means that even the longest and most difficult ventures have a starting point; something which begins with one first step. That is why I often say that a single session is frequently the start of something rather than the end of something. We can rarely solve problems fully in one session, but we can help clients take away something small, but meaningful, that can help them along their life path, knowing, of course, that they can always

---

1 https://en.wikipedia.org/wiki/A_journey_of_a_thousand_miles_begins_
with_a_single_step.

return for more help. It is thus an error to avoid encouraging clients to make small steps in SST.

DON'T STUDY SST FAILURES

The single-session mindset suggests a number of ways that therapists can practise in an SST context. However, following these suggestions does not guarantee that the client will inevitably benefit from the session. Thus, it is important to learn from situations where SST does not go well as well as when it does. Consequently, choosing not to learn from SST failures is an error.

DISREGARD REAL-LIFE ISSUES

In order to help the client with what they are struggling, it is vital to understand their problem in context. In doing so, it is important to appreciate any real-life issues that they are facing. When communicating an understanding of these real-life issues, I have found it useful to help the client see that they have a choice to feel healthily bad about a real-life adversity or unhealthily disturbed about it (Dryden, 2022a). Communicating that it is healthy to feel bad about something bad is a real aid for clients who think that such events should not bother them. I would not be able to do this if I disregarded my clients' real-life issues. I agree with Hoyt and Cannistrà (2021), therefore, that doing so is an error.

INSIST ON ONE MODEL OF THERAPY

In Chapter 42, I discussed what I called the pluralistic nature of SST. Given the variety of issues that clients bring to SST, it would be a mistake to only draw upon one model of therapy and a therapist who does this is trying to fit the client into their model rather than adjusting one's way of working to fit the client.

IGNORE THE CLIENT'S CULTURE

I learned quite early in my career as an SST therapist to be sensitive to a client's culture. Thus, clients from India have different ideas of what respecting their parents means than do clients from the UK, for example. Operating on the latter with the former (or vice versa) is itself disrespectful and will lead to poor results.

THINK THAT TO 'RESOLVE A PROBLEM' IS THE ONLY GOAL OF SST

In my view, most clients come to SST to resolve a problem, but this is not universally the case. I detailed in Chapter 22, the different types of help the SST therapist might offer the client and, from a working alliance perspective, SST is more effective when there is congruence between the type of help the client is looking for and the type of help the therapist offers. Thus, while the goal of SST is often the resolution of a problem this is not always the case and, for the SST therapist to assume that it is, is both inflexible and an error.

NEGLECT PROPER TRAINING, SUITABLE SUPERVISION AND PROPER ADMINISTRATIVE SUPPORT

Proper SST Training, suitable SST supervision and proper administrative support are like the soil in which plants grow. Get them right and the SST practice plant will flourish; get them wrong or fail to provide them altogether and the plant will wither and die (see Chapter 41).

COMMON CONCERNS THERAPISTS HAVE ABOUT SST

Therapists new to SST usually bring a conventional therapy mindset to SST and in doing so express several concerns about SST. In this chapter, I will list some of these common concerns and provide brief responses to them.

SST IS NOT THERAPY

This point is made by therapists who consider that the defining nature of therapy is that is an encounter that lasts a certain length of time and certainly more than a single session. However, SST can be regarded as therapy since it fulfils all the criteria of therapy, namely: (1) the therapist engages with the client to help the person improve some aspect of their mental health; (2) the relationship is ethical and based on informed consent concerning what can and cannot be achieved from SST; and (3) the client determines whether the single session is sufficient or if they require further help (see Young & Jebreen, 2019).

REAL THERAPEUTIC CHANGE HAPPENS SLOWLY AND GRADUALLY

Real therapeutic change can, of course, happen gradually, but it can also happen quickly. Also, the change that happens in a single session is often the initial step in a change process that the client maintains after the session has ended. Can we really say that this first step does not involve 'real' change?

            DOI: 10.4324/9781003386353-108

EFFECTIVE THERAPY IS BUILT UPON THE THERAPEUTIC ALLIANCE, WHICH TAKES TIME TO DEVELOP

The same point that I have made above is also relevant here. While a therapeutic alliance may take time to develop, it often occurs quickly over the course of a single session (see Simon et al., 2012; Young & Bhanot-Malhotra, 2014).

RELATIONAL DEPTH CANNOT BE ACHIEVED IN SST

While it is probably true that a relationship of depth cannot be achieved in SST, sometimes moments of relational depth occur (see the Rogers–Gloria interview – Burry, 2008). This notwithstanding, there is no evidence that developing a relationship of depth in SST would enhance its outcome, even if this were possible.

SST IS A QUICK FIX

A quick fix is generally regarded as an easy remedy or solution, especially a temporary one that fails to address the underlying problem. By this definition, SST is not a quick fix. First, the SST therapist does not attempt to address the client's underlying problem. Rather, they attempt to address the client's nominated problem, that is, what the client deems to be a priority. Second, the therapist does not purport to develop a temporary solution to the client's nominated problem. Rather, they work with the client to develop an effective solution to the problem and to initiate a process of change which can be taken forward by the client after the session has finished.

SST IS A STICKING PLASTER SOLUTION

A sticking plaster is a piece of flexible material with an adhesive backing for covering cuts or small wounds. It therefore protects the client from further harm and promotes healing. Contrast this with a sticking plaster solution which is deemed to be a temporary and inadequate solution to a serious problem. In SST we would agree with the former and not the latter. The therapist works to protect the client from harm and collaborates with them to find a way forward that would promote both healing and growth either from the session itself or from further help if the client requests it.

SST MEANS THAT PEOPLE WILL NOT GET WHAT THEY NEED THERAPEUTICALLY

Planned SST (also called SST by design) was developed in response to the way clients used services. The fact that the modal number of sessions that clients have in an agency is one, and the fact that clients generally are satisfied with this session (Hoyt & Talmon, 2014b), tells us that many clients are looking to be helped very quickly. SST was developed to meet this need. Also, given that SST *also* includes the provision of further help if needed means that SST does give clients what *they* think they need rather than what their therapists think they need. The only limiting factor concerns what services agencies provide. As such failure to provide certain services is a limitation of the agency, not of SST.

SST MEANS A RESTRICTION ON THERAPY SESSIONS

This concern is similar to the one discussed above, and similar arguments apply. Very few, if any, agencies would stipulate that a client can only have one session and no more. As repeatedly stressed in this book, the nature of SST is that the therapist and client contract to work with one another on the understanding that if the client needs further help after the single session, then they can have it. Any restriction on the number of sessions the client can have is set by the agency and not by the nature of SST. Thus, if after a single session, the client and therapist determine that the person would benefit from ongoing therapy, then they can have it if the agency provides it. If the agency does not provide this service, how is this evidence of SST restricting the client?

PEOPLE IN CHARGE OF FUNDING PUSH SST BECAUSE IT SAVES MONEY

The therapeutic purpose of SST is to provide help at the point of need. When SST is introduced into an agency it has the effect of reducing waiting lists for agencies and waiting time for clients. However, there is little evidence that it saves agencies money, and thus if fundholders introduce it because they think it does, then, in my view, they are doing the right thing for the wrong reason. What the introduction of SST does do, in my opinion, is that it improves the efficiency of an agency and improves the morale of therapists who want to help people quickly and now can.

SST MEANS ONE SESSION AND ONE SESSION ONLY

As I discussed in Chapter 1, if one takes the term 'single-session therapy' literally it does seem to mean a therapy which lasts for a single session. As we have seen, however, this is not its nature, as described in Chapter 1 and reiterated throughout the book (e.g., see the above section on 'SST means a restriction on therapy sessions'). There are times when SST *does* mean one session and no more (e.g., one-off therapy demonstrations, second opinions, and when the *client* says at the outset that they only intend to come one time). However, these situations are in the minority and SST is, as has been said, designed to help the client take away what they want from the session on the understanding that more help is available if requested by the client. Because of the confusion that surrounds the term 'single-session therapy', I refer to my general SST approach as 'ONEplus Therapy', which I think is clear about the dual nature of SST (see Chapter 1 for a discussion of this point).

SST IS FIVE, TEN OR MORE SESSIONS 'DISTILLED' INTO ONE

Therapists who are accustomed to providing manual-based or protocol-based therapy, where therapy procedures are outlined session-by-session, think that they have to distil the number of sessions that they usually offer into a single session. This, understandably, is disconcerting if, indeed, it was true, which fortunately it isn't. As I discussed in Chapter 44, SST has its own process with beginning, middle and ending phases, and this process does not require the therapist to cram or distil several sessions into one. It requires the therapist to identify the client's goal for the session, co-create a focus and use this focus to help the client to walk away from the session with something meaningful that they can take forward into their life.

SST IS ONLY APPROPRIATE FOR SIMPLE PROBLEMS

What we have learned from the experiences of therapists who practise SST in open-access or walk-in settings is that people come to those settings for help with a variety of problems, both simple and complex, and in general they get the help that they were looking for. People who think that SST is only appropriate for simple problems generally have not practised it and look at SST through a conventional therapy lens and not with the single-session mindset described in Chapter 14.

SST IS NOT FOR VULNERABLE CLIENTS

A similar argument to the above can be used when responding to the concern that SST is not for 'vulnerable' clients. If a client comes to SST in a state of risk or vulnerability, the therapist works with them to address their concerns with the goal of making them safe and less vulnerable. In SST we focus on the individual and not categories of people and as the term suggests 'vulnerable' clients is a category. I would argue that SST is indicated for a client who is a state of vulnerability or risk given that they are likely to be seen more quickly than if SST was not available and based on the notion that SST includes more help being available for the person who is not left high and dry at the end of the session.

SST PRACTITIONERS THINK THAT SST IS THE ANSWER TO EVERYTHING

In my experience of therapists in the SST community, they are characterised by humility and are aware of what SST can do and what it can't do. SST therapists hold that SST works best when integrated into an agency that delivers several services. We do not think that SST should replace any of these services. If it were true that SST practitioners think that SST is the answer to *everything*, we would argue for all services to be replaced by SST which we do not.

SST IS THE SAME AS CRISIS INTERVENTION

Clients come to SST when they are in crisis, and they come to SST when they are not in crisis. Therefore, single-session-based crisis intervention is one way in which SST can be delivered, but it is not the same as SST.

SST IS EASIER TO PRACTISE THAN LONGER-TERM THERAPY BECAUSE IT IS BRIEF AND FOCUSED

Some therapists think that because SST is brief and focused, then it is easier to practise than longer-term therapy. However, such therapists are the ones that have not had much experience in SST. It could easily be argued that because SST is brief and focused then it is harder to practise than longer-term therapy. Different therapists, both experienced and non-experienced in SST, will have different views on this issue.

FREQUENTLY ASKED QUESTIONS ABOUT SST AND WALK-IN THERAPY

FREQUENTLY ASKED QUESTIONS ABOUT SST IN GENERAL

I have the made the point several times in this book that SST challenges conventional thinking about therapy and, as such, therapists who are first introduced to SST have numerous questions about it and its different facets. I have written a book on the 50 most frequently asked questions that are posed to me at the training sessions that I have given internationally over a ten-year period (Dryden, 2022c). In Table 100.1, I list these questions, some of which I have answered in this book. However, for full responses to these FAQs about SST, I refer the reader to Dryden (2022c).

FREQUENTLY ASKED QUESTIONS ABOUT WALK-IN THERAPY IN PARTICULAR

Walk-in therapy poses numerous challenges to what most therapists hold dear about the theory and practice of psychotherapy. Slive and Bobele (2011c) have listed several FAQs that they are asked whenever giving training courses in walk-in therapy. Because these questions reveal clinicians' preoccupations (as well as misconceptions) about walk-in therapy, they are worth considering together with Slive & Bobele's (2011c) responses. You will note that there is some overlap between FAQs about walk-in therapy, in particular, and about SST in general.

DOI: 10.4324/9781003386353-109

Table 100.1 Frequently asked questions about SST (Dryden, 2022c)

The nature of single-session therapy

1. What is single-session therapy?
2. Why is it called single-session therapy if further sessions are available?
3. What are the differences, if any, between single-session therapy (SST) and one-at-a-time (OAAT) therapy?
4. Is single-session therapy psychotherapy? Is it counselling?
5. Is single-session therapy an approach to therapy?
6. What is meant by single-session thinking?

The foundations of single-session therapy practice

7. How can a therapy agency integrate single-session therapy into its overall service delivery?
8. Can a therapist form an effective therapeutic relationship with a client in single-session therapy?
9. How Can a Therapist Develop a Relationship of Depth with Their SST Clients?
10. How is a client's suitability for SST assessed?
11. Is it possible to practise SST when a therapist is required to carry out an assessment?
12. Why would a client seek single-session therapy?
13. Is SST suitable for a client who wants to explore a problem rather than solve a problem?
14. Which client problems are suitable and which are unsuitable for SST?
15. Can SST be used with clients who have severe, complex or chronic problems or is it only suitable for simple problems?
16. What does a therapist need to know about a client beforehand to practise SST?

The practice of SST

17. Is single-session therapy for all clients?
18. Can a therapist work productively in SST with a client who cannot easily pinpoint a specific problem they wish to tackle?
19. Can clients get what they need from SST?
20. Which client factors contribute to a good outcome or a poor outcome in SST?

(continued)

Table 100.1 (Cont.)

---

21. What does a client need to know about SST beforehand to get the most from the session?
22. Can a client be helped to prepare for the session in SST?
23. What is the best way to start a session in SST?
24. Are sessions in SST longer than sessions in ongoing therapy?
25. How does a therapist manage risk in SST?
26. Which therapist factors contribute to a good client outcome from SST and which therapist factors contribute to a poor client outcome?
27. What tips can you give to help therapists become focused and stay focused in the session?
28. What do therapists most struggle with when practising SST?
29. Can all therapists practise SST?
30. Is SST easier to practise than longer-term therapy?
31. Is there a protocol to be followed while practising SST?
32. Suppose the modal number of sessions is one and 70–80% of these clients find that session sufficient given their current circumstances. Given that in most therapies, the first session is taken up with history-taking and assessment rather than therapy, does this mean that these clients who attend once are helped by a single session of history-taking and assessment?
33. How can a therapist best bring a single session to an end?
34. How does a therapist know when to offer a client further help at the end of a single session?
35. In Which Formats and With Which Client Groups Can SST Be Used?
36. Can clients be harmed in SST?

Critical questions about SST

37. Treatment protocols are based on the idea that therapy for specific conditions should have a set number of sessions (e.g., 12 or 16 sessions). Doesn't this conflict with SST?
38. Doesn't SST involve a therapist cramming several sessions into one?
39. Isn't SST crisis intervention?
40. Does SST only lead to superficial change, given that real change happens slowly and gradually?
41. Doesn't SST help clients deal with their presenting problems rather than with their real underlying problems?

Table 100.1 (Cont.)

42. Isn't SST just a sticking-plaster solution or a quick fix?
43. Does SST restrict clients' access to therapy?
44. Isn't SST used for purely pragmatic reasons such as to bring down waiting lists and to save agencies money? If so, what are the implications for clients and therapists?

Miscellaneous questions
45. Is SST on the curriculum of therapy training courses?
46. What training is necessary to practise SST?
47. What challenges have you faced when practising SST?
48. Which ideas have you personally found most useful in SST?
49. How should SST services be disseminated?
50. Can single-session thinking be applied to areas of work other than therapy?

Question: **Don't some clients have problems that are too severe and too chronic for a single session walk-in service?**

Answer: If this happens, the person could be redirected to a more appropriate resource. On the other hand, people with such problems may seek help for more manageable problems. For example, a person with a borderline personality disorder may walk-in for a single session on interview technique to help with an upcoming job interview.

Question: **Aren't there some clients who want something that a walk-in therapy session can't give them?**

Answer: Yes, but because a client is encouraged to tell the therapist what they want from the session, if this happens the therapist makes clear that the desired service is not provided together with information about where such help is available.

Question: **What about clients who want to walk in again and again?**

Answer: The general response is that this is proof that the walk-in service is doing its job and that the person has formed an alliance with the service and not with any particular therapist.

Question: **How can a walk-in service respond to at-risk clients?**

Answer: When a walk-in service is established, it is important that it forms working arrangements with appropriate local agencies. When risk is apparent, it is assessed and responded to. When this is the case, the person's strengths and the resources available to them are also assessed and incorporated into an agreed safety plan.

Question: **Can't a walk-in service be overwhelmed with more clients than it can handle?**

Answer: When this happens, the agency will do some triaging with people at risk being given an appointment. Anyone not seen will be encouraged to come back at the earliest opportunity. This is not a common occurrence.

Question: **Isn't this a superficial, band-aid approach?**

Answer: Bandages promote healing and prevent the spread of infection, so as Slive and Bobele (2011c: 19) respond, 'Yes. Thank you for the compliment'.

Question: **Is walk-in therapy primarily for low-income and minority groups?**

Answer: As Slive and Bobele (2011c: 19) note, 'Whether a walk-in single session is a good fit depends on the person and the context; it is not an issue of whether walk-in is a better or lesser service'. In the United Kingdom, low-income and minority groups underutilise standard mental health services. So, if such groups decide to use walk-in services, with their emphasis on prompt help at the point of need, this should be a cause for celebration rather than criticism.

AFTERWORD

PERSONAL LESSONS LEARNED FROM PRACTISING SST

The literature on SST is replete with noted figures passing on the hard-earned lessons that they have gained from practising single-session therapy (e.g., Bloom, 1992; Hoyt, 2018; Talmon, 1990). While these lessons are worth learning, it should be remembered that these were learned by people who practise SST in their own way. Please bear this in mind when I discuss in this afterword the lessons that I have personally learned from practising SST in my own way. In doing so, please note that I will only include a point if I have learned the lesson after making a mistake or after some kind of struggle.

DON'T RUSH

When I first started to practise SST, I felt under pressure to work quickly. This pressure came from myself as I thought, at the time, that as I had a lot to do in SST (a misconception which I discuss below), and I did not have much time to do it, I had to rush. The result was that I did not help my clients very effectively. Listening to digital voice recordings of my early SST work confirmed what I felt was the case – I was rushing the client through the process with poor results. I then resolved to take my time and used Mesut Özil, who at that time played for Arsenal in midfield, as a role model as he was known for his ability to create time for himself on the football pitch. My effectiveness increased as I slowed down.

SPEND TIME CONDUCTING AN ACCURATE ASSESSMENT OF THE CLIENT'S PROBLEM

When I was in 'rushing' mode while conducting SST, one of the activities to which I gave insufficient time and attention was conducting an accurate assessment of the client's nominated issue. I am an SST therapist who believes in the value of understanding the client's problem before working towards goal-setting and finding a solution to bridge between the two (see Chapter 56). As such, identifying what for the client is the adversity that lies at the heart of their problem is particularly important because it encourages the development of a bespoke solution to the client's *accurately* understood problem rather than an 'off the peg' solution to the client's *reasonably* understood problem. When I do a public demonstration of SST, people often remark on how much time I devote to problem assessment, but the feedback of the client is generally positive in that they attest to the accuracy of the assessment and state that it helped us to find a good solution to the problem.

DON'T OVERLOAD THE CLIENT

When I was in 'rush' mode when practising SST, the main reason for this was that I believed there were several points that I had to cover. The consequence of this was that I overloaded the client with too much information or covered too many points with them. The feedback from my early clients was that they ended the session confused. One said that their head was spinning at the close. When this happens, then it is unlikely that the person will solve their problem. Consequently, I learned not to overload the client and that, most often in SST, less is more (see Chapter 10).

JUST ONE THING

When I first started to practise SST, I felt the urge to have my clients go away from the session with as much as possible so that they got the most out of the process. I call this the 'Jewish Mother Syndrome'. For example, my own mother was only happy if, after a visit, I left having eaten everything put in front of me, with more food 'for later'! In the same way as a well digested meal is more nutritious than overeating, I learned that my SST clients who left the process having digested one important therapeutic point, principle or method generally got more out of the process than those armed with a plethora of such points, principles and/or methods, but without having digested any of them. From then on, I learned to have my SST clients leave the process with the 'one thing' that would make a difference to them (Keller & Papasan, 2012) and stopped throwing everything, including the kitchen sink, at them. However, if they take away more than one thing, that is OK too.

ENSURE THAT THE CLIENT IS IN ACTIVE PROCESSING MODE

If the client is to get the most out of the single session, then it is important that they actively process the conversation that they are having with their therapist. Initially, I was too concerned with what I believed I had to cover in the session to ensure that the client was actively processing what we were discussing and, from the feedback that I was getting, it was clear that the client's processing of the material was being compromised. When I realised this, I made appropriate adjustments to ensure that the client gets into and remains in an active processing mode. Thus, periodically, I check with the client that we are on track and that I am making myself clear. I also strive to help the person to engage emotionally with the issues being discussed without them getting overwhelmed with their emotions. This will help them engage at a level of cognitive-emotional processing that will facilitate problem-solving.

ENCOURAGE THE CLIENT TO GET IN THE RIGHT FRAME OF MIND FOR THE SESSION AND TO REFLECT ON IT AFTERWARDS

In this modern technological age, people are easily distracted. They tend to check their mobile phones constantly, text or WhatsApp their friends frequently, surf the net on their iPads and computers and listen to music on a variety of devices. I noticed that when people attended for their single session, at the beginning of the session, they were not as focused as I wanted them to be on what we were there for. It took me precious minutes to get them focused. As a result, I now ask people to turn off all devices 30 minutes before the session and go somewhere where they can get in the right frame of mind for the session. Remember that I have already encouraged them to prepare for the session by completing a pre-session questionnaire (see Chapter 49). In addition, after the session has ended, I again encourage the person to go somewhere to be by themself and for 30 minutes to reflect on the session they have just had. I suggest to the person that during this reflection period they consider what they have learned from the session and how they are going to implement what they have learned. Then, they can turn their devices back on.

ENCOURAGE THE CLIENT TO DIGEST AND IMPLEMENT LEARNING BEFORE MAKING ANOTHER APPOINTMENT

As I discussed in Chapter 1, one way of conceptualising SST is that it is a way of working that helps the client get the most out of their first session knowing that it *might* be the only session that they have. I have experimented with several ways of addressing the issue of whether or not the person needs further therapy after the session has finished. Based on this experience, I suggest that the client spend some time (1) reflecting on the session, (2) digesting what they learned from the session and how they can apply this learning and (3) implementing this learning or the solution they chose in the session outside the session. To aid this longer-term reflection and implementation process, I give clients the option of receiving a digital voice recording and/or transcript of the session (see Chapter 85).

REFERENCES

Appelbaum, S. A. (1975). Parkinson's Law in psychotherapy. *International Journal of Psychoanalytic Psychotherapy*, 4, 426–436.

Barber, J. (1990). Miracle cures? Therapeutic consequences of clinical demonstrations. In J. K. Zeig & S. G. Gilligan (Eds.), *Brief Therapy: Myths, Methods and Metaphors* (pp. 437–442). New York: Brunner-Mazel.

Baumeister, R. F. & Bushman, B. (2017). *Social Psychology and Human Nature*. Boston, MA: Cengage Learning.

Bennett-Levy, J., Butler, G., Fennell, M., Hackman, A., Mueller, M. & Westbrook, D. (Eds.). (2014). *Oxford Guide to Behavioural Experiments in Cognitive Therapy*. Oxford: Oxford University Press.

Bloom, B. L. (1981). Focused single-session therapy: Initial development and evaluation. In S. Budman (Ed.), *Forms of Brief Therapy* (pp. 167–216). New York: Guilford Press.

Bloom, B. L. (1992). *Planned Short-Term Psychotherapy: A Clinical Handbook*. Boston, MA: Allyn and Bacon.

Bordin, E. S. (1979). The generalizability of the psychoanalytic concept of the working alliance. *Psychotherapy: Theory, Research and Practice*, 16, 252–260.

Burry, P. (2008). *Living with the 'Gloria Films': A Daughter's Memory*. Ross-on-Wye, Herefordshire: PCCS Books.

Cannistrà, F. (2022). The single session therapy mindset: Fourteen principles gained through an analysis of the literature. *International Journal of Brief Therapy and Family Science*, 12(1), 1–26.

Colman, A. (2015). *Oxford Dictionary of Psychology*. 4th edn. Oxford: Oxford University Press.

Cooper, M. & McLeod, J. (2011). *Pluralistic Counselling and Psychotherapy*. London: Sage.

Cooper, S. & 'Ariane' (2018). Co-crafting take-home documents at the walk-in. In M. F. Hoyt, M. Bobele, A. Slive, J. Young, & M. Talmon (Eds.), *Single-Session Therapy by Walk-In or Appointment: Administrative, Clinical, and Supervisory Aspects of One-at-a-Time Services* (pp. 260–269). New York: Routledge.

Cummings, N. A. (1990). Brief intermittent psychotherapy through the life cycle. In J. K. Zeig & S. G. Gilligan (Eds.), *Brief Therapy: Myths, Methods and Metaphors* (pp. 169–194). New York: Brunner/Mazel.

Cummings, N. A. & Sayama, M. (1995). *Focused Psychotherapy: A Casebook of Brief Intermittent Therapy Through the Life Cycle.* New York: Brunner-Mazel.

Daniels, D. (2012). *Gloria Decoded: An Application of Robert Langs' Communicative Approach to Psychotherapy.* Other Thesis, Middlesex University. Available from Middlesex University's Research Repository at http://eprints.mdx.ac.uk/9787/.

Davis III, T. E., Ollendick, T. H. & Öst, L.-G. (Eds.). (2012). *Intensive One-Session Treatment of Specific Phobias.* New York: Springer.

de Shazer, S. (1988). *Clues: Investigating Solutions in Brief Therapy.* New York: Norton.

de Shazer, S. (1991). *Putting Difference to Work.* New York: Norton.

Doran, G. T. (1981). There's a S.M.A.R.T. way to write management's goals and objectives. *Management Review,* 70(11), 35–36.

Dryden, W. (1985). Challenging but not overwhelming: A compromise in negotiating homework assignments. *British Journal of Cognitive Psychotherapy,* 3(1), 77–80.

Dryden, W. (1991). *A Dialogue with Arnold Lazarus: 'It Depends'.* Milton Keynes: Open University Press.

Dryden, W. (2006). *Counselling in a Nutshell.* London: Sage.

Dryden, W. (2011). *Counselling in a Nutshell.* 2nd edn. London: Sage.

Dryden, W. (2015). *Rational Emotive Behaviour Therapy: Distinctive Features*. 3rd edn. Hove, East Sussex: Routledge.

Dryden, W. (2016). *When Time Is at a Premium: Cognitive-Behavioural Approaches to Single-Session Therapy and Very Brief Coaching*. London: Rationality Publications.

Dryden, W. (2017). *Single-Session Integrated CBT (SSI-CBT): Distinctive Features*. Abingdon, Oxon: Routledge.

Dryden, W. (2018a). *Very Brief Therapeutic Conversations*. Abingdon, Oxon: Routledge.

Dryden, W. (2018b). *Cognitive-Emotive-Behavioural Coaching: A Flexible and Pluralistic Approach*. Abingdon, Oxon: Routledge.

Dryden, W. (2020). *Single-Session Coaching and One-at-a-Time Coaching: Distinctive Features.* Abingdon, Oxon: Routledge.

Dryden, W. (2021a). *Single-Session Therapy @ Onlinevents.* Sheffield: Onlinevents Publications.

Dryden, W. (2021b). *Rational Emotive Behaviour Therapy: Distinctive Features.* 3rd edn. Abingdon, Oxon: Routledge.

Dryden, W. (2021c). *Seven Principles of Doing Live Therapy Demonstrations.* London: Rationality Publications.

Dryden, W. (2022a). *Single-Session Integrated CBT (SSI-CBT): Distinctive Features.* 2nd edn. Abingdon, Oxon: Routledge.

Dryden, W. (2022b). *I Wish You a Healthy Christmas: Single-Session Therapy in Action.* Sheffield: Onlinevents Publications.

Dryden, W. (2022c). *Single-Session Therapy: Responses to Frequently Asked Questions.* Abingdon, Oxon: Routledge.

Dryden, W. (2023). *Single-Session Therapy and Regret.* Sheffield: Onlinevents Publications.

Ellis, A. (1977). Fun as psychotherapy. *Rational Living,* 12(1), 2–6.

Ellis, A. & Joffe, D. (2002). A study of volunteer clients who experienced live sessions of rational emotive behavior therapy in front of a public audience. *Journal of*

Rational-Emotive & Cognitive-Behavior Therapy, 20, 151–158.

Fay, A. (1978). *Making Things Better by Making Them Worse.* New York: Hawthorn.

Flaxman, P. E., Blackledge, J. T. & Bond, F. W. (2011). *Acceptance and Commitment Therapy: Distinctive Features.* Hove, East Sussex: Routledge.

Foreman, D. M. (1990). The ethical use of paradoxical interventions in psychotherapy. *Journal of Medical Ethics*, 16, 200–205.

Frank, J. D. (1961). *Persuasion and Healing: A Comprehensive Study of Psychotherapy.* Baltimore, MD: The Johns Hopkins University Press.

Frank, J. D. (1968). The influence of patients' and therapists' expectations on the outcome of psychotherapy. *British Journal of Medical Psychology*, 41, 349–356.

Freud, S. & Breuer, J. (1895). *Studien Über Hysterie.* Leipzig and Vienna: Deuticke.

Goldfried, M. R. (1988). Application of rational restructuring to anxiety disorders. *The Counseling Psychologist*, 16, 50–68.

Goulding, M. M. & Goulding, R. L. (1979). *Changing Lives through Redecision Therapy.* New York: Grove Press.

Haley, J. (1989). *The First Therapy Session: How to Interview Clients and Identify Problems Successfully* (audiotape). San Francisco: Jossey-Bass.

Hauck, P. A. (2001). When reason is not enough. *Journal of Rational-Emotive & Cognitive-Behavior Therapy*, 19, 245–257.

Hayes, A. M., Laurenceau, J.-P., Feldman, G., Strauss, J. L. & Cardaciotto, L. (2007). Change is not always linear: The study of nonlinear and discontinuous patterns of change in psychotherapy. *Clinical Psychology, Review*, 27, 715–723.

Hoyt, M. F. (2011). Foreword. In A. Slive & M. Bobele (Eds.), *When One Hour is All You Have: Effective Therapy for Walk-in Clients* (pp. xix–xv). Phoenix, AZ: Zeig, Tucker, & Theisen.

Hoyt, M. F. (2018). Single-session therapy: Stories, structures, themes, cautions, and prospects. In M. F. Hoyt, M. Bobele, A. Slive, J. Young & M. Talmon (Eds.), *Single-Session Therapy by Walk-In or Appointment: Administrative, Clinical, and Supervisory Aspects of One-at-a-Time Services* (pp. 155–174). New York: Routledge.

Hoyt, M. F., Bobele, M., Slive, A., Young, J. & Talmon, M. (Eds.). (2018a). *Single-Session Therapy by Walk-In or Appointment: Administrative, Clinical, and Supervisory Aspects of One-at-a-Time Services.* New York: Routledge.

Hoyt, M. F., Bobele, M., Slive, A., Young, J. & Talmon, M. (2018b). Introduction: One-at-a-time/single-session walk-in therapy. In M. F. Hoyt, M. Bobele, A. Slive, J. Young & M. Talmon (Eds.), *Single-Session Therapy by Walk-In or Appointment: Administrative, Clinical, and Supervisory Aspects of One-at-a-Time Services* (pp. 3–24). New York: Routledge.

Hoyt, M. F., & Cannistrà, F. (2021). Common errors in single session therapy. *Journal of Systemic Therapies,* 40(3), 29–41

Hoyt, M. F., Rosenbaum, R. & Talmon, M. (1990). Effective single-session therapy: Step-by-step guidelines. In M. Talmon, *Single Session Therapy: Maximizing the Effect of the First (and Often Only) Therapeutic Encounter* (pp. 34–56). San Francisco: Jossey-Bass.

Hoyt, M. F., Rosenbaum, R. & Talmon, M. (1992). Planned single-session psychotherapy. In S. H. Budman, M. F. Hoyt & S. Friedman (Eds.), *The First Session in Brief Therapy* (pp. 59–86). New York: Guilford Press.

Hoyt, M. F. & Talmon, M. (Eds.). (2014a). *Capturing the Moment: Single Session Therapy and Walk-In Services.* Bethel, CT: Crown House Publishing.

Hoyt, M. F. & Talmon, M. (2014b). What the literature says: An annotated bibliography. In M. F. Hoyt & M. Talmon (Eds.), *Capturing the Moment: Single Session Therapy and Walk-In Services* (pp. 487–516). Bethel, CT: Crown House Publishing.

Hoyt, M. F., Young, J., & Rycroft, P. (Eds.). (2021). *Single Session Thinking and Practice in Global, Cultural and Familial Contexts: Expanding Applications.* New York: Routledge.

Hymmen, P., Stalker, C. A. & Cait, C.-A. (2013). The case for single-session therapy: Does the empirical evidence support the increased prevalence of this service delivery model? *Journal of Mental Health,* 22(1), 60–67.

Iveson, C. (2002). Solution-focused brief therapy. *Advances in Psychiatric Treatment,* 8, 149–157.

Iveson, C., George, E. & Ratner, H. (2014). Love is all around: A single session solution-focused therapy. In M. F. Hoyt & M. Talmon (Eds.), *Capturing the Moment: Single Session Therapy and Walk-In Services* (pp. 325–348). Bethel, CT: Crown House Publishing.

Jacobson, N. S., Follette, W. C. & Revenstorf, D. (1984). Psychotherapy outcome research: Methods for reporting variability and evaluating clinical significance. *Behavior Therapy,* 15, 336–352.

Jones-Smith, E. (2014). *Strengths-Based Therapy: Connecting Theory, Practice and Skills.* Thousand Oaks, CA: Sage Publications.

Kazantzis, N., Whittington, C. & Dattilio, F. (2010). Metaanalysis of homework effects in cognitive and behavioral therapy: A replication and extension. *Clinical Psychology: Science and Practice,* 17, 144–156.

Keller, G. & Papasan, J. (2012). *The One Thing: The Surprisingly Simple Truth Behind Extraordinary Results.* Austin, TX: Bard Press.

Kellogg, S. (2007). Transformational chairwork: Five ways of using therapeutic dialogues. *NYSPA Notebook,* 19 (4), 8–9.

Kellogg, S. (2015) *Transformational Chairwork: Using Psychotherapeutic Dialogues in Clinical Practice.* Lanham, MD: Rowman & Littlefield.

Kopp, S. (1972). *If You Meet the Buddha on the Road, Kill Him: The Pilgrimage of Psychotherapy Patients.* Palo Alto, CA: Science and Behavior Books.

Kuehn, J. L. (1965). Encounter at Leyden: Gustav Mahler consults Sigmund Freud. *Psychoanalytic Review*, 52, 345–364.

Lambert, M. J. (2013). The efficacy and effectiveness of psychotherapy. In M. J. Lambert (Ed.), *Bergin and Garfield's Handbook of Psychotherapy and Behavior Change.* 6th edn (pp. 169–218). New York: Wiley.

Lazarus, A. A. (1981). *The Practice of Multimodal Therapy.* New York: McGraw-Hill.

Lazarus, A. A. (1993). Tailoring the therapeutic relationship, or being an authentic chameleon. *Psychotherapy: Theory, Research, Practice, Training*, 30, 404–407.

Lemma, A. (2000). *Humour on the Couch: Exploring Humour in Psychotherapy and in Everyday Life.* London: Whurr.

Leyro, T. M., Zvolensky, M. J. & Bernstein, A. (2010). Distress tolerance and psychopathological symptoms and disorders: A review of the empirical literature among adults. *Psychological Bulletin*, 136, 576–600.

Malan, D. H., Bacal, H. A., Heath, E. S. & Balfour, F. H. G. (1968). A study of psychodynamic changes in untreated neurotic patients: I. Improvements that are questionable on dynamic criteria. *British Journal of Psychiatry*, 114, 525–551.

Malan, D. H., Heath, E. S., Bacal, H. A. & Balfour, F. H. G. (1975). Psychodynamic changes in untreated neurotic patients: II. Apparently genuine improvements. *Archives of General Psychiatry*, 32, 110–126.

Miller, S. D., Duncan, B. L. & Johnson, L. D. (2002). *The Session Rating Scale 3.0.* Chicago, IL: Authors.

Miller, W. R. & C. de Baca, J. (2001). *Quantum Change: When Epiphanies and Sudden Insights Transform Ordinary Lives.* New York: Guilford.

Minuchin, S. & Fishman, H. C. (1981). *Family Therapy Techniques.* Cambridge, MA: Harvard University Press.

Murphy, J. J. & Sparks, J. A. (2018). *Strengths-Based Therapy: Distinctive Features.* Abingdon, Oxon: Routledge.

National Trust. (2017). *Places that Make Us: Research Report.* Swindon, Wiltshire: National Trust. Available at: www. nationaltrust.org.uk/documents/places-that-make-us-research-report.pdf.

Norcross, J. C. & Cooper, M. (2021). *Personalizing Psychotherapy: Assessing and Accommodating Patient Preferences.* Washington, DC: American Psychological Association.

O'Hanlon, W. H. (1999). *Do One Thing Different: And Other Uncommonly Sensible Solutions to Life's Persistent Problems.* New York: William Morrow.

O'Hanlon, W. H. & Hexum, A. L. (1990). *An Uncommon Casebook: The Complete Clinical Work of Milton H. Erickson M.D.* New York: Norton.

Paul, K. E. & van Ommeren, P. (2013). A primer on single session therapy and its potential application in humanitarian situations. *Intervention,* 11(1), 8–23.

Pugh, M. (2019). *Cognitive Behavioural Chairwork: Distinctive Features.* Abingdon, Oxon: Routledge.

Pugh, M. (2021). Single-session chairwork: Overview and case illustration of brief dialogical psychotherapy. *British Journal of Guidance & Counselling,* DOI: 10.1080/03069885.2021.1984395

Quick, E. R. (2012). *Core Competencies in the Solution-Focused and Strategic Therapies: Becoming a Highly Competent Solution-Focused and Strategic Therapist.* New York: Taylor & Francis.

Ratner, H., George, E. & Iveson, C. (2012). *Solution Focused Brief Therapy: 100 Key Points and Techniques.* Hove, East Sussex: Routledge.

Reinecke, A., Waldenmaier, L., Cooper, M. J. & Harmer, C. J. (2013). Changes in automatic threat processing precede and predict clinical changes with exposure-based cognitive-behavior therapy for panic disorder. *Biological Psychiatry,* 73, 1064–1070.

Rescher, N. (1993). *Pluralism: Against the Demand for Consensus.* Oxford: Oxford University Press.

Riemer, M., Stalker, C. A., Dittmer, C., Cait, C.-A., Laurier, W., Horton, S., Kermani, N. & Booton, J. (2018). The walk-in counselling model of service delivery: Who benefits most? *Canadian Journal of Community Mental Health*, 37(2), 29–47.

Rogers, C. R. (1951). *Client-Centred Therapy*. London: Constable.

Rosenbaum, R., Hoyt, M. F. & Talmon, M. (1990). The challenge of single-session therapies: Creating pivotal moments. In R. A. Wells & V. J. Giannetti (Eds.), *Handbook of the Brief Psychotherapies* (pp. 165–189). New York: Plenum Press.

Rosenthal, R. & Jacobson, L. (1968). *Pygmalion in the Classroom: Teacher Expectation and Pupils' Intellectual Development*. New York: Holt, Rinehart & Winston.

Rubin, Z. (1973). *Liking and Loving: An Invitation to Social Psychology*. New York: Holt, Rinehart & Winston.

Scamardo, M., Bobele, M. & Biever, J. L. (2004). A new perspective on client dropouts. *Journal of Systemic Therapies*, 23(2), 27–38.

Seabury, B. A., Seabury, B. H. & Garvin, C. D. (2011). *Foundations of Interpersonal Practice in Social Work: Promoting Competence in Generalist Practice*. 3rd edn. Thousand Oaks, CA: Sage Publications.

Sharoff, K. (2002). *Cognitive Coping Therapy*. New York: Brunner-Mazel.

Simon, G. E., Imel, Z. E., Ludman, E. J. & Steinfeld, B. J. (2012). Is dropout after a first psychotherapy visit always a bad outcome? *Psychiatric Services*, 63(7), 705–707.

Slive, A. & Bobele, M. (Eds). (2011a). *When One Hour is All You Have: Effective Therapy for Walk-In Clients*. Phoenix, AZ: Zeig, Tucker & Theisen.

Slive, A. & Bobele, M. (2011b). Walking in: An aspect of everyday living. In A. Slive & M. Bobele (Eds.), *When One Hour is All You Have: Effective Therapy for Walk-In Clients* (pp. 11–22). Phoenix, AZ: Zeig, Tucker, & Theisen.

Slive, A. & Bobele, M. (2011c). Making a difference in fifty minutes: A framework for walk-in counselling. In A.

Slive & M. Bobele (Eds.), *When One Hour is All You Have: Effective Therapy for Walk-In Clients* (pp. 37–63). Phoenix, AZ: Zeig, Tucker, & Theisen.

Slive, A. & Bobele, M. (2014). Walk-in single session therapy: Accessible mental health services. In M. F. Hoyt & M. Talmon (Eds.), *Capturing the Moment: Single Session Therapy and Walk-In Services* (pp. 73–94). Bethel, CT: Crown House Publishing.

Slive, A. & Bobele, M. (2018). The three top reasons why walk-in single sessions make perfect sense. In M. F. Hoyt, M. Bobele, A. Slive, J. Young & M. Talmon (Eds.), *Single-Session Therapy by Walk-In or Appointment: Administrative, Clinical, and Supervisory Aspects of One-at-a Time Services* (pp. 27–39). New York: Routledge.

Slive, A., McElheran, N. & Lawson, A. (2008). How brief does it get? Walk-in single session therapy. *Journal of Systemic Therapies*, 27, 5–22.

Steenbarger, B. N. (2003). *The Psychology of Trading: Tools and Techniques for Minding the Markets*. Hoboken, NJ: John Wiley & Sons.

Swaminath, G. (2006). Joke's a part: In defence of humour. *Indian Journal of Psychiatry*, 48(3), 177–180.

Talmon, M. (1990). *Single Session Therapy: Maximizing the Effect of the First (and Often Only) Therapeutic Encounter*. San Francisco: Jossey-Bass.

Talmon, M. (1993). *Single Session Solutions: A Guide to Practical, Effective and Affordable Therapy*. New York: Addison-Wesley.

Talmon, M. (2018). The eternal now: On becoming and being a single-session therapist. In M. F. Hoyt, M. Bobele, A. Slive, J. Young & M. Talmon (Eds.), *Single-Session Therapy by Walk-In or Appointment: Administrative, Clinical, and Supervisory Aspects of One-at-a-Time Services* (pp. 149–154). New York: Routledge.

Talmon, M. & Hoyt, M. F. (2014). Moments are forever: SST and walk-in services now and in the future. In M. F. Hoyt & M. Talmon (Eds.), *Capturing the Moment: Single Session Therapy and Walk-In Services* (pp. 463–486). Bethel, CT: Crown House Publishing.

Weakland, J. H., Fisch, R., Watzlawick, P. & Bodin, A. M. (1974). Brief therapy: Focused problem resolution. *Family Process*, 13, 141–168.

Weir, S., Wills, M., Young, J. & Perlesz, A. (2008). *The Implementation of Single Session Work in Community Health.* Brunswick, Victoria, Australia: The Bouverie Centre, La Trobe University.

White, M. (1989). The externalizing of the problem and the re-authoring of lives and relationships. In *Selected Papers* (pp. 5–28). Adelaide, Australia: Dulwich Centre Publications.

Young, J. (2018). SST: The misunderstood gift that keeps on giving. In M. F. Hoyt, M. Bobele, A. Slive, J. Young & M. Talmon (Eds.), *Single-Session Therapy by Walk-In or Appointment: Administrative, Clinical, and Supervisory Aspects of One-at-a-Time Services* (pp. 40–58). New York: Routledge.

Young, J., Klosko, J. S. & Weishaar, M. E. (2003). *Schema Therapy: A Practitioner's Guide*. New York: Guilford Press.

Young, K. (2018). Change in the winds: The growth of walk-in therapy clinics in Ontario, Canada. In M. F. Hoyt, M. Bobele, A. Slive, J. Young & M. Talmon (Eds.), *Single-Session Therapy by Walk-In or Appointment: Administrative, Clinical, and Supervisory Aspects of One-at-a-Time Services* (pp. 59–71). New York: Routledge.

Young, K. & Bhanot-Malhotra, S. (2014). *Getting Services Right: An Ontario Multi-Agency Evaluation Study*. Available at: www.excellenceforchildandyouth.com.

Young, K. & Jebreen, J. (2019). Recognising single-session therapy as psychotherapy. *Journal of Systemic Therapies*, 38(4), 31–44.

Zlomke, K. & Davis, T. E. (2008). One-session treatment of specific phobias: A detailed description and review of treatment efficacy. *Behavior Therapy*, 39, 207–223.

INDEX

Note: Page numbers in *italic* denote figures and in **bold** denote tables.

Acceptance and Commitment Therapy (ACT) 188
acceptance-based change 184, 188
accessibility 143, 149, 268, 270
action planning 243–245
active-directive approaches 68, 75, 83, 107–108
Adler, Alfred 10
administrative support 123, 143, 145, 299
adversities 172–173, **174**; adversity focus 172–173; adversity-related goals 105–106, 177–178; first and subsequent responses to 197–198, **198**, **199**
advertising, walk-in therapy 273, 274–277
affect change 185
'African Violet Queen' case 11–12, 34–37
agencies 122–124, 302, 303, 305; client–service alliance 272–273; contra-indications for SST 144–145; delivery by appointment 49–50; delivery format 51; embedded approach 50, 64, 137–138; follow-up 255, 256–258; indications for SST 142–144; one-at-a-time

therapy (OAATT) 6, 7, 22–23, 39, 249, 259–262, 269, 273; organisational factors 122–124, 142–145, 299; policy on further help 249; service evaluation data 143, 255–256, 258; waiting lists 8, 22–23, 32, 39, 40, 82, 259, 262, 270; *see also* walk-in therapy
American Psychological Association (APA) 56
amygdala 214
aphorisms 114–115, 129, 242
applicant role 132, 149
appointment, service delivery by 49–50
Apprentice, The (TV programme) 99
approaches *see* therapeutic approaches
Arts University Bournemouth 273
assertive boundary setting 182
assessment: criteria-based 137–138; problem 19, 27, 41, 50, 120, 204; risk 73, 138, 269
attitudinal change 185–186, 187, 229, 235
Auden, W.H. 214
'authentic chameleon' concept 113, 140

avoidance: of discomfort
180–181; of issues 179–180

Barber, J. 284
'BASIC I.D.' framework 184–185
bearability: of discomfort
180–181; of distress 181
beginning phase of sessions 133,
162–164, 234, 279; *see also*
pre-session preparation;
therapeutic focus
behavioural change 185,
186–188
behavioural goals 177
behavioural rehearsals 237–238
behavioural solutions 234,
236–238
Bentine, Michael 20–21, 40, 229
'Big I–Little i' technique 208, *209*
Bloom, Bernard 13
Bobele, Monte 15, 55, 57,
268–269, 270–271, 306, 310
Bordin, E. S. 160
Bouverie Centre, Victoria,
Australia 15, 65
Brian (anger with wife case) 230
brief encounters 20–21
brief intermittent therapy 30–31
brief narrative therapy 278–280
Burry, Pamela 286

C' de Baca, J. 97
Cannistrà, F. 42, **46**, 47, 295
'Capturing the Moment'
conferences 15–16, 67, 109
Caravan Drop-in and
Counselling Service,
Piccadilly, London 276–277
case conceptualisation 120
case formulation 19, 41
chairwork 181, 226–228, 238

change *see* therapeutic change
Chinese farmer story 216–217
clarity 99–100
client-centred focus 73–74
client criteria question 137–138
client-driven therapy 74–75
client feedback xiii, 77, 134, 247,
252, **253–254**, 255, 258, 280
client goals 59–60, 74–75,
104–106, 160, 175–178, 299;
adversity-related 105–106,
177–178; behavioural 177;
definition 175; emotional
177–178; end-of-session
44–45, 296; finding instances
already happening 202–203;
focusing on 102, 176; outcome
markers 194–195; problem-
related 233; progress markers
195, 196; 'SMART' 176
client-initiated SST 52–53, 74
client-led therapy 43–45
client role 132
client–service alliance 272–273
client–therapist alliance 25, 28,
63, 69, 120, 133, 160–161, 233,
301
clients: benefits of walk-in
therapy 270–271;
characteristics of 'good'
127–130; choice of therapy
length 6, 38–39, 75; core
values 209; culture 299;
dropping out 28–29, 38,
53, 95, 157; empowerment
48; expectations 22–23,
97–98, 128, 158, 296; external
resources 31, 45, 48, 83,
86–87, 210–211; first contact
with 131–132, 149–150; help-
seeking roles 131–132, 149;

implementation 243–245;
intentionality 96; interrupting
169–170; lack of information
231–232; morale 46, 134, 296;
'noticing change' logs 196;
openness 76, 96; previous
solution attempts 204–206;
problem maintenance factors
179–183; rapid engagement
with 113; readiness 80–81, 82,
128–129; reflection 250–251;
role models 212–213, 237;
satisfaction 25, 61–62, 64, 95,
271; self-help/self-change
34–37, 48; strengths 31, 45,
48, 83–85, 210–211, 279;
stuckness 90–91, 167,
289–291; summarising 100,
103, 117–118, 133–134,
239–240, 280; take-aways
45–46, 89, 103, 133–134,
229–230, 241–242;
termination of therapy 28–29,
38, 53, 95, 157; types of help
sought 44, 69; vulnerable 304;
weaknesses 83, 85; working
alliance 25, 28, 63, 69, 120,
133, 160–161, 233, 272–273,
301; see also adversities;
client goals; techniques
and methods; therapeutic
change
clinical demonstrations 10–11,
55, 66, 283–284; see also
filmed training tapes
Cluedo (game) 169
cognitive behavioural solutions
235, 237, 238
cognitive behavioural therapy
(CBT) 19, 35, 68, 73, 108,
188, 235, 237; see also

Single-Session Integrated
Cognitive Behaviour Therapy
(SSI-CBT)
cognitive change 185–186
cognitive solutions 234–235, 237
Colman, A. 185
common concerns 61–64,
300–305
common errors 295–299
complex problems 43, 63–64,
88–89, 296, 304
constructive approaches 67–68,
75, 107
constructive responses to
adversities 197–198, **198**,
199
continuing professional
development (CPD) 143
contra-indications for SST: client
criteria question 137–138;
service 144–145; therapists
140–141
core values, client's 209
corrective dialogues 227–228
Counselling Session Rating
Scale (CSRS) 252, **253–254**
COVID-19 pandemic 4, 86,
276
crisis intervention 19, 305
criteria-based assessment
137–138
criteria for SST: client criteria
question 137–138; service
contra-indications for SST
144–145; service indications
for SST 142–144; therapist
contra-indications for SST
140–141; therapist indications
for SST 139–140
culture 299
Cummings, Nicholas 30–31

de Shazer, S. 104
delivery format 4, 51, 86
demonstration sessions 10–11,
    55, 66, 283–284; *see also*
    filmed training tapes
distress, unbearability of 181
Doran, G. T. 176
dos and don'ts 116–121
doubts, reservations and
    objections (DROs) 61–64, 123,
    142, 145, 300–305
drop-outs 28–29, 38, 53, 95, 157
duration of therapy *see* therapy
    length
dynamic poles 126

earnings 124
Ellis, Albert 10–11, 12, 34–37,
    56, 66, 220, 285
embedded approach 50, 64,
    137–138
emotional goals 177–178
emotional impact 114–115,
    207–209
emotional problems 172, **174**
end-of-session goals 44–45, 296
end-of-session summaries 100,
    103, 118, 133–134, 239–240
ending phase of sessions
    133–134, 234, 246–247; action
    planning 243–245; discussing
    further help 103, 134, 247,
    248–249; dos and don'ts
    117–118, 121; ending well 46;
    summarising 100, 103,
    117–118, 133–134, 239–240,
    280; take-aways 45–46, 89,
    103, 133–134, 229–230,
    241–242; unfinished business
    121, 246; *see also* post-session
    phase

enquirer role 131–132, 149
environment-focused change
    190–191, 200–201
environmental solutions 234
Erickson, Milton 11–12, 34–37
ethics 50, 223; informed consent
    7, 132, 149, 285, 300
exceptions to problems 200–201
expectations 22–23, 97–98, 128,
    158, 296
expertise, use of 107–108
explorer role 131
exposure therapy 65
external dialogues 226–227
external resources 31, 45, 48, 83,
    86–87, 210–211
externalising conversations 280

facing issues 179–180
feedback: client xiii, 77, 134, 247,
    252, **253–254**, 255, 258, 280;
    outcome evaluation data 143,
    255, 258; service evaluation
    data 143, 255–256, 258;
    see also second opinions
fees 124
filmed training tapes 12, 56,
    65–66, 285–287
Fishman, H. C. 217
flexibility, therapists 113–114,
    139–140, 295
flexible thinking 181–182
focus *see* therapeutic focus
follow-up 134, 195, 233, 247,
    255–258, **257**, 268–269
Foreman, D. M. 223
Frank, Jerome 46, 97, 296
frequently asked questions 306,
    307–309, 309–310
Freud, Sigmund 9–10
'Friday Night Workshop' 10–11

friend technique 224–225
future orientation 78–79

gateway approach *see* embedded approach
Gestalt therapy 12, 68, 108
Ghost Town (film) 119
'Gloria' films 12, 56, 65–66, 285–287
goal-setting 44–45, 104–106
goals, client 59–60, 74–75, 104–106, 160, 175–178, 299; adversity-related 105–106, 177–178; behavioural 177; definition 175; emotional 177–178; end-of-session 44–45, 296; finding instances already happening 202–203; focusing on 102, 176; outcome markers 194–195; problem-related 233; progress markers 195, 196; 'SMART' 176
goals, therapist 57–58, 160
Gustav Mahler 10

Hauck, P. A. 182
Hayes, A. M. 62
healthy negative emotions 178
help-seeking roles 131–132, 149
homework assignments 89, 243
Hoyt, Michael 5, 6, 14–15, 17, 25, 38, 39, 40, 43, 48, 67–68, 75, 88, 107, 108, 131, 150, 162, 194, 295
humour 130, 220–221
Hymmen, P. 3–4, 194

imagery 114–115, 129, 181, 187, 208
imagery change 185, 188
implementation 243–245

implementation obstacles 245
indications for SST: client criteria question 137–138; service 142–144; therapists 139–140
individual-focused change 184–188, 190–191
inferences: definition 185; testing 182, 187
inferential change 186, 229, 235
informed consent 7, 132, 149, 285, 300
inner strengths 31, 45, 48, 83–85, 210–211, 279
intentionality 95–96
intermittent therapy 30–31
internal dialogues 227
international symposia 15–16, 67, 109
interruption 169–170
Iveson, C. 78

Jacobson, L. 97
'Jewish Mother Syndrome' 32–33, 312–313
Joffe, D. 11
Jones-Smith, E. 83

Kaiser Permanente Medical Center, California 14–15, 24, 258
Kellogg, S. 226, 227
Kopp, Sheldon 108
Kronich, Aurelia Öhm- 9
Kuehn, J. L. 10

Lambert, M. J. 61
language use 208
Laozi 297
Lazarus, Arnold 113, 140, 184–185

Lemma, A. 130
length of sessions 41, 65–66, 297
length of therapy *see* therapy
　length
Leon (public speaking anxiety
　case) 168
'less is more' principle 32–33
Linda (environmental solutions
　case) 234
listening 119–120, 126
Lorna (criticism case) 173

Malan, David 12–13, 127
Malcolm (sweating case) 167
markers for change 194–195;
　outcome markers 194–195;
　progress markers 195, 196
'maybe one, maybe more'
　principle 5–6, 42–43
meaningful places 214–215
memorable phrases 229–230, 242
mental rehearsals 236–237
Mental Research Institute (MRI)
　Brief Therapy Center, Palo
　Alto, California 204
meta-disturbances 173
metaphors 114–115, 129
micro demonstrations 283
Miller, S. D. 252
Miller, W. R. 97
mindful acceptance 232
Minuchin, S. 217
misinformation 231–232
modification-based change 184,
　188
morale, client 46, 134, 296
Moshe, Talmon 14–15
Murphy, J. J. 84

narrative therapy, brief
　278–280

National Health Service, UK
　265, **266**
National Trust 214
negative emotions, healthy and
　unhealthy 178
Niebuhr, Reinhold 184
non-attendance 28–29, 38, 53,
　95, 157
'noticing change' logs 196

O'Hanlon, W. H. 11–12, 34–37
one-at-a-time therapy (OAATT)
　6, 7, 22–23, 39, 249, 259–262,
　269, 273
one-session treatment (OST)
　65, 180
ONEplus therapy 7–8, 303
online therapy sessions 4, 51, 86
open-access (walk-in) therapy
　15, 39, 51, 55, 157; advertising
　273, 274–277; benefits for
　clients 270–271; case for
　270–271; client criteria and
　137, 138; complex problems
　304; definitions 268–269;
　follow-up 268–269; frequently
　asked questions 306, 309–310;
　further help 157, 249;
　pathway to help 265, **267**;
　session structure 278–280;
　summarising 280; therapist
　satisfaction 271; training 273;
　use of term 15, 263; working
　alliance 272–273
openness 76–77, 96
optimism **110**, 111, 126, 246
organisational factors 122–124,
　142–145, 299
Öst, Lars-Göran 65
outcome evaluation data 143,
　255, 258

outcome markers 194–195
Özil, Mesut 120

parables 216–219, 242
paradox 222–223, 232
parameters, agree or review 157–159
Pat (weight loss case) 200–201
pathways to help 265, **266**, **267**
Perls, Fritz 12, 56, 66, 285, 286–287
person-centred therapy 12, 73
phobias: one-session treatment (OST) 65, 180; Vera (elevator phobia case) 34–37, 81, 89, 96
physical take-aways 89, 241–242
pivot chords 192–193
places, meaningful 214–215
planned SST 38–39, 52–54, 95, 157
pluralism 125–126, 298
pluralistic perspective 42–43, 113–114, 140
polar bear technique 232
post-session phase 134; client feedback xiii, 134, 247, 252, **253–254**, 255, 258, 280; follow-up 134, 195, 233, 247, 255–258, **257**, 268–269; further help 103, 134, 157, 158, 247, 248–249, 255, 302; implementation 243–245; outcome evaluation data 255, 258; recordings and transcripts 158–159, 242, 250–251; reflection 250–251; service evaluation data 143, 255–256, 258
pre-session preparation 132–133, 151; questionnaires 49, 84, 86, 132–133, 151, **152–153**, 162,

210, 279; risk assessment 73, 138, 269; telephone calls 86; walk-in therapy 269, 279
private practice: follow-up 256, **257**; options for further help 248–249; therapist earnings 124
problem assessment 19, 27, 41, 50, 120, 204
problem-focused approach 73, 79, 162–163, 165–167, 204–206
problem maintenance factors 179–183
problem-related goals 233
problematic responses to adversities 197–198, **198**, **199**
problems: complex 43, 63–64, 88–89, 296, 304; definition 175; emotional 172, **174**; exceptions to 200–201; previous problem-solving attempts 204–206; reframing 166, 173, 229, 235
progress markers 195, 196
psychoanalysis 9–10
psychodynamic therapy 12–13, 68, 108

quantum change 21, 62–63, 97–98
questionnaires: follow-up 256–258, **257**; pre-session 49, 84, 86, 132–133, 151, **152–153**, 162, 210, 279

Rational Emotive Behaviour Therapy (REBT) 12, 68, 108, 173, 177–178
Ratner, H. 200
readiness 80–82; client 80–81, 82, 128–129; therapist 81–82

real-life issues 298

recordings of sessions 158–159, 242, 250–251

reductio ad absurdum technique 222–223

reflection, post-session 250–251

reframing problems 166, 173, 229, 235

rehearsing solutions 102, 236–238

Reinecke, A. 238

relational depth 301

Rescher, N. 125

resources *see* external resources

rigid thinking 181–182

rigidity, therapists 140–141

risk assessment 73, 138, 269

Rita (criticism at work case) 202–203

Robin (work-related anxiety case) 191

Rogers, Carl 12, 56, 66, 73, 285, 286

role models 212–213, 237

role-play 182, 187, 228

role-play demonstrations 283–284

Ronseal approach 3–4

Rosenbaum, Robert 14–15, 25, 192

Rosenthal, Howard 286

Rosenthal, R. 97

Sarah (second opinion case) 289–291

Scamardo, M. 29

second opinions 56, 288–291

self-disclosure, therapists 76–77, 213

self-help/self-change 34–37, 48

sensation change 185, 188

service delivery 49–51, 137–138; by appointment 49–50; client–service alliance 272–273; delivery format 4, 51, 86; embedded approach 50, 64, 137–138; organisational factors 122–124, 142–145, 299; service contra-indications for SST 144–145; service evaluation data 143, 255–256, 258; service indications for SST 142–144; *see also* walk-in therapy

service-wide support 123, 142, 144

Session Rating Scale (SRS) 252

sessions *see* SST sessions; therapy length

Sharoff, K. 212–213

Shostrom, Everett 12, 285–287

significant others: previous solution attempts 204, 205–206; as role models 213; support of 196

silent assent 182

Simon, G. E. 25, 29, 161, 272

simple solutions 64, 88–89

Single-Session Integrated Cognitive Behaviour Therapy (SSI-CBT) 112, 137, 172–173, 177–178, 242, 244

Single-Session Therapy (SST): challenge to established beliefs 61–64; client-initiated 52–53, 74; clinical demonstrations 10–11, 55, 66, 283–284; common concerns 61–64, 300–305; common errors 295–299; conducive environment 122–124; in context 109–110, **110**;

definitions 3–8; development of 9–16; dos and don'ts 116–121; filmed training tapes 12, 56, 65–66, 285–287; frequently asked questions 306, **307–309**, 309–310; future orientation 78–79; mindset 42–47, **46**, 82; one-at-a-time therapy (OAATT) 6, 7, 22–23, 39, 249, 259–262, 269, 273; planned 38–39, 52–54, 95, 157; pluralistic nature of 125–126, 298; for second opinions 56, 288–291; therapist–client jointly initiated 53–54; therapist-initiated 54; types of help 44, 69; unplanned 38, 53, 95, 157; use of time 40–41, 102; what it is not 17–19; *see also* clients; criteria for SST; service delivery; SST process; SST sessions; therapeutic approaches; therapists; walk-in therapy

skills development: clients 187; *see also* supervision; training

Slive, Arnold 15, 55, 57, 268–269, 270–271, 306, 310

small steps 297–298

'SMART' goals 176

solution-focused approach 73, 78–79, 89, 163, 175, 200–204

solutions 133, 233–235; agreeing on 233; behavioural 234, 236–238; cognitive 234–235, 237; cognitive behavioural 235, 237, 238; definition 175; environmental 234; implementation of 243–245; previous solution attempts 204–206; rehearsing 102,

236–238; simple 64, 88–89; types 234–235

'sooner is better' principle 32

Sparks, J. A. 84

SST by default (unplanned SST) 38, 53, 95, 157

SST by design (planned SST) 38–39, 52–54, 95, 157

SST mindset 42–47, **46**, 82

SST process 131–134; beginning phase 133, 162–164, 234, 279; clarity about 99–100; first contact with clients 131–132, 149–150; middle phase 133; *see also* ending phase of sessions; post-session phase; pre-session preparation

SST sessions: beginning phase 133, 162–164, 234, 279; delivery format 4, 51, 86; length of 41, 65–66, 297; 'less is more' principle 32–33; middle phase 133; parameters 157–159; planning for time available 102; possibility of further sessions 5–6, 42–43, 158, 248–249, 302; power and integrity of 109, **110**; recordings and transcripts 158–159, 242, 250–251; 'sooner is better' principle 32; structure 101–103, 234, 259–262, 278–280; summarising 100, 103, 117–118, 133–134, 239–240, 280; take-aways 45–46, 89, 103, 133–134, 229–230, 241–242; working alliance 25, 28, 63, 69, 120, 133, 160–161, 233, 272–273, 301; *see also* client goals; ending phase of sessions; techniques and methods; therapeutic change; therapeutic focus

Steenbarger, B. N. 192–193

stories 114–115, 129, 216–219, 242

'stranger on the train phenomenon' 20

strengths 31, 45, 48, 83–85, 210–211, 279

strengths-based approaches 83–85, 163–164

structure of session 101–103, 234, 259–262, 278–280

stuckness 90–91, 167, 289–291

summaries 100, 103, 118, 133–134, 239–240

supervision xiii, 123–124, 143, 145, 286, 291, 299

supportive role models 213

Swaminath, G. 220–221

take-aways 45–46, 89, 103, 133–134, 229–230, 241–242

Talmon, Moshe 4, 5, 9, 22, 24, 25, 40, 43, 48, 53, 67, 97, 109, 112, 123, 124, 126, 128, 176–177, 194, 195, 200–201, 258

Tavistock Clinic, London 12–13, 127

techniques and methods: action planning 243–245; agree markers for change 194–195; agree on solution 233; aphorisms 114–115, 129, 242; assess previous solution attempts 204–206; chairwork 181, 226–228, 238; corrective dialogues 227–228; emotional impacts 114–115, 207–209;

external dialogues 226–227; externalising conversations 280; find exceptions to the problem 200–201; find instances of goal already happening 202–203; focus on second responses to adversity 197–198, **198**, **199**; friend technique 224–225; humour 130, 220–221; imagery 114–115, 129, 181, 187, 208; internal dialogues 227; interrupting clients 169–170; language use 208; memorable phrases 229–230, 242; metaphors 114–115, 129; mindful acceptance 232; 'noticing change' logs 196; parables 216–219, 242; paradox 222–223, 232; physical take-aways 89, 241–242; pivot chords 192–193; polar bear technique 232; providing information 231–232; reframing problems 166, 173, 229, 235; rehearsing solutions 102, 236–238; role models 212–213, 237; role-play 182, 187, 228; stories 114–115, 129, 216–219, 242; summarising 100, 103, 117–118, 133–134, 239–240, 280; topophilia 214–215; utilise client's core values 209; utilise client's strengths and external resources 210–211; visual representations 208, *209*, 242

telephone: follow-up calls 256, **257**; pre-session 86; therapy sessions 4, 276 termination of therapy: unplanned 28–29, 38, 53, 95, 157; *see also* ending phase of sessions

therapeutic approaches 67–68; active-directive approaches 68, 75, 83, 107–108; constructive approaches 67–68, 75, 107; problem-focused approach 73, 79, 162–163, 165–167, 204–206; solution-focused approach 73, 78–79, 89, 163, 175, 200–204; strengths-based approaches 83–85, 163–164

therapeutic change: acceptance-based strategies 184, 188; accepting costs of 36–37; affect change 185; attitudinal change 185–186, 187, 229, 235; 'BASIC I.D.' framework 184–185; behavioural change 185, 186–188; client empowerment 48; clinically significant change 62–63; cognitive change 185–186; environment-focused 190–191, 200–201; established beliefs about 61–64; expectations of 97–98, 128, 158, 296; imagery change 185, 188; individual-focused 184–188, 190–191; inferential change 186, 229, 235; initiating quickly 34–37; modification-based strategies 184, 188; 'noticing change' logs 196; objective versus subjective measures 61–62, 63; outcome markers 194–195; progress markers 195, 196; quantum change 21, 62–63, 97–98; self-help/self-change 34–37, 48; sensation change 185, 188; speed of 34–37, 62–63, 300; therapy length and 20–21, 34

therapeutic focus 114, 165–167; adversity focus 172–173; client-centred focus 73–74; co-creation of 45, 102; problem-focused approach 73, 79, 162–163, 165–167, 204–206; solution-focused approach 73, 78–79, 89, 163, 175, 200–204; working focus 168–171

therapeutic relationship *see* working alliance

therapist–client jointly initiated SST 53–54

therapist-initiated SST 54

therapists: as 'authentic chameleon' 113, 140; benefits of walk-in therapy 271; characteristics of 'good' 112–115; clarity 99–100; common concerns 61–64, 300–305; common errors 295–299; continuing professional development (CPD) 143; contra-indications for SST 140–141; earnings 124; expectations 97–98; flexibility 113–114, 139–140, 295; goals 57–58, 160; helpful attitudes for 109–111, 110; indications for SST 139–140; intentionality 95–96; interrupting clients 169–170; listening 119–120, 126; openness 76–77; optimism 110, 111; pluralistic perspective 42–43, 113–114, 140; rapid engagement with clients 113; readiness 81–82; rigidity 140–141; as role models 213; satisfaction 271; self-disclosure 76–77, 213; skill deficits 141; SST mindset 42–47, **46**, 82; supervision xiii, 123–124, 143, 145, 286, 291, 299; training xiii, 26, 122–123, 142, 143, 144, 145, 299; use of expertise 107–108; working alliance 25, 28, 63, 69, 120, 133, 160–161, 233, 272–273, 301; *see also* techniques and methods; therapeutic approaches; therapeutic change

therapy agencies 122–124, 302, 303, 305; client–service alliance 272–273; contra-indications for SST 144–145; delivery by appointment 49–50; delivery format 51; embedded approach 50, 64, 137–138; follow-up 255, 256–258; indications for SST 142–144; one-at-a-time therapy (OAATT) 6, 7, 22–23, 39, 249, 259–262, 269, 273; organisational factors 122–124, 142–145, 299; policy on further help 249; service evaluation data 143, 255–256, 258; waiting lists 8, 22–23, 32, 39, 40, 82, 259, 262, 270; *see also* walk-in therapy

therapy demonstrations 10–11, 55, 66, 283–284; *see also* filmed training tapes

therapy length: client choice 6, 38–39, 75; client expectations and 22–23; client satisfaction and 25, 95; difficulty predicting 27; intermittent therapy 30–31; modal number of sessions 24–25, 252, 295, 302; possibility of further sessions 5–6, 42–43, 158, 248–249, 302; session length 41, 65–66, 297; therapeutic change and 20–21, 34; unplanned termination 28–29, 38, 53, 95, 157

therapy sessions *see* SST sessions; therapy length

'Three Approaches to Psychotherapy' *see* 'Gloria' films

time 40–41, 102

Tom (work-related anxiety case) 192–193

topophilia 214–215

training xiii, 26, 122–123, 142, 143, 144, 145, 299; *see also* filmed training tapes

transcripts of sessions 158–159, 242, 250–251

unfinished business 121, 246

unhealthy negative emotions 178

university counselling services 6, 22–23, 32, 39, 249, 259–262, 273

unplanned SST 38, 53, 95, 157

Vera (elevator phobia case) 34–37, 81, 89, 96

Very Brief Therapeutic Conversations (VBTCs) 11, 66

Via Character Strengths Survey 83
visual representations 208, *209*, 242
vulnerable clients 304

waiting lists 8, 22–23, 32, 39, 40, 82, 259, 262, 270
Walk-in Counselling Clinic, Ottawa, Canada 274–276
walk-in therapy 15, 39, 51, 55, 157; advertising 273, 274–277; benefits for clients 270–271; case for 270–271; client criteria and 137, 138; complex problems 304; definitions 268–269; follow-up 268–269; frequently asked questions 306, 309–310; further help 157, 249; pathway to help 265, **267**; pre-session preparation 269, 279; session structure 278–280; summarising 280; therapist satisfaction 271; training 273; use of term 15, 263; working alliance 272–273
Watts, Alan 217
Weakland, J. H. 204
Weir, S. 5, 74, 77, 123
wise rabbi story 218–219
working alliance 25, 28, 63, 69, 120, 133, 160–161, 233, 272–273, 301
working focus 168–171; *see also* therapeutic focus
workshops *see* therapy demonstrations
written reminders 89, 242

'You have to get its attention first' story 217
Young, Jeff 24, 43, 63–64, 137–138, 227, 269
Young, Karen 278

Zoom therapy sessions 4, 51, 86

Printed in the United States
by Baker & Taylor Publisher Services